PENGUIN BOOKS

TRIUMPH

TRIUMPH

Life After the Cult:
A Survivor's Lessons

Carolyn Jessop

WITH LAURA PALMER

PENGUIN BOOKS

PENGUIN BOOKS

Published by the Penguin Group
Penguin Books Ltd, 80 Strand, London WC2R ORL, England
Penguin Group (USA) Inc., 375 Hudson Street, New York, New York 10014, USA
Penguin Group (Canada), 90 Eglinton Avenue East, Suite 700, Toronto, Ontario, Canada M4P 2Y3
(a division of Pearson Penguin Canada Inc.)
Penguin Ireland, 25 St Stephen's Green, Dublin 2, Ireland (a division of Penguin Books Ltd)
Penguin Group (Australia), 250 Camberwell Road, Camberwell, Victoria 3124, Australia
(a division of Pearson Australia Group Pty Ltd)
Penguin Books India Pvt Ltd, 11 Community Centre, Panchsheel Park, New Delhi – 110 017, India
Penguin Group (NZ), 67 Apollo Drive, Rosedale, Auckland 0632, New Zealand
(a division of Pearson New Zealand Ltd)
Penguin Books (South Africa) (Pty) Ltd, 24 Sturdee Avenue, Rosebank,
Johannesburg 2196, South Africa

Penguin Books Ltd, Registered Offices: 80 Strand, London WC2R ORL, England

www.penguin.com

First published in the USA by Broadway Books, an imprint of the Crown Publishing Group,
a division of Random House, Inc. New York 2009
First published in Great Britain by Viking 2010
Published in Penguin Books 2011

1

Printed in Great Britain by Clays Ltd, St Ives plc

ISBN: 978-0-141-04705-8

www.greenpenguin.co.uk

This book is dedicated to everyone who gave their all to protect the FLDS children in the aftermath of the raid on the YFZ Ranch. People drove themselves past the point of exhaustion day after day and week after week because they believed FLDS children deserve to live in freedom and security like every other American child.

This book is also dedicated to my children—Arthur, Betty, LuAnne, Patrick, Andrew, Merrilee, Harrison, and Bryson—who center my life in a love that knows no bounds and grows stronger every day. And to Brian Moroney, who makes me laugh and never lets me forget that I am loved unconditionally, I dedicate this book to you, too. You help make our family a triumph.

Acknowledgments

Kris Dahl, my agent at International Creative Management, remains a shining example of what it means to be at the top of your game.

My collaborator, Laura Palmer, has come through again for me as always with her talent and kindness. We make a great team.

Diane Salvatore, publisher at Broadway Books, brought her passion, intellect, and commitment to ensure that this book would be the best it can possibly be. Lorraine Glennon, my editor, brought more steadfastness and dedication to this manuscript than I thought was humanly possible. Diane and Lorraine were backed up by their incomparable assistants, Hallie Falquet and Annie Chagnot.

David Drake, the head of publicity at Broadway, makes excellence look easy and is a gift to every author he supports. Ellen Folan, the publicist for *Triumph* has the competence to match her enthusiasm.

Jean Traina has my grateful thanks for designing the elegant cover on this book. Janet Biehl proved that the art of copyediting is far from dead.

Last, but in no way least, Laura Neely, Kris Dahl's assistant at ICM, is almost peerless in her ability to keep up with everything essential in an author's life, from the moment negotiations begin until manuscripts are completed. Thank you.

I met some of the finest people I have ever known in Texas during the raid. The love and dedication for the FLDS children expressed by the team at CASA, the Children's Advocacy Center of Tom Green County, Inc., was miraculous. CASA is headed by executive director, Debra R. Brown, and ably managed by program director, Shirley Davis, and case managers Paulette Schell, Connie Gauwain, Judy Morehouse, and Valerie Trevino.

Kathy and Randy Mankin, publishers of *The Eldorado Success,* demonstrate week after week that a shoestring budget doesn't mean you can't do accurate and honest journalism. Their dedication in pursuing the facts, wherever they may lead, is exceptional. I am proud to know them.

Lisa Jones and Natalie Malonis have been the attorneys who stood up with me when I stood up to Merril in court. I could not have had more superb help. Thank you.

Jeff Schmidt worked relentlessly as an attorney in pursuit of justice and protection for the FLDS children. He is one of the unsung heroes of that time. Sharing his dedication to the welfare of children is Charles Childress, who helped and supported this book. Nick Hanna came through for me and my family.

Dan and Leenie Fischer, Sam Brower, and Gary Engels have all dedicated much of their lives to confronting the crimes of the FLDS.

Doris Besikof has been enormously supportive of me and I am grateful for her expertise and guidance on legal questions. Kathleen Cochran, in San Diego, helped my family have one of our happiest times together.

Crystal and Chuck Maggelet have been wonderful and supportive friends here in Salt Lake City. Thanks to Jan Johnson, who helped me get started as a writer. Venus Cederstom was always there for me as a good neighbor and a great friend during one of the toughest times in my life.

Thank you Stan, Mollie, and Hannah Helfand for graciously including us in Emilie's bat mitzvah, which helped me see how religion can be such a positive influence on life. I'd also like to thank Frank and MJ Chmelik for making me feel welcome at Brian's Claremont McKenna College reunion. Thanks, too, to Jacqueline McCook for providing the photographs of the Harvard reunion I attended with Brian. My love and gratitude to Brian's mother, Edith Moroney, for accepting all of us into her life.

Dr. Lisa Sampson is always on call for my family. I know Harrison, my most vulnerable child, is safe in her care. Angela Barrett-Locker, Harrison's case manager, is dedicated to making his life all it can be. Thanks are also due to Freyja and Shad Robison who welcomed Harrison into their home with love and support whenever I had to be away and to Cindy Nelson who provides love and care to Harrison each morning.

I also want to thank my children: Arthur, LuAnne, Patrick, Andrew, Merrilee, Harrison, and Bryson, who all sacrificed a lot of time with me so this book could be written; and to my eldest daughter, Betty, who returned to the FLDS but has never left my heart. Grateful thanks to my dad, Arthur Blackmore, who stepped up for me in my child-support case. Finally, I would like to thank Brian Moroney for showing me what unconditional love is.

Preface

In *Escape,* the memoir I published in October 2007, I told the story of my dramatic, middle-of-the-night flight from the Fundamentalist Church of Jesus Christ of Latter-Day Saints (FLDS), the Mormon polygamous cult that I'd been born into thirty-five years earlier. I was elated when *Escape* was published, staggered when it went as high as number two on the *New York Times* nonfiction best-seller list, and utterly convinced that that was the end of the story. My children and I were enjoying our freedom and flourishing in our new lives.

Then on April 3, 2008, I abruptly collided with the past I thought I'd put so firmly behind us. That's the date when law enforcement officers representing the state of Texas, acting on a telephone tip from a girl calling herself Sarah Barlow, surrounded the FLDS compound near Eldorado, Texas. That dramatic night was the beginning of months of upheaval in my life unlike any I had experienced while escaping from the cult.

The raid was shocking, alarming, yet it also filled me with hope. Perhaps, I thought, the crimes committed by the FLDS against its women and children would finally be revealed to the rest of the world.

Like the millions of Americans who watched the crisis play out on television, I was sickened when I saw the faces of the children being removed from the Yearning for Zion (YFZ) Ranch. I shuddered to imagine the fear and trauma they must have been feeling as they left the only world they had ever known. But even as I viewed the same dramatic footage as everyone else, I saw it from a unique perspective because I was intimately familiar with the major players. For seventeen years I had been married to Merril Jessop, the FLDS leader who was running the YFZ Ranch. When I was eighteen, I was forced to marry him, a man thirty-two years my senior, as the price I had to pay before I could go to college. We had never even spoken to each other. I became his fourth wife, and we had eight children in fifteen years.

We lived in Colorado City, Arizona (just across the border with Utah), in an FLDS community of ten thousand people. I fled before Merril relocated to the compound in Texas, which had been built for the sect's most elite members. I'd heard Warren Jeffs, the "prophet" of the FLDS, talk about moving his followers to "The Center Place." I knew it would be an isolated enclave cut off from the rest of the world, and I was sure that if my family were ever forced to live in such a place, I would never be able to protect my children from the radical extremism that Jeffs preached. That was just one motivation among many for my desperate desire to get out.

But even though I fled the FLDS, I never stopped loving my step-children. I had reason to believe that at least eight of them were on the YFZ Ranch, and my heart was torn apart by what they might be going through. I also realized that if I hadn't escaped, I could easily have been one of the distraught FLDS mothers crying on TV. I knew many of the women who were being interviewed. Some were good mothers who loved their children but were trapped in a world of systematic degradation, exploitation, and abuse.

With so many people I cared about involved, I started working behind the scenes with the authorities to help them understand the religious culture they were dealing with. I tried to help the dedicated child-care advocates who were suddenly struggling to care for and cope with hundreds of FLDS children who'd been separated from their mothers.

I've written *Triumph* to tell what I know about what went right—and what went terribly wrong—with the raid in Texas.

But I also wrote *Triumph* to explain why I was able to break through the crippling and destructive elements of the FLDS mind control into which I'd been indoctrinated since birth. I have been asked over and over, "What made you different? Where did you find the determination to get yourself out with all your children? How did you hold on to your courage?"

Just recently I was in Texas to testify in one of the criminal trials resulting from the Texas raid. I met a woman who'd left the FLDS rather than be forced into a second marriage with a man she abhorred. She had no children, so she had only herself to get to safety. Yet she told me how hard it had been for her and how overwhelmed she'd been with fear and doubt when she first got out. She questioned everything about her decision. "I even questioned if I was turning against God," she confided. "I had so many, many questions. I can't imagine what it would have been like if I'd had crying children, begging me to allow them to return."

She was right—it *was* hard, at times almost crushingly so. But I can honestly say I never looked back after I made it to safety. I never questioned myself or wondered if I did the right thing. I had periods of confusion about where I was going in my life and how I would get there. Living in a homeless shelter for a time with my eight children—one of whom is profoundly disabled—was one of the most difficult challenges I encountered. But I never doubted that I'd done the right thing; nor did I feel guilty about leaving the FLDS.

The woman I met in Texas had left the FLDS suddenly, when an opportune moment presented itself. So she faced a host of massive changes all at once. That's sometimes the way transformation happens.

But my message in *Triumph* is about how you can transform your life in simple, gradual, and consistent ways, especially when you don't have money, support, or a guarantee that you can get where you're trying to go.

I did not completely change the way I viewed my world in one moment. My shedding of decades of FLDS mind control came in stages. Looking back now, I can see that I was transforming my life years before I fled. It happened incrementally. Sometimes it was a day at a time, sometimes just an hour. But each moment was a building block that led me to the next stage in my journey, and then the next. Working gradually helped me amass the psychological and emotional strength I needed to trust myself. (About the need to keep my children safe, I had no doubts whatsoever.)

We live in a culture where everything happens so fast that we often forget that our lives do not—and usually cannot—transform themselves overnight. In my life there were no quick fixes. My experience was traumatic, but the tools I used are available to anyone who wants to find a new and better direction.

I hope no one reading *Triumph* will ever be in a situation as desperate as mine. I lived in a world that was so rigidly controlled that if I had been caught reading a book like this one, it would have been confiscated and destroyed. I would have been punished for having contact with the evil outside world. My life in the FLDS was so extreme and dangerous that when I decided to leave, I had no margin for error. Each choice and every strategy I pursued had to be careful and deliberate.

But at some point nearly everyone, no matter what her situation, has to face change that is terrifying and overwhelming. I had virtually no money (I left with twenty dollars in my wallet), but I radically changed my life through a series of ordinary steps that anyone can take. What worked for me can serve as a guide for others.

Change is often so frightening that we resist, deny, and run away

from what we know we need to do, deadening ourselves to other possibilities. It's not easy to tackle our monsters and confront our fears.
When I fled from the FLDS with my eight children, it was like leaping
off a cliff. I had no idea where we would land or what might happen
to us. Survival was my primary goal. But I did more than survive: my
life with my family became a triumph. It is by no means perfect; my
heart aches for my daughter Betty, who returned to the FLDS two days
after turning eighteen. But I am filled with gratitude and the wisdom
that I have worked so hard to earn.

As I've crisscrossed the country over the past few years promoting
Escape, the question I get asked more than any other is "How did you
do it?" It's not just women who want to know. Men also show up at
my readings and events, and they too shake their heads and ask the
same question.

The questions got me pondering: What *were* the tools of my
transformation? My path was never sure, but I feel I now have some
answers. I'd like to share them with you. May my triumph help create
yours.

PART ONE

Taking On the FLDS

The Raid

It was Thursday, April 3, 2008. I was home in West Jordan, Utah, folding laundry in my bedroom, when my cell phone rang.

"Carolyn, it's Kathy. Something is going on at the ranch. Law enforcement is at the gate, and the country road has been shut down."

Kathy Mankin and her husband, Randy, publish *The Eldorado Success,* the local newspaper in Eldorado, Texas, the town nearest to the Yearning for Zion Ranch, a $20 million compound spread across seventeen hundred acres in West Texas. The YFZ Ranch is owned and operated by the Fundamentalist Church of Jesus Christ of Latter-Day Saints, the polygamous Mormon cult in which I'd spent my entire life until fleeing in April 2003. My ex-husband, Merril Jessop, had been running the ranch since becoming one of the highest-ranking men in the FLDS in 2006.

Kathy and Randy had been covering the FLDS since 2003, when the ranch was bought under false pretenses as a corporate retreat and lodge. On March 24, 2004, with the headline "Corporate Retreat or Prophet's Refuge?" the Mankins broke the news to the residents of Eldorado—a town of roughly two thousand residents, thirteen churches, three restaurants, and an aging motel—that their new neighbors were members of an extreme polygamous sect. Kathy and I had been in touch since 2006, when she called to find out what might be going on at the ranch and to broaden her knowledge of the FLDS. This time, though, her voice sounded urgent.

"Randy asked one of the law enforcement officers where they were all coming from, and he said they were coming in from everywhere," she told me. She said it was hard to get information because law enforcement was keeping the media out of the area. She was worried about an ugly showdown if the FLDS did not cooperate.

My phone rang nonstop for the rest of the night. It soon became clear that Merril was in a major confrontation with the law. Since the national media had no idea what was going on yet, we couldn't turn on the TV for information. All I knew were the bits and pieces that my callers told me.

Of course I knew just how dangerous this situation could become. It was no secret within the FLDS that members would be proud to die for the prophet. In fact, Warren Jeffs, the now-imprisoned leader of the FLDS, once asked at the regular monthly meeting for FLDS men how many would be willing to die for him. As the rest of the community learned immediately afterward—this was the kind of news that spread like wildfire—every single one of the men stood. Then again, no one would have dared not to.

My greatest fear was that whatever was happening at the YFZ Ranch could explode into another Waco, the Texas town where seventy-six people died back in 1993, when the Branch Davidian compound, run by the self-styled prophet David Koresh, burned to the ground after being raided by federal agents. Footage of that raid circulated among the FLDS as an example of how corrupt the government had become. FLDS leaders blamed the government for killing everyone at Waco.

I had eight stepchildren on the YFZ Ranch who were younger than eighteen and several more who were adults. I had taught a few of FLDS leader Warren Jeffs's wives when I was a schoolteacher, and

I was concerned that they might be on the ranch, too. Severing my-self from the FLDS did not mean I stopped caring about those I'd loved when I was there. It was a constant source of guilt that I'd been unable to protect those loved ones as much as I'd managed to protect my own children. In the nearly six years since I'd fled, my life—and my children's—had steadily improved. Knowing firsthand how joyful life could be made me yearn even more that those still mired in the cult might one day cut themselves loose.

But my deepest concern was for my daughter Betty, who'd broken my heart when she returned to the FLDS in 2007 immediately after turning eighteen. For about a month we lost all contact but gradually began talking again by phone. Our last conversation, just four days earlier, had lasted forty-five minutes. She was not living on the YFZ Ranch but was cooking and cleaning for her half-brothers, who were working on construction jobs outside Texas. She never talked about why she wasn't on the ranch with her father, whom she idolized, but I suspect Merril wanted to make sure she was truly committed after living for four years "on the outside." My heart froze as I contemplated what this new crisis might mean for our still-shaky relationship. But above all I felt relief that Betty wasn't at the ranch.

It was an endless night. When the calls stopped, my mind didn't. Something huge was unfolding in Texas. What terrified me most was that Merril was in charge of the hundreds of children inside the com-pound. Merril saw himself as invincible and had never been reason-able or accountable to anyone. He was a bully and a coward. And that, of course, made him even more dangerous. He was careful to protect his own safety, but if he felt desperate and trapped, he was capable of doing something stupid.

After a sleepless night, I got up the next day, April 4, and began calling everyone who might know something. I learned that the ranch had been surrounded because the Child Protective Services (CPS) for Texas wanted to talk to a young girl named Sarah Barlow, who'd made a call to an abuse hotline on March 29, 2008. The girl had begged for help, claiming she was forced to marry at sixteen, became pregnant, and was repeatedly raped and beaten by her fifty-year-old husband.

Initially Merril refused to allow the CPS workers on the YFZ Ranch because, he insisted, there was no one there by the name of Sarah Barlow. But after resisting for hours, Merril apparently realized that the Texas Rangers weren't backing down. So he finally allowed them and their deputies to enter. They were followed by a team from CPS, who began searching the compound for "Sarah," the young girl who'd made the call. When they could not find her, the CPS team wanted to talk to all the teenage girls on the premises who were younger than seventeen.

Of the twenty girls CPS interviewed, five were named Sarah. One had had a baby at sixteen but she said she was not Sarah Barlow. CPS found other girls under eighteen who were pregnant. Under Texas law, it is a crime to engage in sexual contact with someone younger than seventeen who is not a legal spouse. I was told that the girls generally refused to answer questions; the few who did talk were defiant in their insistence that no age was too young to get married.

The Texas Supreme Court decision that was reached six weeks later described the reception CPS got at the ranch: "When the Department arrived at the YFZ Ranch, it was treated cordially and allowed access to children, but those children repeatedly 'pled the Fifth' in response to questions about their identity, would not identify their birth dates or parentage, refused to answer questions about who lived in their homes and lied about their names—sometimes several times. Answers from parents were similarly inconsistent: One mother first claimed that four children were hers, and then later avowed that they were not. Furthermore, the Department arrived to discover that a shredder had been used to destroy documents just before its arrival."

Law enforcement officers who accompanied CPS onto the ranch noticed pregnant young girls being herded from one house to another on the compound. A lawyer involved with the case later told me that the state always suspected that it never got all the children from the ranch because some had been whisked away.

By Saturday, April 5, CPS had taken 167 children into custody. I was on the phone when the news bulletin appeared on TV, announcing that district judge Barbara Walther had ordered the removal of young girls from the ranch. Moments later there was a shot of a bus filled with young girls leaving the compound. One of the heads I saw bobbing up and down through the bus window had bright red hair. My heart almost stopped. I was sure it was my fourteen-year-old stepdaughter; she would be terrified at being removed from the only world she had ever known.

What had begun as a simple investigation of a distress call by a young woman named Sarah had exploded into a human tragedy and a major national news story.

Once again Merril revealed his stupidity. If he'd only cooperated with authorities at the beginning and provided one of the Sarah Barlows for questioning, the raid on the ranch could probably have been avoided. The interview would have been fruitless, and there would have been no grounds for law enforcement to search all the homes on the ranch. The officers might have wanted to do more questioning, but CPS would never have discovered as much as it did.

As for CPS, along with not being equipped to handle all the children who were removed from the ranch, it never found the Sarah Barlow who'd made the call. Suspicion was building that the call was a hoax. All the same, evidence suggested that the YFZ Ranch was a hotbed of child abuse. As this evidence was presented to Judge Walther, she ordered more and more children removed.

By Monday, April 7, Judge Walther had ordered 401 children into temporary protective custody based on a determination of significant risk of harm. In addition, 133 women had now left the compound. The men, meanwhile, were told to remain on the ranch while the investigation continued.

Kathy told me that the small community of Eldorado was spinning from the shock of seeing hundreds of children being pulled from the YFZ Ranch. The residents had had no idea there were so many children sequestered on the ranch since, as Kathy said, the women and children were never seen in town, only the men. All anyone knew was that the ranch was a closed polygamous community that kept to itself.

The raid was now the largest child custody case anyone could remember in U.S. history. Unfortunately, CPS was not remotely prepared to provide for the hundreds of children suddenly in its care. Emergency workers were being called in from other areas of Texas to help. The Eldorado community began collecting emergency relief to provide food, toys, cribs, and other items the children needed.

"They should have kicked out the men and left the children undisturbed," Kathy said angrily. "Those kids should not be traumatized like this."

She was right, but I knew there was plenty of trauma going on inside the ranch, too. One of the major reasons I fled the FLDS was because fourteen-year-old girls were routinely forced to marry and my daughter Betty was thirteen at the time. And in the months before my escape, the FLDS was becoming even more fanatical. Warren Jeffs, who'd ascended to the official leadership of the FLDS in 2002 after his father, Rulon Jeffs, died, was splitting up families and talking about sending "worthy" FLDS members to "The Center Place." At that point in time, none of us knew what he meant by "The Center Place" but I thought it sounded terrifying.

During the nearly two years, from 2005 to 2006, when Warren Jeffs was on the run (a status that eventually earned him a place on the FBI's Ten Most Wanted list), my husband, Merril Jessop, became one of the most powerful leaders in the cult. If I'd stayed married to him, my eight children and I would almost surely have been forced to move to the compound in Texas, where we would have been completely cut off from the outside world. Even worse, my handicapped son, Harrison, would have been unable to get the medical care and therapy he needed to survive.

Merril had ten children under the age of twelve when we got married, and he fathered twenty more over the next seventeen years. It had been nearly five years since I'd seen any of the stepchildren I'd helped raise, and I knew their world had only grown less safe. With Warren Jeffs's 2006 arrest and conviction (he's now serving two five-years-to-life sentences for being an accomplice to rape), his followers became more convinced than ever that he was being persecuted like Jesus Christ, just as he'd predicted.

As I watched the crisis at the YFZ Ranch on TV, fear and hope were my dueling emotions. I was frightened about what might happen to the children and heartsick that they might have to endure yet more pain. At the same time I hoped that maybe, just maybe, the long legacy of abuse and crimes against FLDS women and children might finally be drawing to a close.

More than almost anything else, I wanted to see those children saved.

The Drama Unfolds

My days soon became a blur. My book, *Escape*, had raised my profile, making me the media's go-to person for commentary on FLDS matters. I did a late-night interview with CNN's Anderson Cooper from a Salt Lake City studio. Afterward I got a call from Shannon Price, the woman who worked for Dan Fischer, the former FLDS member and dentist who founded the nonprofit Diversity Foundation to help the hundreds of "lost boys" who'd been kicked out of the FLDS as teenagers (mainly so the old men wouldn't have to compete with them for young girls). Shannon, who lived in Salt Lake City, asked if I'd be willing to go to Texas with her. "The authorities need help understanding the FLDS," she said. "They're in over their heads. The local sheriff would like a few of us to come down and assist."

As the ex-wife of the man in charge, I knew I'd have valuable insights. But Shannon was leaving in two hours, and I needed more time.

Information continued to pour in with every phone call. More children were being removed from the ranch, and a search warrant had been issued for the temple, the most sacred site on the compound. On Merril's orders, FLDS men barred its entrance. The Texas Rangers broke the massive front doors to enter; once inside, they had to break down other doors.

The most symbolic was the door that Warren Jeffs had decreed only God could walk through. That did not really impress the Texas Rangers, who blew it wide open. There they discovered a room surrounded by a thick wall of limestone and an enormous vault door. They went to court to get a search warrant to enter.

I was back home looking into what it would take to fly to Texas when Crystal Maggelet called. She and I had met the year before, and she was very moved by my story. She'd been following the news on television and wanted to know how I was doing. Crystal is a part owner of one of the largest private companies in the state, Flying J, and she also runs several hotels, the Crystal Inns. I told her I was trying to figure how to get to Texas to see my stepchildren, and Crystal immediately said her husband, Chuck, would fly us on his private plane. We'd leave the next day, Sunday, and land on a rural landing strip a mile outside of Eldorado. I brought my daughters LuAnne and Merrilee with me. LuAnne was especially eager to see her half-siblings and wanted to reassure them about life outside the FLDS.

My older children, Arthur, 20, LuAnne, 17, Patrick, 15, and Andrew, 13, were pleased that their half-siblings might get some protection but also concerned about how they'd react to being suddenly removed from the only life they'd ever known. By contrast, my two youngest—Bryson, 6, and Merrilee, 10—were mostly oblivious to what was happening because they had so little memory of their past. Merrilee was far more interested in her current friends than in anyone from the FLDS. When Bryson, my baby, once saw pictures of several FLDS girls on TV, he said they looked like "a whole bunch of Bettys." (Betty continued to wear FLDS clothing after we escaped, except when she ran track in high school.)

My boyfriend, Brian, was completely supportive. He spent as much time as he could at my house in case I had to travel or do interviews. The raid was as much of a shock for him as it was for me. We had been together for almost four years, and Brian knew, from seeing how damaged my children had been, what the reality of FLDS life was. He was furious about the emotional and physical neglect that so many kids endured and especially hated the fact that these children had been pulled out of public school and were being brainwashed in FLDS via homeschooling.

Brian's dad had been career military, and Brian couldn't fathom why the same basic human rights that his father had fought for overseas were being denied to children here at home. Brian could never understand why the government was not upholding its moral obligation to protect children from abuse. He got so outraged about some of the things I told him that happened to women and children in the FLDS that I would have to give him the information in small doses. But Brian also understood that sometimes our justice system fails. He tried to prepare me for the worst in case that happened this time.

The flight was a thrill for the three of us. Merrilee and LuAnne had fun teasing Chuck while he was piloting the plane. Kathy Mankin was waiting for us when we landed. We piled into her car, which was loaded in the back with dishes from feeding the media who had descended on the town and were hanging out at her newspaper's office. Satellite trucks were lined up for blocks. Most of the media were camped out as close to the children as they could get, but many were leaving at about the time I got to town because the state had just moved the children from Eldorado to Fort Concho, a restored historic fort.

Almost immediately I touched base with Shannon, who was on the scene in Eldorado, talking to authorities and trying to help any way she could. "Things are pretty intense," she said. "I need to talk to Sheriff Doran before you come over. Stay where you are until I call back." When she called back, she said there was no way I could bring LuAnne and Merrilee into the investigation area. She said I would be allowed through the gates only if she met me. Kathy drove me over.

One of the CPS workers met me outside the Schleicher County

Civic Center, where the investigation was taking place. I asked her about seeing my eight stepchildren, whom I believed had been taken into custody. She said the investigation made that impossible at the moment. But she also said that CPS needed my help in understanding the FLDS. I followed her into a large metal building overflowing with law enforcement and CPS workers. I was asked to sit at the end of a long table. She disappeared.

The place felt like a command center in a war zone. The FLDS had always been a law unto itself, and when Texas seized the children from the ranch, it was tantamount to a declaration of war. The FLDS is one of the largest closed polygamous groups in the United States, with tentacles throughout the western United States and into Canada and Mexico. Its members don't see themselves as being subject to the laws of their country. They had no qualms about taking on the nation's second-largest state. I knew all this but doubted that the people working the crime scene did.

I was starting to feel numb, but even so I could not entirely block out the intense emotions that penetrated the atmosphere. An officer approached me and asked me to follow him to a room in the rear of the civic center. He introduced me to Brooks Long, the Texas Ranger in charge of the raid.

Long was a tall and rugged-looking man who apologized for his appearance, saying he'd been working around the clock since the raid began almost four days earlier. He'd been told I had relatives in custody and wanted to know if I'd be willing to answer a few questions. Without elaborating, he told me that because of what they'd found when they initially broke into the temple, they now needed to go back to the judge for another warrant to search a room they'd been unable to get into with the first warrant.

Long asked me about my relationship to those living at the YFZ Ranch. I explained that I had been married to Merril Jessop for seventeen years and had eight children with him. Long was stunned. "I am talking about Fredrick Merril Jessop, the man in charge of the ranch," he said. "Is he the man you are claiming you were married to?"

"Yes, he was my husband. I was married to him, along with six other wives."

"When did you leave him?"

"I didn't. I escaped with all of my children nearly five years ago."

"How did you get away?"

"It's a long story. Mark Shurtleff, the attorney general of the state of Utah, got involved and helped me eventually get custody of my children."

Long was calm but intensely focused. "If you were married to Merril, there are some things I need to know from you. Were you ever involved in a setting where you had an intimate relationship with other people watching?"

It was my turn to be shocked. I told him I'd never heard of anything like that ever happening when I was in the FLDS.

The questioning continued, and I could tell they'd found something in the temple that had set off alarms. Long asked me several questions about the reason I was married to Merril. Then he said, "You know, when you get a search warrant to look for pot, and find crack cocaine, methamphetamines, and other illegal things you didn't have the warrant to search for, it's still all evidence of a crime, even if that wasn't what you went in looking for."

Long stopped for a few seconds and then shook his head. "How can I help these poor people? How can I get them to tell me the truth so I can protect them?"

"This is why I came down here," I said. "I've been begging CPS to let me see my stepchildren in custody. I brought my two daughters along so they could see their half-siblings. They haven't seen one another for years. When I first left the FLDS, it was very difficult for my children. But now they've adapted to a better life and emerged from the trauma of their past. If my stepchildren could see how happy my daughters are now, maybe this wouldn't be so difficult and scary for them."

"You've asked to see your stepchildren and were told no?" Long was incredulous.

"They are telling me there is no way I will be allowed to see them. Eight are in custody, and I can give CPS the names, ages, and descriptions."

Long was adamant. "You can see your stepchildren. I'll make that happen."

He left and came back with another man. We sat down, and I gave him the names of my eight stepchildren and their mothers. He wrote down the information and then left to talk to some people. He came back and asked me more questions. Then he left again to talk with CPS workers. It was starting to feel like an endless cycle.

Finally it looked like the reunion might happen. I was told that as soon as my stepchildren were located, I'd be able to see them. I said I wanted to make sure my daughters were with me when the children were found, so I called Kathy, who said she'd drive the girls over.

I waited. And waited some more. The man I'd been talking to never returned. I don't think he had the heart to break the news to me himself.

"I understand you want to see your stepchildren, and you have every right to do so," said the woman who finally showed up to crush my hopes. "We're about reuniting families and keeping them together. But this case is under investigation, and sometimes the criminal side can overrule CPS when they feel that it's in the best interest of the criminal case. So we are not allowing anyone to see family right now. This may change, and if it does, you can come back."

"I flew here with my two daughters from Utah. My daughters haven't seen their half-siblings for several years."

"I'm sorry, but you can't see them until we're through with the investigation. That is a CPS standard."

I couldn't believe it. The last thing I wanted to do was contaminate their investigation, but none of this made any sense. I walked like a zombie to where Kathy was waiting with LuAnne and Merrilee.

"Brooks Long, who's in charge of the investigation, has the power to overrule CPS, and he did. I don't know what happened," I told Kathy and the girls. "CPS still turned everything around, and they're refusing to allow me to see the kids."

Kathy was indignant. "We can get this overturned," she said. "There's probably a judge who'll issue a court order." But it soon became apparent that overturning the CPS decision wouldn't be easy. Kathy thought if I could stay for several days there might be a chance.

I wasn't sure. From what I'd witnessed in that large building bursting with law enforcement (all of whom appeared to be as stressed as they were sleep deprived), I certainly didn't want to interfere. They seemed confused about what they were dealing with. That was no surprise to me: the FLDS has been a secretive group for decades. True, other cults in the United States are multigenerational, but they're not as dangerous and destructive as the FLDS. The newer cults are composed of people who led normal lives and then decided to join a cult. Most FLDS members, by contrast, have been born into the cult and have only superficial knowledge, if any, of the outside world. The FLDS doesn't believe in recruiting members; it's up to the women to produce children to carry on the work of God. It perpetuates its own, and this makes it a very different phenomenon for the authorities. Taking on the FLDS was like taking on a small nation-state.

I desperately wanted to see my stepchildren. But Texas was now engaged in a massive child abuse investigation involving more than four hundred children. In a gesture typical of his generous spirit, Chuck, our pilot, offered to stay if I wanted to keep the pressure on CPS. He said he didn't want me to decide to go home simply because he needed to get back.

But I had a nagging feeling that I would only be wasting my time if I stayed and fought. Knowing Merril, I would have bet money that he'd ordered everyone to be noncompliant. If so, CPS may not have known who my stepchildren were because they didn't have accurate information. Trying to find them could be impossible and would only create more stress for an already overwhelmed staff attempting to hold an explosive situation together.

It was hard for CPS to appreciate how rigidly controlled these children were. When I lived in the FLDS, if the prophet gave the word to fast and pray for a day, we did. No questions asked. We believed that God would answer the prophet's prayers only if he had an obedient and faithful people. If even one person broke the fast, that could mean that the prophet's prayers went unanswered.

The children had been drilled into a lifestyle of utter submission, too. If these kids were told that the prophet wanted them not to eat for three days, they would not touch a single morsel because that could jeopardize everyone else. God might require the group to pay an enormous price for the disobedience of one of its members, so they dared not disobey.

I later learned that the FLDS mothers weren't allowing their children to give out any information to the people trying to help them. As a result, CPS had no way of knowing many of the children's names. I don't know if they were ever able to find birth certificates for some of the younger ones. Over the course of several weeks, former FLDS members who went to Texas attempting to see relatives in custody were all turned away. Some even went to Texas governor Rick Perry's office begging to see relatives. One woman told me all she got from the governor was a hug.

Less than eight hours after we touched down, we were already on our way back home. LuAnne and Merrilee were crushed. They couldn't understand why they were prevented from seeing their half-siblings. Stories started circulating that several of the young girls they knew were pregnant and many had babies. All of my children were concerned about their half-sisters, especially one who had disappeared right after we left. She was thirteen, and we all feared she had been forced to marry Warren Jeffs. We also lost contact with Betty during this time. None of us could get her to answer her phone or return a text message. It was weeks into the raid before she contacted any of her siblings. When she did, she made it clear she had no interest in talking to me. I was upset but not surprised.

Even though our Texas trip was a disappointment, my children were excited about the possibility of seeing their half-siblings some-time soon. They hoped Texas authorities would protect the kids from their father. Maybe now that the state was involved, Merril would be unable to force his sons to work construction jobs at an early age and sell his daughters in marriage to gain influence and power. My kids wanted their half-siblings to have the chance to go to public schools and play sports just like they now did.

Their current attitudes did not spring up overnight, of course. When we first escaped, my children were badly shaken and angry at me for taking them from the life they were used to. Growing up, they had almost no exposure to the outside world, and so they had no idea what we were doing or why. But after nearly five years of freedom, they now felt they had wonderful lives. Even in the worst times, they said their new lives were far better than their old. Like me, they fervently hoped that the state of Texas would give their half-siblings the same opportunities I'd fought to give them.

And at first that's what seemed to be happening. Brooks Long got his search warrant for the temple from the judge. But this time it wasn't just Texas authorities searching the temple; it was also the Feds. Reporters said truckloads of documents and other material were hauled out of the temple.

I knew how obsessed Warren Jeffs was with documenting his behavior, especially his underage marriages. Now that volumes of information were in the custody of authorities, perhaps the crimes of the FLDS would be publicly exposed. It was my most intense hope.

By the time I got back home on Monday morning, the FLDS public relations blitz had been launched in full force. Willie Jessop was recruited to become its spokesman. I'd been a classmate of his in school. In every interview he stayed on message: the FLDS was being persecuted for its religious beliefs. Photos taken by FLDS mothers with cell phones were widely distributed to the media, showing their purported mistreatment in shelters. Before long the strategy seemed to be working: newspapers ran front-page articles that often seemed to accept the FLDS side of the issue without challenge.

One morning LuAnne came into my bedroom and picked up *The Salt Lake Tribune*. After scanning the article I'd been reading, she threw the paper on my bed and shouted, "That *bitch*!" Plastered across the paper's front page was a large photograph of my grown step-daughter Monica, 34, LuAnne's half-sister. The story said Monica had gone shopping and left her small children at home with her sister. When she returned, her children had been removed from the Eldorado compound. Monica insisted she was a good mother who'd never harmed her children and that the state had no right to remove them without evidence of abuse. A reader who knew nothing about the FLDS would be inclined to agree.

LuAnne was furious. "She can be so self-righteous about not hurting her own children, but she didn't have anything against hurting me," she said. I had no idea what she was talking about and was unprepared for what followed. "When you were at work, she spanked me real hard every single day. One day she said, 'Why aren't you crying? I spanked you real hard.' I said, 'I'm used to it; you do it all the time.'"

I was livid. I'd had no idea that Monica had been spanking LuAnne. She and I took a moment to talk about what happened. LuAnne said she never dared tell me about the abuse while we were still in the FLDS because she feared what Monica would do if she found out she'd told. I never saw marks on LuAnne, but we were required to wear long sleeves, and children bathed in private with the doors closed. So it would have been entirely possible for me not to have a clue—especially if LuAnne didn't want me to know.

Once my children felt safe, about three years after we escaped, they started telling me many stories of abuse. They opened up about spankings and having their heads smashed against other children's heads. I heard about episodes of intense hair pulling and about their being forbidden to eat meals. As incredibly hard as it was for me to hear these stories, I also felt relieved that they were able to talk about them. I was eager to help them begin to recover.

Now, as the events in Texas dragged on, every day triggered new emotions in every member of my family. Although we were hundreds of miles away, we felt like we were in the epicenter of the story because we knew so many of the players. Even as I struggled to hold my family together through the storm of events, I was besieged with questions and interview requests from the media.

I felt obligated to do as many interviews as I could. I had a unique perspective and could put things in context for people who were otherwise clueless about the FLDS. I was determined to share my hard-earned expertise to help educate the public about the cult's crimes against women and children. What made it more difficult was the state's refusal to release information to the public about criminal evidence they'd uncovered at the ranch. Yes, a legal case was being built and couldn't be compromised, but it left me feeling like a voice crying out in the wilderness. The pressure on me was relentless. I was physically and emotionally exhausted but determined to keep going because I had been married for seventeen years to the man who was at the center of this ongoing national news story. If I didn't speak out, who would?

A Voice from the Past

Perhaps the most dramatic day for me since the raid on the YFZ Ranch was Monday, April 14, 2008. That's when Judge Walther separated the mothers from their children, who'd been moved from Fort Concho and were now staying at the San Angelo Coliseum. The only mothers who could remain with their kids were those whose children were eighteen months or younger. Once separated, the children were eventually placed in sixteen group shelters and foster homes throughout Texas.

With this development, the FLDS public relations machine went into overdrive: As they boarded buses, the mothers held up signs reading "HELP US" or "OUR CHILDREN HAVE BEEN STOLEN." The news media showed wrenching images of sobbing mothers who said they'd been separated from their children.

I did newspaper, radio, and television interviews nonstop. By late in the day, I was ready to collapse from exhaustion when I got a call from a producer for Anderson Cooper's CNN show inviting me to be a guest that night. The producer was desperate because Cooper was going to interview women from the ranch and needed another viewpoint to balance the broadcast.

I agreed to do the show and headed back to the studio in Salt

Lake City where I had done live shots. I'd just done another interview and was only a few minutes away. But when I got there, the studio was locked and everyone gone. My publicist called and said they'd interview me by phone, so I did it from the car.

I knew most of the mothers on the ranch but wondered if I could tell who was speaking if I couldn't see her face. I could hear Anderson asking one of the mothers a question. I was nervous about reacting to someone I couldn't see.

But I instantly recognized Cathleen, one of my former "sister wives." I could never forget her voice. Angry feelings bubbled to the surface. Emotions coursed through every cell of my body when I heard her talk about being separated from her children. Here's an excerpt from a CNN transcript:

CATHLEEN: So, we need the public to know that an injustice has been done against us. In the land of the free, in the home of the brave, we are being treated like the Jews were when they were escorted to the German Nazi camps.

COOPER: You're saying you are being treated like people sent to concentration camps?

CATHLEEN: Yes, we have been treated that way in a country that professes to be free, in the land of the free and the home of the brave. And we have been persecuted for our religion.

COOPER: Just for accuracy's sake, do you actually know what happened to the Jews during World War II? Because it does not seem to be the same, just factually speaking.

CATHLEEN: I do. I do. I am forty-two years old. I'm very studied in history. I have a college degree.

Anderson asked her a few more questions about the raid, and then it was my turn. He was surprised to learn that I was wife number four and Cathleen was number five. I explained on-air what she did the night I fled.

CAROLYN: She's also the one who told on me when I was trying to escape. So, in the land of the free and the home of
the brave, why is it that she felt so urgent to go to Merril
in the middle of the night and tell him that I had my children up, and I was leaving? I nearly didn't make it out
because she made that phone call. And, so, she believes in
freedom. Where's my rights as a mother to take my children
and flee if I believe we are at risk?

COOPER: What do you think should happen now?

CAROLYN: I think that every case needs to be heard. I think
that it all needs to go to a court. And if there's crimes that
have been committed against children, then a judge is
going to have to rule in the best interest of protecting
a child. And this, by the way, is not about religious persecution. It never has been from the beginning. Nor is it
about polygamy.

   The officers did not go in there because they had a
call that there was polygamy going on in that compound.
They had a cry for help from a child. And they went in
to investigate that cry for help. And when they got in,
whether they found that child or not, that's why they went
in. And they did find other children that were being
abused, and that, either way, having sex with a sixteen-
year-old in the state of Texas is a felony. They found—
they found felony cases of child abuse.

Brian taped the CNN interview. When I got home, we watched it
with some of the children. Since I'd done the interview on my cell
phone, it was the first time I'd seen Cathleen since the raid. She had

aged far beyond her years; she also looked more miserable than I could ever have imagined.

The children watching TV with us didn't know I was going to be on *Anderson Cooper 360°* that night. They were focused on several of their half-siblings who were being interviewed at the ranch. (In a big about-face, in response to Judge Walther's ruling that moms be separated from their children, the FLDS let reporters and camera crews onto the compound.) When Cathleen started talking, my children were shocked because she had changed so much. Seeing their half-siblings separated from their mothers reminded them that if I hadn't gotten us out, they could have ended up in the custody of Texas. I could have been one of the moms crying on TV, like Cathleen. Hearing Cathleen and me on CNN taking opposing sides was a revelatory moment for them. They realized that the comfort of their own beds and their public school were gifts I had given them. For five years they'd been living normal lives, protected from the fate that their half-siblings were now enduring.

I had been in such shock since the raid hit that I hadn't really stopped to think about the fact that I could easily have been in Cathleen's position at this very moment. As I contemplated that awful fate, I nearly wept with pure gratitude.

When I woke Bryson and Merrilee the next morning, the fact that we were together and safe as one family seemed nothing short of a miracle. I drove them to school, kissed them goodbye, and then waited for the moment I loved—when they turned and waved to me before entering their school. I could never take such a moment for granted. I had always felt that a higher power was involved with my success in escaping the FLDS, as well as with getting custody of my children. Too many events had lined up and happened in just the right way. One misstep, and I surely would have failed. Now more than ever before, I realized that if I hadn't taken those necessary steps, a higher power couldn't have protected us. I easily could have ended up as one of the zombielike women on the YFZ Ranch.

My heart hurt for them all, but especially the children. A mother has the right to teach her children about religion. But she doesn't have a right to injure them or allow others to do so, even if she believes that the man hurting her children is a prophet of God.

A Public Relations Blitz

It turned out that some of the women seen sobbing on the news were never in the coliseum and that the state didn't have their children in custody. At least that was the view of Debra Brown, the executive director of the Children's Advocacy Center of Tom Green County. In that position, Brown is also responsible for CASA, or Court Appointed Special Advocates, which was in charge of monitoring the welfare of the children for Judge Walther. "I think those ladies were brought in to perform for the cameras," Brown told me. "The women shown on TV were not the mothers we were working with at the coliseum. We had some very upset mothers because their children had been taken, but they were not the moms being shown on TV. It was weird when that happened. We were like, 'Who the hell are those people?'"

This made perfect sense to me: the FLDS must have brought women in from Colorado City, Arizona, who were capable of doing a better job of crying on camera than the actual mothers, who were too distraught. After all, if the latter had been allowed to tell the truth about what they were feeling, they might have said things that would have caused problems for the FLDS.

CASA works on behalf of the court as its eyes and ears to determine the validity of claims made by Child Protective Services about whether children should be returned to their parents or remain in state custody. CASA was alerted to what was happening on the ranch on the evening of April 3 because of the possibility of abuse. Based in San Angelo, about forty-five miles from the ranch, this particular branch of CASA had a full-time staff of only four and soon was dealing with hundreds of women and children. Initially Judge Walther had asked if it could handle a dozen.

"We were totally in uncharted territory," said Shirley Davis, CASA's program director. "None of us really knew anything about polygamy. We'd heard some stories about Warren Jeffs when he was on the FBI list. But none of us had any idea about the number of people on the ranch." Within hours, CASA began assembling dozens of volunteers who worked practically around the clock for the next seven days, backed up by an outpouring of support from churches and other charities.

The FLDS children were different from any whom CASA had worked with before. They had no concept of fun. "When we'd ask them what they did for fun, they'd say work," recalled Paulette Schell, a CASA case manager. "Or they'd pick up rocks and dig ditches." Some of the children at Fort Concho asked for gardening tools "so they could go outside and pick weeds."

"The pregnant teenagers were really tough," added Debra Brown. "Some acted like you were ridiculous, rolling their eyes, flipping their hair as they looked you up and down."

At one point Shirley Davis got a call from a CASA worker who was supervising some FLDS girls who'd been temporarily settled in nearby Midland, Texas. "They had a group of difficult girls who wanted makeup," Davis said. "The worker told me, 'Shirley, I don't know what to do.' I said, 'I'm going to tell you. You go to Wal-Mart and fill up a basket full of makeup, and you send me the bill.' She said, 'You're going to give them makeup!' And I said, 'You bet I'm going to give them makeup!'"

Davis treasured the sweetness of some of the older teenagers she got to know. "They were hilarious," she said. "They had awesome senses of humor sometimes and could be giggly little girls until their brothers or other FLDS males walked into the room. Then it all disappeared."

Debra Brown told me at one point that she'd have much preferred to work with mothers addicted to crack cocaine than with the FLDS moms. Most addicted moms understand at some level that what they are doing is wrong and that society will not tolerate their injuring their children. They realize that they have to cooperate with the state and that if they don't, they could lose their children. In contrast, FLDS mothers truly believe not only that what they are doing is right, but that God is on their side. In their eyes, state workers are agents of the devil whom God will punish. They also believe that the state has no right to interfere with their religious beliefs, even if those beliefs violate the law.

Brown also explained that the courts ordered the children to be separated from their mothers because the mothers were actively and aggressively interfering with the investigation. The day before that decision, Judge Walther ordered all cell phones confiscated from FLDS women and children because some of them were talking to reporters and sending pictures from their cell phones, making an already chaotic situation more unmanageable.

Another problem for CPS was that mothers would remove the identification bands from their child and trade with a band from another child, so that state workers would be unable to identify the children whose DNA they had taken. The mothers also coached the children on what to say. One CPS worker I spoke to said that the mothers didn't even try to swap name bands with children of roughly the same age. Nor did they bother to hide what they were doing. They were deliberately disruptive because they thought the state had no right to do what it was doing.

All the mothers were told that if they wanted to be reunited with their children, they should go to a shelter and cooperate with the state in its investigation. If they did that, they would be given the necessary help to get their children back. Only six women went to the shelter to fight for their children. Once again I shuddered to think that I could easily have been one of those desperate women if I'd not escaped.

Stories circulated among former FLDS members that Merril had sent a message through his attorneys to those six mothers, warning that any woman who cooperated with Texas would have her children taken from her by the priesthood. This was an ongoing reality in the FLDS and a far more terrifying threat to most of the women than the state of Texas.

The public sympathy that was building for the FLDS was deeply distressing to those of us who were former members. We all knew that Warren Jeffs took children from their biological mothers and re-assigned them to other mothers. This practice went unchallenged because of the entrenched belief that everything Jeffs did was based on revelations from God. But Merril exploited the separation of the FLDS women from their children to maximum advantage since it touched a primal fear in any parent.

The airwaves were saturated with FLDS mothers claiming the state had stolen their children, which prompted public outrage. The problem was that the public was projecting its own parenting values onto the FLDS—values that had no relevance to the way the FLDS conducted family life. The FLDS works to break the bonds between a mother and child. When I was married to Merril, any of his wives could discipline another's children. My kids did not call me "Mom" until we escaped. We were "Mother Carolyn, Mother Barbara, Mother Tammy, Mother Cathleen, Mother Ruth, and Mother Foneta." We did minimal hugging and kissing of our children. Showing physical affection was seen as bestowing individual worth on a child, some-thing only a father could do.

When the media was allowed into the YFZ Ranch shortly after the raid, I was struck by the absence of toys. How could there be over four hundred children and no toys? A portrait of Warren Jeffs hung over each bed, as well as over all the desks at school, but there was nothing to suggest that children lived there. That was another big change from when I was in the FLDS. We had toys and play equipment, and the only picture of Warren Jeffs was in the living room.

The absence of a well-organized media campaign to counter the FLDS's PR blitz meant that the public didn't get a balanced view of the world inside the YFZ Ranch. Most of the information recovered during the raid was part of the criminal investigation, but it was shared with CPS. So CPS couldn't claim it didn't know what the investigators found. My fear was that the state of Texas didn't completely understand the FLDS or the games it played. I knew the FLDS would do whatever it took to turn public opinion against the state.

A FLDS website was quickly set up to solicit donations from the public based on the FLDS claim that it was being persecuted for its religious beliefs. When I clicked on it, I became seriously worried that the FLDS was going to win its media war. The public has so little awareness of how destructive polygamy can be to women and children. Merril painted himself as a martyr, when in fact he was a criminal. I knew some of the mothers who appeared on TV and was convinced they were lying. I understood that they wanted their children back, but I thought they should cooperate with the state.

Texas was also flooded with attorneys ad litem, lawyers who volunteered and then were appointed by the court to represent the interests of the children in the legal proceedings. Many of the ad litems had seen the crying mothers on TV and were extremely sympathetic toward the FLDS because they felt that Texas had overstepped its bounds. Most had no background in family law.

Not only did the state have the media to deal with, but it also had only fourteen days from the time the children were initially seized to defend its actions in court and present sufficient evidence to keep the children in custody.

The first day of the hearing in Judge Walther's courtroom in San Angelo, April 17, came with a mob of attorneys ad litem and parents representing over four hundred children. All of them were required to be in the courtroom. Every motion had to be reviewed by every attorney. It was a tedious day with endless objections. No one involved with the case had any idea of how Judge Walther might rule. Even members of CASA felt that the judge might return the children, though no one could think of a case with this level of abuse in which the judge had returned the children.

In the end, even with the endless objections and the complexities of such a mammoth case, Judge Walther ruled that there was sufficient evidence to keep the children in state custody.

This courtroom drama was followed a few weeks later by another one, this time centered on my stepson Daniel Jessop, 24, one of Merril and Barbara's sons. Danny was one of the few FLDS fathers who showed up for a custody hearing. He made a perfect poster boy for the FLDS because he was not in a plural marriage. His wife, Louisa Bradshaw Jessop, was "a disputed minor" whose newborn baby, along with her two older children, was in state custody while Texas determined whether she had been of legal age when she married Danny. It was finally established that Louisa, while a minor at the time of her marriage (she was seventeen), was older than the legal marrying age in Texas.

The FLDS argued that Texas overreached in removing all the children from the ranch during the raid simply because it found a few young girls who appeared to have been sexually assaulted. But those girls had nothing to do with Daniel's young children. If Texas was concerned with underage marriages, the FLDS attorneys argued, why take babies and toddlers away from their mothers? Needless to say, this argument resonated with a lot of people.

...I happened to know that Daniel Jessop's children ...uch at risk because he'd sexually molested my daughter ...she was four years old. I did not find this out until 2006, and I immediately reported him to the state of Arizona and got her into therapy. The state conducted a complete investigation of the evidence and awarded crime victim's assistance to pay for psychological counseling. Although investigators concluded that the molestation occurred, certain issues complicated prosecuting the crime. For one thing, Daniel Jessop was no longer in Arizona, and we didn't know where he was living. The authorities also told me it could be hard to get a conviction because my daughter was so young when the crime occurred. I didn't want to put her through a trial if there was any chance he'd be acquitted, because she'd feel victimized again. She was shocked when he turned up on television. "Mom, I saw Danny on TV," she told me. "I couldn't believe the stuff he said." She'd been taught about sexual abuse at school and knew not only that it was wrong but that the state had the right to remove a child from his or her parents if the child was being hurt in any way.

I will always regret that I had no advance knowledge that my stepson, Daniel, was going to take the stand. If I'd known, I would have insisted that the Texas attorneys question him about the investigation that Arizona had done about his molestation of my daughter. I made phone calls to Texas officials and told them about the case. But I was never able to connect with anyone who had an interest in pursuing it.

It was insane to me that the FLDS would use Danny Jessop as a poster boy after what he'd done to my daughter. But on reflection, I decided that having a child molester represent the FLDS was all too appropriate.

In Custody

With Judge Walther's ruling, the state of Texas, which already had some twelve thousand children in its foster care system, now had 439 more. Over the next six weeks foster care and other placement-related costs would soar to more than $3 million. The ultimate cost far exceeded that amount.

FLDS children brought a unique set of challenges. They needed services that the traditional system was not prepared to handle because they had grown up under the mind control of a religious cult. A lot of them exhibited out-of-control behavior. I know this because after Judge Walther's ruling, I received many calls from their guardians seeking my input and guidance, which I was happy to provide.

I knew what a treacherous and uphill battle these caretakers faced. Once people heard about my willingness to share what I knew about the FLDS and its child-rearing practices, my cell phone rang nonstop. It quickly became clear that there were things no one was talking about publicly. Caretakers were discreet in phrasing their questions because they did not want to give out confidential information. But after thirty-five years in the FLDS and seventeen as the wife of Merril Jessop, I knew the culture inside and out. It meant a lot to me to be able to transform my pain into a way to help children who'd had only the most minimal exposure to the outside world.

One of the biggest issues was that many of these kids had no respect for women. This was common in the FLDS culture but hard for outsiders to grasp. That lack of respect, combined with racial prejudice (another part of FLDS dogma), meant that many CPS workers had no authority whatsoever. The only way a woman could get some children to cooperate was by having a white male stand beside her demanding that the children be respectful. The worst scenario was when an African American woman was placed in charge. This was a surefire disaster. FLDS children are indoctrinated to believe that all people of color were put on the earth to preserve evil and will burn in hell when they die.

I've seen tapes of Warren Jeffs's racist preaching on YouTube. In one of his rants he says, "You see some classes of the human family that are black, uncouth, or rude and filthy, uncomely, disagreeable or low in their habits, wild and seemingly deprived of nearly all the blessings of the intelligence that is generally bestowed upon mankind." (Inflammatory statements like this about blacks and homosexuals led the Southern Poverty Law Center to declare the FLDS a hate group—the first time it ever gave a religious sect that designation.)

Warren Jeffs's views on race were even more extreme than those of the traditional FLDS, and he actively encouraged people to hate African Americans and other nonwhite races. I had been raised with more traditional FLDS teachings and was distraught that my children were being exposed to such incendiary racism.

Although I wasn't raised with Jeffs's radically extreme teachings, I was taught from an early age that people of color were a disgrace to God and had to come to earth with darkened skin because their spirits in the preexistence weren't deemed worthy enough to be incarnated into a white body. It was common for children in the FLDS, when I was growing up, to be taught that Abraham Lincoln was evil because he freed the slaves and called slavery and polygamy twin evils. And this was when FLDS children still attended public schools!

Warren Jeffs is still viewed by the FLDS as its prophet. In a conversation with his brother that was recorded on a jail surveillance tape on January 25, 2007, Jeffs said, "I am not the prophet. I never was the prophet, and I have been deceived by the powers of evil." The day before in a recorded telephone conversation from prison, Jeffs said that he had not held the priesthood since he was twenty and had "committed immoral acts" with a sister and daughter. Of course, many of his true believers are convinced that he was tortured in prison to make such statements. Jeffs used to preach that he would be persecuted like Jesus Christ, so many of his followers thought his arrest was a fulfillment of his prophecy.

In my conversations with the caretakers of the YFZ children, I tried to explain how racist the FLDS is so they could better understand the children's exasperating behavior. The boys in custody would be obedient if a white male was in charge, but if it was a woman, they sometimes called her names such as *slut, bitch,* or *whore*; both boys and girls were often physically violent with those caring for them. When I was married to Merril, he encouraged his children to be disrespectful of and abusive to his wives. He saw it as a way to control his family. If the children in custody believed in the name of God that it was all right to beat their mothers, then I knew how readily they would believe it was godly to beat others. So just imagine how some of these children would treat a total stranger who they were convinced was evil. Of course, these kids could also turn on the manners when they had to.

The social structure in Merril's family had always been defined by female relational aggression, or the "queen bee syndrome." I had no reason to think that anything had changed when Merril moved his family to the YFZ Ranch. Barbara, Merril's favorite wife, was the queen bee, with total and complete authority. We all had to answer to her. Sometimes the queen bee changes when the husband marries a new wife. But in Merril's family Barbara always remained the queen bee despite the six other wives he had when I was married to him.

Even though men have all the power in the patriarchal world of the FLDS, they sometimes defer to the queen bee to keep peace. And sometimes queen bees compete with their men, but it's a delicate balancing act. A queen bee must be very subtle in her manipulation of her husband. Merril could have replaced Barbara as his favorite wife or subverted her queen bee status, but he had no reason to because she controlled him so deftly. She convinced him that she was helping him maintain control and would make him feel threatened by his other wives' actions. I never knew if Merril was unaware of the crimes she was committing against his family or simply didn't care. He did enjoy the conflict that her abuse generated. Merril fed off the tension that anger created.

I knew that there was no way the children in state custody would obey a CPS or CASA worker over the commands of one of the queen bees. This was a problem that Debra Brown immediately recognized. "We really wanted the children separate from the mothers and from the older children," Brown said. "There's a real pecking order there."

"When you tried to talk to one, you were immediately surrounded, and there was a spokesman," added Brown's colleague, Shirley Davis.

Another issue faced by those dealing with the children was that queen bees could not be removed, and a similar hierarchy operated among daughters in a large FLDS family. If, for example, one of the queen bee daughters moved or was married off, a middle bee would emerge and take control. In FLDS families, the middle bees are the eyes and ears on the ground for the queen bee. The middle bees can also be other wives who act as supplicants to keep the queen bee in power in exchange for additional status.

The other daughters and mothers who are not in the queen or

middle bee position are powerless and must submit to the demands of their superiors. In Merril's family, Tammy was Barbara's faithful middle bee. Cathleen and I were her victims because we both refused to be Barbara's lackeys.

This entire system was deeply entrenched, and I knew it would give the state workers hell when they ran into it. These workers obviously had experience with families in crisis, but rarely were they part of a highly structured social system in which females aggressively controlled one another. I could tell by the number of phone calls I was getting that the CPS workers were feeling the stress. Shortly after the judge ruled that the children would not be going back to the ranch immediately, CPS organized a two-day workshop for the heads of the various departments who were working directly with the children. I was invited to participate in the workshop and flew back to Texas to provide information about the FLDS lifestyle, belief system, and social structure, and to alert the workers to areas in which the children were at risk of trauma.

The mood at the workshop was a mixture of concern and tension. Those responsible for the more than four hundred children clearly took their work very seriously. Other cult experts attended, and we sat around a table and took turns talking and asking questions. There were also psychologists, doctors, and attorneys.

CPS officials made it clear that while they were seeking answers for the FLDS children, they could not shortchange the other twelve thousand children in their custody. I wasn't sure that anyone at the workshop truly understood that this was not just an added burden—it was an epic moment. For one of the first times in history, children from this closed religious community had been given the protections—guaranteed by the Constitution—that are the birthright of every American.

I feared Texas might walk away from this problem if it became too complicated. Rarely does anyone tackle the FLDS and win. I am the only woman I know who made it out with all her children and won full custody. The FLDS is as rich as it is ruthless, and it is hard to stand up to their well-funded and withering assaults.

What made me optimistic during the workshop was the genuine interest that so many CASA workers had in preventing these children from further injury and trauma. It was obvious to me that they chose to do this work because in their heart of hearts they believed that even children born into a closed religious community had the right to be protected.

The state workers who were allowed to give media interviews were unable to provide the public with information about what they had witnessed while working with the FLDS. I spoke freely about the abuse that had occurred to my children before I left. The FLDS was pouring everything it had into its public relations campaign to convince the public that its members were being persecuted for their religious beliefs. (Its spokespeople never mentioned that polygamy is a felony; they framed it as a religious and lifestyle choice.) Their strategy seemed to be that FLDS members' rights as Americans were being violated—they were the victims, not the children. If they could win that point in the court of public opinion, they felt confident they'd get the children back.

One of the television interviews I saw during this time was with my stepdaughter Monica. She became Warren Jeffs's fifth wife in her twenties. I attended her wedding. Another of my stepdaughters, Monica's sister Millie, was married to Warren Jeffs at seventeen.

In the interview Monica was asked if she thought it was all right for young girls to be involved in underage polygamous marriages. She became defiant. "We don't do that in our religion," Monica said. She showed no remorse about lying in public. She actually not only knew of her husband's underage brides but went to the weddings and gave them her full support.

As I watched interview after interview, I was struck by how

accelerated the level of FLDS mind control had become since 2003, when I fled. Many of the FLDS mothers who were paraded before the camera were my stepdaughters. I immediately noticed that they spoke in a monotone, deliberately mimicking the voice of the prophet, Warren Jeffs.

Members of the FLDS believe their prophet is the closest man on earth to God. If you want to become like God, you must first become like his prophet. The FLDS members had taken that belief to an entirely new level—they were now speaking with the tone of voice and using the same facial expressions as their leader. It was like watching a roomful of Warren Jeffses with female faces. Five years earlier my stepdaughters had all spoken like themselves. I wondered what, if anything, was left of their former selves.

My children had an equally difficult time watching their half-siblings on TV. "It felt like they had all vanished from my life" was how LuAnne described it. Although she expressed relief that they were still alive and seemed reasonably well, she bristled when they talked on camera about how "blessed" they were because of their religion. "I think I'm the one who is blessed because I had a mother who protected me from abuse they think is normal," LuAnne said. "I remember feeling the very way they feel, but it was only because I never had a chance to feel any other way. It tears me apart to hear them when they don't know what it's like to be free."

LuAnne had been working as a bagger for an Albertsons supermarket for more than a year before the raid; now, with all the media coverage, she started getting more questions about polygamy from co-workers. Stories of her father's family were spread all over the country. LuAnne was determined to continue with her life and made every effort to keep her composure and maintain some form of normalcy. But she understood why there was so much curiosity about the FLDS. She worked really hard to take everything in stride and always be responsive to people's questions.

One day one of LuAnne's fellow baggers asked, "When you were living in the FLDS, did you ever see your moms get into catfights?"

"Yes, I watched them fight all the time," she responded. "Sometimes it was more interesting than others. But since my mom moved us to Salt Lake and my dad moved his entire family to Texas, they're in different states now. So if I want to see my moms have a catfight, I just turn on the TV and watch it on CNN." (LuAnne was thinking of the back-and-forth that Cathleen and I had on *Anderson Cooper*.)

The media seemed particularly obsessed with the pioneer clothing that FLDS women wore. I was often asked why they dressed that way. With their long dresses, long underwear, and hair piled high on their heads, FLDS women look like they are racing headlong into the nineteenth century.

It looks bizarre to me now, but I wore clothing like that for thirty-five years. Thankfully, though, when I was growing up I did not have to wear long underwear, which a lot of us hated. It was hot and uncomfortable and made us look like big blobs. It did not become mandatory until I was in my thirties, courtesy of an edict that came from the prophet Rulon Jeffs, Warren's father. Then when Warren took over in 2002, after his father died, things got even worse. Even children had to wear long underwear as soon as they were potty-trained. Warren Jeffs also banned red, bright purple, and any fluorescent color. (When he was captured by a Nevada state trooper in 2006, the Cadillac Escalade he was driving was red—yet another example of his complete and utter hypocrisy.)

We were told that wearing long underwear was preparation for the sacred underwear we might one day wear as temple garments. The FLDS considers these garments to be the ultimate in holy attire. For any ceremony or endowment that takes place in the temple, special garments are worn. In fact, whenever a change of any kind was presented to us, the explanation was always religious. We were always told that we were being rewarded for being righteous and faithful and had proven ourselves worthy of living a higher form of God's law.

The FLDS clothing sets women apart while also desexualizing them, by flattening their chests and hiding their natural shape. Whenever the dress code became more restrictive, Warren Jeffs always said that it was a sign that "God loves you so much he wants you to be more like him." So FLDS women, who had so few rights to begin with, had even more of their individuality stripped away. The clothing we wore was like a fence drawn around us to make us off limits.

With so much media interest in the clothing, the FLDS decided to cash in. Its "Captive FLDS Children" website soon had a display of prairie-style clothing for sale.

From Bad to Worse

I was sickened, but not surprised, when the news broke on April 30, 2008, that forty-one of the boys removed from the YFZ Ranch showed signs of having had broken bones. Some of them were "very young," according to child protection officials. Debra Brown said CASA requested body scans to determine exactly how many of the children had ever had broken bones, but none were ever done.

Physical abuse was not uncommon in Merril's family during the years I was married to him. I'd seen boys hit with large boards and kicked hard enough to cause fractures. One boy was kicked so violently, he flew across the room. But it wasn't just abuse; there was medical neglect as well. One night when my son Patrick was six, he fell off a bunk bed. Merril refused to let me take him to the doctor. I was sure his arm was broken; Merril, who had never gone beyond the eighth grade, insisted it was not. Pat was in agony. I sat up with him all night and gave him pain medication. As a mother in the FLDS, I did not have the freedom to take my child to the doctor without my husband's permission! I waited for three days until Merril went out of town to take Pat to the clinic. By then Pat was unable to use his arm. As it turned out, it was broken and needed to be set.

Rod Parker, the attorney who has been representing the FLDS since 1990, tried to dismiss the reports about broken bones by saying that if they were true, then the boys would have been taken to hospitals for treatment. Sadly, it rarely happened that way.

Boys are also abused by being forced to quit school and work construction jobs from an early age. They have no choice. Merril's son Johnson, who was living at the compound at the time of the raid, had told my children a few months earlier that he'd been in a severe accident while working construction and almost had to have his leg amputated. (It got trapped under scaffolding.) Men in the FLDS use their sons as slave labor to make money off them in their construction businesses. The boys work from sunrise to sunset. My oldest son, Arthur, was forced to quit school at twelve. He would go to work at 5:00 a.m. and come back at dark. Twelve- to sixteen-hour days were not unusual. By the time we escaped six years ago, Arthur had been out of school for three years and resisted returning. On two early occasions he had to be taken to school in handcuffs. Now he's about to start his junior year in college.

Along with the report about the broken bones, Texas officials released a photo of a young girl of about twelve being kissed on the mouth by Warren Jeffs. The face was blurred to protect her identity, but I knew who she was. It was my stepdaughter, the girl with the bright red hair whom I thought I'd seen on a bus leaving the compound.

I first saw the photo during an interview with Nancy Grace, who had a show on CNN at the time. When Nancy asked for my comments, I was not only shocked but felt sick to my stomach. Some questioned whether the picture was real; maybe she had just been posing with the prophet. But anyone in the FLDS knows that a man never kisses any female unless she belongs to him in marriage. Such behavior is completely taboo.

My children reacted violently to the photo. Whatever loyalty to their father that any of them had left ended once and for all. My daughter LuAnne was hit especially hard. She loved her half-sister, and it was devastating for her to think that she had been so badly injured by being married to Warren Jeffs when she was twelve. I could see from LuAnne's face how stricken she was. She now knew at a cellular level that what I had been telling her for almost six years was true. After realizing the condition her half-siblings were in, her entire attitude toward school changed, and she decided to become an attorney. I think she started feeling responsible for the loved ones from whom she had been separated. Her search for a way to keep others from being injured like her half-sister had begun.

It was depressing to realize how much worse things had gotten since we escaped. I was distraught that I had no legal way to protect my stepchildren. Even the knowledge that I'd been able to protect my own did nothing to ease my despair that a little girl I cared about had been injured.

At times I felt overwhelmed by everything that was happening in Texas. But Brian, as always, came through for me in every way. This was the first time in my life when I could rely on a man for emotional strength, support, and protection.

I had major concerns about the FLDS children in state care. Clearly they had been injured by abuse and not just by mind control. Sexual abuse does long-term damage to a child's brain. More than four hundred children were also at risk of ending up in the foster care system indefinitely. Texas usually had only one year to reunite each of the children with their parents. If the reunification was unsuccessful, the state would have custody of the children until they turned eighteen.

I did interviews almost every day during the crisis. Brian helped me process the developments of each day. Despite the demands of his own corporate job, he listened and gave me input on what I might be able to do next. Not only had he fallen in love with a woman with eight children, he also had to grapple with the impact of the FLDS in our lives. The events unfolding in Texas were making Brian even more outraged—as an American, as a father, and as a deeply moral man.

Among the Missing

What was also terribly upsetting for me during these frantic weeks was that I had lost contact with Betty once again. I had no way of knowing where she was, since apparently she was no longer living and working as a housekeeper for her half-brothers. I felt ill at the thought that she might have been taken to the YFZ Ranch.

Betty was more valuable than ever to the FLDS now. Not only was she Merril's most prized daughter, but she was also my child and could be used against me. I was doing a lot of media interviews, and *Escape* was also educating the public about the cult's mind control. I was a problem for the FLDS, and now my daughter was being pulled into the middle of it.

Along with the moment-by-moment blows during the crisis, I was dealing with constant phone calls. I had been to Texas several times, and I was working with the state on issues concerning the children. CPS workers committed to helping the children called often. But as the crisis wore on, I also heard from people seeking missing family members. Sometimes the questions were about specific children they hoped might be in state custody. Often they were about a sister with children who had disappeared. Did I have any way of knowing if she had been on the Texas compound during the raid? The state was, of course, looking for relatives to place the children with if the parents were ultimately deemed unfit. Within a month, non-FLDS relatives were mobilizing to get FLDS children back to Utah and Arizona from Texas.

Who were these people? Some were part of an extended network of people who were former FLDS but had relatives in custody. Many of these extended family members wanted to offer their hearts and their homes. Many were willing to offer a place not only for children but also for their mothers. There were substantial obstacles to making such offers a reality, but the goodwill of those who wanted to help protect the children was as genuine as it was deep. Many people who had left the group understood how severe conditions were after Warren Jeffs assumed power. I heard about many, many offers from people who wanted to bring the children into their homes and help with counseling and any other support that was needed.

My conversations with CPS in Texas confirmed that the situation for the FLDS children was looking up. The state was extremely interested in placing them in long-term care with a relative, even if the relatives were out of state, as was the case for most of the Texas children. One of the greatest advantages that a former FLDS relative could provide for a child was an understanding of the belief system into which he or she had been indoctrinated. Most former FLDS had also experienced the abusive nature of the FLDS lifestyle, so they understood on a personal level the devastation it can do to an individual. Some of the offers were coming from individuals who wanted to take in younger siblings or half-siblings to raise.

The most heartbreaking calls were from former FLDS members who were desperately searching for a missing family member. These were people who had vanished during Warren Jeffs's reign of terror. Missing. Gone. Disappeared. It began happening in Colorado City, Arizona, and Hildale, Utah, shortly after Jeffs took over. We suspected the missing were being sent to FLDS compounds in the West or in

Canada. But no one knew for sure. It was terrible enough when a family went missing, but the anguish was compounded when no one knew where they went.

Often a family was moved during the night. Their neighbors would wake up the next morning and see a new family moving in next door. No one was told where the other family had gone—only that the family had been reassigned to live somewhere else because they'd been blessed by the prophet with a mission. Families were usually not allowed to take anything with them. The instructions were to leave their possessions behind for the family that would take their place. People knew not to ask questions in the FLDS.

Sometimes entire families disappeared, but often it would be just one family member. Parents would not know where a child had gone, only that he or she had been called by the prophet and sent on a mission. The older kids were often used as labor, which we'd find out about only after they returned.

The upsurge in these disappearances happened after I fled the FLDS. I learned about it from friends who stayed behind but also because I was serving on the United Effort Plan (UEP) trust, which had been taken over by the state of Utah in 2005. No one in the FLDS owned their own homes. All were held jointly by the trust. When the court ordered them seized, the state then controlled these homes. An advisory board was established to oversee the trust and to suggest how its assets would be utilized. (I was one of six people chosen out of thirty who applied.) So we were aware when houses were suddenly evacuated. The FLDS would try to move a family in immediately, but that wasn't always possible. At one point twelve homes were empty, and no one knew what had happened to those families.

Warren Jeffs would sometimes evict a man from the community and give his family to another man. Other stories circulated that Jeffs would kick out a woman, take her children, even nursing babies, and give them to "a more worthy mother." It's indicative of his absolute power that there wasn't a revolt. Children were sometimes severed from both parents. This was happening before I left the FLDS, but at first it was mostly the men who were kicked out. Warren Jeffs commanded my former sister wife Cathleen's father, Nephi, to leave his family. Nephi's third wife was then married to Merril; that meant Cathleen and Grace, her stepmother, were sharing the same man. Grace got into trouble with Merril, so he took her children from her and moved them to Texas. She was told to remain in Colorado City and repent.

Many of the wrenching phone calls I received confirmed the stories that had been leaking out of the community over the previous several years. People were indeed missing, and their distraught family members had been unable to communicate with them. The sixty-four-million-dollar question for a family member was, which compound has my missing loved one been taken to? The hope for such families was that if their children had been taken to the YFZ Ranch, they'd now be in state care.

One of the calls I received during this time still haunts me. When I said "Hello," I heard a young girl on the other end. Her voice seemed to tremble as she stumbled over her words. "I didn't think you would answer the phone. I thought I would only get an answering machine."

I laughed. "You're in luck that you didn't get my voicemail," I said. "My phone has been ringing off the hook, and I have to call most people back." She didn't respond to my lightheartedness.

"I heard you've been in Texas working with the authorities." She paused for a long time. Then she asked, "Have you seen my mother?" The question was phrased one word at a time between sobs. "She got me to my uncle's before she disappeared." The girl's sobbing was becoming uncontrollable. "Oh, I didn't realize this was going to be so hard," she said. Words could not make it past her tears.

I tried to make her feel safe. "It's all right, honey," I reassured her.

"Crying is just fine. I can listen as long as you need. But I need to know who your mother is."

She regained enough composure to say, "I will call you back later. I can't talk right now. It's too hard."

I knew it was important to keep her on the phone. In my experience, these callers rarely called back. I didn't know who this girl was. All I knew was how terribly upset she was and that I'd be powerless to help her if she hung up.

"Being upset is all right, and time is not an issue for me," I said. "I want to help you find your mother."

Her voice was carried by waves of sobs. "I have to go. I can't talk about this."

The line went dead. I threw my cell phone across the bed. This was the most distressing call yet. If she had only told me her mother's name, I might have had a chance of finding her. I might have been able to refer her to someone in CPS who could have helped locate her siblings. Her number did not show up on my cell phone, so I could not track her.

Losing that call reinforced how powerless I felt. Hearing about the abuse of my stepchildren and the trauma that this young girl was facing because her mother had been stolen from her was almost too much. How could such things happen?

She never called back. It would be an entire year before I got an e-mail from a source. The girl did find her mother, who was finally reunited with most of her children and is now out of the FLDS. All the public saw and heard were the faces and the emotional appeals from crying FLDS mothers who were given due process as granted by the Constitution. The invisible mothers, the ones who disappeared and had their rights to their own children savaged by Warren Jeffs, are not only still invisible but also still silent. The law failed to protect these women, who had no ability to protect themselves. Had the media been able to tell this story, I wonder if it might have kept public opinion from swinging wildly to the side of the FLDS.

As it turned out, some of the children in state custody were found to have none of their actual biological parents living at the ranch. CASA told me that a surprising number of mothers showed up after the children were in custody admitting they had not been on the ranch at the time of the raid. They all had different explanations. The lifestyle on the ranch was so restrictive—women were not free to come and go—that it's plausible that once women were separated from their children, they had a hard time getting them back.

While CPS and CASA workers were dealing with the disturbing realities of what had been discovered on the YFZ Ranch, the media reports were becoming increasingly sympathetic toward the FLDS mothers. The weeping and distraught women in their quaint clothes invited the public to imagine their own worst fears of being separated from their children. Religious freedom—fundamental to American identity—is a powerful argument. But few viewers could appreciate that the media were showing just the tip of an iceberg. Beneath the slick FLDS spokesman and the zombie women in their *Little House on the Prairie* dresses was a sadistic and cruel world that perpetuated abuse against women and children.

Public opinion was turning not only against the state but against the state workers as well. CPS staffers who'd worked extremely long shifts, slept on cots, and endured abuse from the most aggressive children in the FLDS were now being called "Nazis" by some. The photos of a twelve-year-old girl passionately kissing Warren Jeffs, a man of fifty who was on the FBI's Ten Most Wanted list when the photograph was taken, seemed to have minimal impact on the wave of pro-FLDS feeling that was building in the public.

The state was starting to think about what the next level of care for the children would require. Until it could determine if parental reunification was possible, the children needed to be moved from temporary foster care to longer-term facilities.

I was feeling cautiously optimistic when, on May 22, 2008, a bomb-shell blew everything apart. The Third Court of Appeals in Austin ruled that Texas had acted improperly in seizing the children because the raid was too broad. The lower court ruling was overturned. This meant the children were going back.

It was unbelievable to me that the children would be returned to their abusers. Was it about money? I knew the raid and its aftermath were costing the state millions of dollars. Now that public opinion was swinging in favor of the FLDS, was Texas looking for a way out of the mess?

The news made me weak. The hope that had been quietly building in me was shattered. I expressed my dismay in every media interview I did after the ruling came down. But I was in an awkward position; so few women ever escape, and almost none with all their children, that I sounded like a lone voice in the wilderness. "If it's really as bad as Carolyn Jessop keeps saying, why don't more flee?" went the senti-ment. Negative stories about me were circulating on the Internet. Some of the statements were so outrageous and made such little sense that I stopped reading them. Did anyone really believe that Texas would take more than four hundred children into custody so I could make money on a book?

The state fought back by challenging the appellate court decision and blocking the orders, issued only hours before, to give the children back to their parents. All state workers were told that if any FLDS parents came to the shelters and wanted to pick up their children, they were not to release any of them until the Texas Supreme Court made its ruling.

My spirits were buoyed, at least for the time being. State workers kept seeking my advice. One who approached me had been working with my stepdaughter Millie and her children. Millie had been married to Warren Jeffs at seventeen. This worker kept shaking her head and saying over and over to me, "They can't let these children go back to that abuse. This can't be happening. We have to do something to stop this. These children have to be protected." She did not go into detail, but it was clear from her distress that she had seen and heard terrible things.

An enormous outpouring of emotion came from those who had witnessed the mind control to which the children were subjected and had heard the children's abuse stories. Those who talked about it with me had horror written on every inch of their face.

What upset me most was that the children who'd told their care-takers the truth about their lives might now be handed back to their abusers. They had opened up because they thought they were going to be protected. Now they ran the risk of terrible reprisals if what they'd said got reported back to the FLDS elders. Never again would they trust anyone non-FLDS who offered them protection. They would forever view those people as evil, interested only in tricking and be-traying them. And that concept would be reinforced by the punishment they'd likely receive for speaking out.

I was often asked by the media what I feared most. I always said my worst fear was that the children might not be given the complete protection they deserved and would be sent back to their perpetrators. Now that fear seemed to be coming true. The only hope was that the Supreme Court would overrule the appellate court and that the state would continue protecting the hundreds of children in its care. I could neither believe—nor accept—that the state of Texas would shove these children into the same dark corner where it found them. Didn't these young citizens deserve the same protections guaranteed to every other child in America? Could their parents' bizarre cult be-liefs, hidden behind the magic word *religion*, supersede the rights guaranteed by the U.S. Constitution? I was thirty-five years old before I ever breathed as a free citizen. How could the abuse of yet another generation be perpetuated when Texas had the power to stop a lot of it right now?

Once you've taken on a highly controlled group, backing down only makes the group stronger. If the FLDS won this war, it would feel empowered to take its crimes to another level. Not only that, but other closed polygamous groups closely monitored what was happening in the FLDS, because it was the largest such group. If this ruling held, they too might up the ante in their behaviors and practices.

If, on the other hand, Texas protected the children in its custody, it would send a message to FLDS members everywhere, as well as members of similar groups, that they could lose their children if they abused them. People would think twice before allowing the leadership of their organizations to injure their children. Texas, I felt, now had a moral obligation to follow through on its actions and protect the more than four hundred children in its care.

A lot of memories came rushing back to me. Until I won full custody of my own children, I had felt like the legal system was set up to protect the perpetrators. As I wrote in *Escape*, my children went on weekend visitations with their father in which he would force them to fast and pray for my death. I felt crushed and unsure if there was any way the system could protect women who were fleeing from abuse. Over the years, however, I had seen such positive change and progress in my own life that I was optimistic about the *potential* in our legal system.

How could a state that likes to brag "Don't Mess with Texas" back down from this confrontation? I was holding my breath for the ruling from the Texas Supreme Court.

A Spinmaster in the Spotlight

In the immediate aftermath of the raid, Willie Jessop stepped into the spotlight and stayed there. (His father was Merril's cousin.) As the unofficial public spokesman of the FLDS, Willie reveled in the limelight and came across as a strong but friendly kind of guy. There was nothing strange or creepy about him, which was good image building for the FLDS.

Willie and I grew up together. He was a classmate of mine throughout school and always more of a follower than a leader. He strayed from the community in his late teens, and we never knew if he was still in the FLDS or not. Some said he had gone to California, lived on the beach, and worked as a limo driver for a wealthy clientele. For whatever reason—maybe because he made such good money in California—the FLDS wanted Willie back. The word around the community was that Rulon Jeffs went out to California and personally encouraged Willie to come home.

Willie did return, and with the money he made he bought a backhoe and went into business with one of his uncles. Willie continued to display his knack for making money and dutifully turned over a percentage of it to the prophet as required. But Willie was not given a wife for a long time. When he was finally assigned in marriage, it was to a woman who wasn't part of the community's inner circle. I think this was difficult for him. The Willie I knew had expensive tastes and built a showcase home for himself that was the talk of the FLDS. My sense is that if he could have chosen for himself, he would have picked a flashier wife.

Many of us in the community thought Willie was something of a joke. He had worked as Warren Jeffs's bodyguard and was known as "Willie the Enforcer." I was surprised when he became the FLDS spokesman because I knew he could be a loose cannon. He might have been a quiet kid, but as an adult he had a notorious temper.

Sam Brower is a licensed private investigator in Utah who'd been hired by attorneys and others in law enforcement to probe the FLDS for the past five years. Brower shared his take on Willie in an interview with a local ABC news station in Arizona on June 6, 2008. "Willie was always the strong arm," Brower said. "He was the guy who showed up just to intimidate people." Brower added, "He's the hatchet man. His role now is to put somebody out there, [and] keep talking to the media and the public while the church leaders vanish."

Willie's job was spin, and he was as smooth as he was masterful. His logic frequently had holes, but the media rarely forced him to deal with his inconsistencies. Initially his line was that no underage marriages occurred within the FLDS, that all marriages in the FLDS were consensual. Then Willie changed his tune. He admitted that a few girls on the ranch were involved in underage marriages and that they'd given birth to babies. But he wondered why there was such an uproar since teen pregnancy was prevalent throughout the United States.

He also claimed that if any girls in the FLDS were married before they were eighteen, it was because they insisted. The FLDS, according to Willie, was being persecuted because of its religious beliefs. He kept reiterating that if the girls had been pregnant and attending a public high school, no one would have thought twice about it.

This was a gross misrepresentation of the truth. If a high school girl were sexually assaulted against her will by a man more than twice her age, her parents would press charges. Even if she claimed to consent, the man could still be charged with statutory rape in most states. Willie certainly knew that no FLDS girl could insist on being married to a man of her choosing. In the FLDS, as he knew as well as I, a girl's only "right" is to be perfectly obedient to the prophet of God.

My daughter LuAnne and I watched several of Willie's interviews. As he talked, she shook her head and told me some of the things Warren Jeffs had taught them in their morning session at the start of school every day. Jeffs emphasized that it was up to the prophet to decide whom a girl should be placed with in marriage. Girls had absolutely no right to set their hearts on a certain man. God, according to Jeffs, required all of his young ladies to get rid of their worldly traditions.

Those of us who had been in the FLDS knew Willie was deliberately misleading the public. Most of the girls seized in the raid who'd been forced to have sex had done so not with someone their own age but with men who were at least twenty years older. This was what Texas was determined to prosecute. The issue that the FLDS tried to shield from public view was that within its closed society was a highly organized conspiracy involving the sexual assault of children through underage marriages with the complete knowledge, tacit or otherwise, of their parents.

It's been alleged that Merril Jessop himself performed the marriage of his twelve-year-old daughter to the fifty-year-old prophet, Warren Jeffs. Even if Barbara, the girl's mother, hadn't taken the infamous photograph of Jeffs kissing her daughter, she most likely was present when it happened. It's a tremendous honor when your daughter marries the prophet, even if she is only twelve. Based on evidence seized in the raid, Merril would eventually be indicted on charges of performing an unlawful marriage ceremony involving a minor. He would turn himself in to authorities on November 25, 2008.

Willie Jessop claimed that it wasn't standard FLDS practice for a girl under eighteen to marry. But on June 2, 2008, he said that if the public had a problem with it, the FLDS was willing to put a stop to all underage marriages. He said the church was "clarifying its policy on marriage" and would advise families to "neither request nor consent" to the marriage of underage girls. "In the FLDS church, all marriages are consensual," he said. "The church insists on appropriate consent."

However indirectly, Willie Jessop seemed to be finally acknowledging the truth.

I was asked in several interviews for my reaction to Willie's announcement. I said I didn't believe the FLDS ever intended to stop underage marriages. I pointed out that Willie was only the spokesman, not the prophet. He had claim to no real power (even though he sought it). What he was saying was spin and propaganda. I also told the interviewers that Willie, like all the rest of us, had heard the recordings of Warren Jeffs instructing the faithful to lie whenever necessary and promising that God would protect them if they did.

As long as Jeffs was considered the FLDS prophet, no one would change his edict on underage marriage. Yes, he was in prison, but most in the FLDS still considered him their leader. He lowered the marriage age, he said, because of the increasing evil in the world, which made underage marriage necessary to preserve the FLDS.

On that point I have to agree with Jeffs, because polygamy will come to a halt only when women stop being willing to participate. If a girl is allowed to mature and make her own decisions, odds are she will choose to marry someone closer to her own age—ideally someone she has dated beforehand—and that never happens in the FLDS. To let young women control their dreams, hopes, and desires held serious risk for the FLDS. The older girls became, the more confident and independent they were about their lives. When I married Merril, most of his daughters would not marry until they were in their twenties. By the time I fled, they were being married at fourteen. A fourteen-year-old who gets pregnant right away is trapped in the FLDS because by the time she is eighteen, the odds are she will have a few kids. Her chances of getting a college education—or even finishing high school—are slim. These women become so isolated from the outside world that they really have no understanding of alternatives.

Warren Jeffs's reign was so much more oppressive than his father's that women and girls started looking for other options. The younger girls knew how much they could lose once they began sinking into the quicksand of polygamy. Jeffs understood that underage marriages were essential in maintaining his power. He needed young girls to marry and have babies to perpetuate the FLDS. Jeffs had, at one point, eighty wives, many of whom were very young. He did not want to be the only one in the FLDS committing these crimes, so he normalized the behavior.

A Terrible Reversal

On April 18, 2008, Judge Walther ordered the FLDS mothers and men living on the YFZ Ranch to provide DNA evidence, and the actual testing began three days later. More than one hundred mothers provided DNA samples so they could be matched with their children. By comparison, only a few men voluntarily gave DNA samples. Most refused to comply with the court order.

The first wave of testing indicated that nearly a hundred children did not match up with any of the DNA samples. The assumption was that this was because none of these children had a parent living with them on the ranch. But most of the children's DNA showed that they were related to each other, with cross matches in several directions. Several of the tests of the unmatched children were sent to a lab that specialized in matching a child's DNA to the mother. These results also revealed that most of the children on the ranch were closely related to one another. How could more than four hundred children be so closely related? Nearly all the people on the ranch were Merril's biological children and grandchildren, his stepchildren and their grandchildren, his siblings, *their* children and grandchildren, his sons-in-law and their families, his daughters-in-law and *their* siblings. Almost every family was linked into Merril's family in one way or another.

Nearly every man on the ranch who wasn't a son or a stepson was married to one of Merril's daughters.

The numbers say it best: CPS removed 468 people from the ranch—439 children and 29 women. But among the 468 there were only eighteen last names.

The DNA began illuminating other disturbing evidence. The children's parents in several cases had married double first cousins. In other cases, full sisters married the same man, making their children half-siblings as well as first cousins. The extensive intermarrying made it extremely difficult to sort out who the children's parents were. The situation went far beyond what is typically demanded of DNA testing and called for more specialized testing.

One consequence of all the intermarrying is that FLDS children have a higher incidence of a rare and catastrophic genetic disease, fumarase deficiency, than children anywhere else in the world. Up until 1990, only thirteen cases were known worldwide, but since then twenty have been reported in the FLDS community I fled, although none on the ranch. Fumarase children are subject to severe mental retardation, epileptic seizures, and encephalopathy.

Warren Jeffs couldn't refuse to come in for DNA testing. The Texas Rangers went to the Arizona jail where he was awaiting trial on charges of arranging two other underage marriages and collected a sample of his DNA. The results established that Jeffs had fathered a baby with a minor on the ranch.

On May 29, 2008, just as the DNA was starting to reveal more and more about the reality of life within the YFZ compound, the Texas Supreme Court issued its ruling: all the children were to be returned to their parents. As upsetting as this news was, I can't say it was entirely unexpected. My first thought was that now the crimes against the children would increase. I was furious that the state of Texas had started something it couldn't finish. If it didn't think it could ultimately protect the children from the ranch, it should have left them there.

But once a state has taken on the FLDS, it *should not* back down. Retreat only feeds the cult's arrogance and pushes its crimes to higher levels.

This was an exceedingly difficult day for all of us who'd spent months working to protect the children. But the FLDS could not declare a complete victory: CPS could still proceed on a case-by-case basis and argue whether it was safe enough for *each* child to be returned. The thorniest issue for both the appellate and the Supreme Court was the removal of *all* the children without adequate evidence that all were in danger. My own feeling, based on conversations I had with CPS staff, is that the agency was so overburdened with providing care for the 439 children in its custody that it lacked the resources to build the abuse case it needed to sway the courts. The children were never given psychological evaluations or sophisticated bone scans that would have established their emotional state or the extent of past broken bones and fractures.

The court said the departures were to begin as soon as possible. Some guidelines were set: parents and children were to be fingerprinted, and parents were to provide addresses for where the children were being taken, along with the names of everyone else who'd be living at that address. Parents and children were not to leave Texas without court approval. Parents were to give seven days' notice of any change of address. All parents were to take CPS parenting classes. CPS retained the right to visit any parent's house unannounced between 6:00 a.m. and 8:00 p.m. each day. CPS could also order psychological, medical, or psychiatric tests for parents as well as children.

All the children were returned to their parents or guardians by 2:00 p.m. on June 4, 2008. After the Supreme Court ruling, CPS had worked out an agreement stipulating that anyone who picked up a child had to be photographed with that child and fingerprinted. But some FLDS members refused to comply even with this requirement. It was a total fiasco.

State workers were despondent as they watched the children depart. There was plenty of regret and blame to go around. I got dozens of calls and e-mails from CPS workers begging me to help them do something. One e-mail I'll never forget came from a woman who had desperately wanted to protect the two young mothers and their children she'd come to know and love:

> When I heard these two mothers were leaving, I rushed up to the center and gave each one a box of pre-addressed and stamped envelopes and cards. I wrote down every way in the world to get in touch with me. I told them that my husband and I, as well as my daughter and her husband, would come get them anywhere—any time of the day or night, at any place.

> My heart was broken when the children left. The life drained right out of their little eyes when they saw their mothers (except for the very young ones). But 4 and 5 and on up knew this was it. Two children in our care (3 and 5 years old) acted out and displayed sexual abuse, and the 5 year old told me "there are naughty men on the land."

> I, my daughter, and my sister want to help. We have homes with room to house someone. My sister is a retired school teacher/principal now working in real estate. We can help these families make the transition into the real world. I have written detailed reports on what was said to me by the children about working in the "garden" or fields in severe heat and cold, the harsh schedule they kept, the lack of education, the sexual abuse, etc. . . . I don't know if it will get to the right place and make a difference.

> I simply cannot let this drop. I have grieved, lost my voice (I think from stress and tiredness), and pray continuously for these families. Please let us know how we can help. Can we help raise money . . . write certain people? Something has got to be done.

Some of the children did not seem particularly happy to see their mothers, and I understood why: FLDS children rarely get attached to their mothers. Once my children reached toddlerhood, my parenting was constantly sabotaged. Any wife in the family could discipline them. (Interference with babies was less because babies take a lot of work, and family members were glad to have anyone else do it.) I'd give my children permission to do something, and then another wife would come along and punish them for doing the very thing I had said was okay. Moreover, most of Merril's children were taught to despise and hate their mothers, so as to enforce their father's power, and many came to believe their mothers deserved any physical or verbal abuse he unleashed. Year after year of this kind of disruption will alter a relationship. My children quickly learned to submit to the person in power, and they soon figured out it wasn't me.

When I was ordered to work full time as a teacher (and turn my salary over to Merril), I had to leave my nursing babies at home. In theory, my sister wives or Merril's daughters would care for them. Invariably I'd race home at lunchtime to nurse, only to find my baby in a diaper drenched with urine. When I'd ask if he'd been fed, one of Merril's daughters would say, "No, we wanted him to be hungry when you got home." It was infuriating. I knew my babies weren't being well cared for when I was at school. But if I complained, I was accused of rebelling against Merril.

Many Americans were taken aback when they saw video clips of the FLDS mothers greeting the children from whom they'd been separated for weeks with handshakes instead of hugs. But such lack of affection is standard for the FLDS. In Merril's family, we were not allowed to kiss and hug our children. When I tried to show affection to mine, they were so ridiculed that I quit. If I hugged them in private, they'd say, "Father doesn't want you to do that" or "That's bad, Mom."

Nor could I have a birthday party for any of my children. Why? Because doing so would mean I was assigning value to my child—a privilege held only by their father. For anyone else, such an action was considered taking glory unto oneself. So daring to hold a birthday party would have been seen as one more act of rebellion against Merril, one more subversion of his power.

While the FLDS drama in Texas was playing out in the media, commentators often remarked on the healthy diets the compound children appeared to have—in marked contrast to the average American child. In my opinion, that was another distortion. True, the kids at the YFZ Ranch weren't eating Happy Meals or junk food. When I was married to Merril, we didn't eat that stuff either. But we were still hungry most of the time. The reasons were not financial; Merril had, and still has, plenty of money. Food was simply another way he exerted control, a way to make us feel powerless and submissive. We ate a high-starch diet that was mostly rice, beans, potatoes, and bread. We had vegetables from the garden in the summer, but not in the winter, and rarely much protein. I was often famished, and I know the children were, too. I once saw a child slapped so hard when he tried to get a slice of bread that he flew into a cupboard.

That kind of violence was not unusual in our home, yet I had no power to stop it. Not all of Merril's other wives were violent, but several were. When I complained, Merril would call me into his office and say, "*You* are the abuser because you are indulging your children in allowing them unhealthy behavior!" Any behavior he didn't approve of was considered abusive.

In my experience, most kids in the FLDS behave like orphans. They usually bond with a sibling of their own age for mutual protection. My eight children were all terrified of Merril and were trained to treat and fear him like a god. But they have shown me how incredibly resilient kids can be. After a lot of work and therapy, we have become a family for the first time. We hug and kiss one another and say "I love you" all the time.

My children had escaped a terrible fate, and naturally I hoped and prayed that somehow the FLDS children in Texas might also be spared. But the Supreme Court decision changed everything. Before the ruling, several of the FLDS mothers had told their children's court-appointed guardians that they would leave the FLDS in order to get their children back. These women said they would get jobs, find apartments, and even divorce their husbands if that's what it took. I know some were sincere because they had already taken steps in that direction. But now it didn't matter. They no longer had options: if they didn't return to the compound with their kids, they could risk being separated from them altogether.

Not surprisingly, hostility arose between many FLDS mothers and those who had worked so tirelessly to help them. Women who until then had been cooperating with the state turned on their attorneys and the state workers assisting them. I learned this from an attorney who was working with one of Warren Jeffs's daughters. The attorney absolutely adored this young woman and wanted to take her and her several children into her own home. But when the ruling came down, the young woman decided that since God had delivered them, she no longer needed the help of anyone in this world.

Because the court's decision gave CPS the right to monitor all the children after they returned and to make unannounced visits, Merril didn't allow all of the families to return to the YFZ Ranch. In the end, only a select few brought their children back. The rest of the mothers were required to live in outside apartments or other homes so the FLDS could keep the ranch off-limits to any child-protection authorities.

Another appalling consequence of the Supreme Court ruling was that my stepson Danny Jessop—the man who had sexually abused my daughter—was back as a media favorite. During one of his many televised interviews, my daughter started shrieking, "I hate him! He is such a liar! He's sitting there with a great big smile on his face and lying."

I'm not the only former FLDS member who feels that Texas

dropped the ball with this case because it never fully understood what it was up against. We all knew the FLDS would push back with everything it had—and that that was a lot more than the state of Texas realized. With assets of over $100 million, the FLDS has, and has always had, deep enough pockets to hire the most talented lawyers it can find.

I was deeply distraught because I knew that more than four hundred children had lost their rights. It was unfathomable to me that the largest custody case in U.S. history had simply gone up in smoke. Children who had been promised safety and protection were turned back to their perpetrators. I saw it as nothing less than a tragedy.

But through my despair I saw the shining faces of the true heroes I met during those long weeks. These were the men and women who had the courage to stand tall through a crisis: the law enforcement officers who worked extremely long hours to investigate heartbreaking crimes, and the CPS staffers who marched unflinchingly into a chaotic and extremely stressful situation day after day. I was amazed at the way the community of Eldorado rallied to collect supplies and offer support for the children. More than a hundred attorneys streamed in from across the state to volunteer their time and talents to help ensure that every child received legal protection. Professionals rallied to put systems and strategies in place so the children would not be further traumatized. CASA tackled a staggering caseload and recruited emergency volunteers to provide additional services for all the FLDS children. Various nonprofits leaped into the fray to offer whatever they could, especially in the area of temporary and long-term care. Dozens of families throughout the western United States generously volunteered to take in women and children from the FLDS.

If the only way to overcome evil is through love, these were the people who really tried, by opening their hearts, committing their talents, and refusing to back down. If only the legal system had underscored their efforts instead of undermining them.

Ms. Jessop Goes to Washington

It's not often that an attorney general tells a U.S. senator that he's full of it—especially when he's the Senate majority leader. But a few weeks after the Texas raid, Senator Harry Reid (D-Nev.), a Mormon convert, told the University of Utah's KUER radio station, "I am a cheerleader for what Texas is doing. Texas is doing what Utah and Arizona should have done years ago."

Mark Shurtleff, the Utah attorney general, who was very supportive of me when I first escaped, lashed back. "Harry Reid is full of crap" was how he put it to Salt Lake City's *Deseret News* on May 4, 2008. He continued in *The Salt Lake Tribune*: "To have him come in, without any knowledge whatsoever, and to accuse Utah of doing nothing is unacceptable. He ought to get educated before he opens his trap, frankly."

Shurtleff did concede an important point to the *Deseret News*. "It's never been that I choose to ignore a felony crime in the state," he said. "It's always been a matter of resources." Shurtleff went on to point out that the more than four hundred children Texas had in state custody were a drop in the bucket compared to the thousands of children who would flood the foster care system in Utah if he took a similar hard-line approach. "If we start prosecuting polygamy just for polygamy, where do we stop?" he told the reporter. "The state of Utah, let alone my office, does not have the resources."

I don't doubt that Utah and Arizona lack the resources to tackle the enormous problems posed by the FLDS in their states. That is why the federal government has to get involved. Both Shurtleff and Terry Goddard, the attorney general for Arizona, sent Harry Reid a four-page letter and a stack of documents defending the actions that Utah and Arizona have taken against the FLDS over recent years. The hatchet was soon buried.

Reid promised both men he would lobby for a federal task force to probe crimes linked to polygamy. Said Goddard, "All is forgiven if he will help us get active federal involvement in cases that they can investigate."

An enormous step was taken in that direction on July 24, 2008, when I raised my right hand and swore that the testimony I was about to give was the truth. Senator Harry Reid, true to his word to bring federal pressure to the crimes of polygamy, convened hearings before the Senate Judiciary Committee. I was the only woman invited to testify.

It was an enormous milestone in my life. I was speaking to senators and to history. I had never had a voice before. The only free speech in the FLDS was the freedom to parrot the words of the prophet. I didn't *dare* say what I really felt about my husband or the prophet because of my fear of retribution and retaliation. Not until a year after my escape did I realize I had rights as an American citizen that were guaranteed and protected by the U.S. Constitution.

Senator Reid's office first approached me about testifying shortly after the FLDS children were sent back to the YFZ Ranch. I was told I'd need to testify only about my knowledge of federal crimes, because the government could not get involved with issues that fell under the state jurisdiction. Reid was planning to sponsor legislation that would create federal programs to assist victims trying to leave closed polygamous communities. He also wanted a special federal task force to investigate crimes related to polygamy.

In the time leading up to my testimony, my children suddenly began getting more phone calls from their half-siblings in the FLDS. Texas, which had been holding grand jury hearings in late July, was on the verge of handing down its first indictments based on evidence seized during the raid. As head of the compound, Merril, my ex-husband, was going to be the focus of intense scrutiny.

I was working on my Senate testimony when the calls to my kids accelerated. They always started out innocuously but quickly moved into questions about me. One of LuAnne's half-brothers called from Texas. "We know your mom has been working with the state, and we know she has been in Texas during the time the children were in state custody," he said.

"The only reason Mom has been in Texas," LuAnne replied, "was because some of the state workers wanted to understand the FLDS culture."

"I hope for your mom's sake that you are telling the truth," he said.

LuAnne was sick of being interrogated and threatened. She challenged her half-brother about his little sister being married to Warren Jeffs when she was twelve.

"What's wrong with that?" he said.

"What's wrong with our little sister being married to some old guy when she's only twelve?" LuAnne asked incredulously.

The conversation abruptly ended.

As these phone calls continued, my children became more assertive in confronting their half-siblings. "If you're calling to bitch about my mom," they'd say, "then I have nothing to say to you."

What really struck all of us was that the kids' half-siblings actually thought my children would turn on me. (In truth, in the immediate aftermath of our escape, they would have.) One of my stepchildren asked LuAnne point-blank why she and her siblings were not doing what Father expected them to do. "Because Father abandoned us, never made any effort to visit us for years, and didn't even give us his telephone number," LuAnne replied.

Merril's son Johnson, who was the same age as LuAnne, said it was not their father's responsibility to maintain a relationship with them, but their responsibility to keep in contact with Merril.

I thought about putting a stop to the calls, but then I realized it was good for my children to practice standing up for themselves. They laughed whenever someone said, "Tell your mother to keep sweet." That FLDS mantra of "proper" behavior seemed silly to them now.

The Senate Judiciary Committee hearing was held on July 24, which seemed surreal since that's one of the most sacred days in the Mormon calendar. Pioneer Day commemorates that date in 1847 when Brigham Young first looked out over the Great Salt Lake Valley and told his followers that they could stop traveling—he'd found his version of the Promised Land. I'd just journeyed in the exact opposite direction, from Salt Lake City to Washington, D.C., where our nation's laws are crafted and enforced. It was also LuAnne's seventeenth birthday, which I was sorry to miss. But she shared my pride in what this moment meant for me.

Dan Fischer was also invited to testify. We discovered that we'd been on the same flight when we bumped into each other in the Washington airport. If Dan hadn't been there to help my eight children and me after we fled, if he and his wife, Leenie, had not been so steadfast in their support, I could never have made a safe transition from the tyranny of the FLDS to another life.

Right after the breakfast I was too nervous to eat, Dan and I shared a cab up to Capitol Hill. It was comforting to have him guide me to Room 226 in the Dirksen Senate Office Building. Several FLDS members were hovering outside the hearing room. One was Dan's little sister, who hadn't spoken to him in years. She was with her husband and looked vulnerable and extremely out of place. Dan reached out and gave her a hug. She told him he should know better than to participate in a hearing like the one that was about to begin.

The FLDS had tried and failed to be included in the hearings. As Senator Reid said, "If you are working on sexual exploitation of children, you don't bring in the people who are exploiting the children to testify." I think the FLDS showed up anyway to harass witnesses and try to hoard the media spotlight.

The hearing, "Crimes Associated with Polygamy: The Need for a Coordinated State and Federal Response," began with a statement by chairman Senator Sheldon Whitehouse (D-R.I.), who said, "As recent events in Texas make clear, this is an issue of particular concern in the West and Southwest and deserves this Committee's attention. Indeed, the Federal government has a great interest in addressing child abuse, sexual abuse fraud, and other federal and state crimes that have originated in polygamous communities."

The first witness was Senator Harry Reid. He said that in his earlier career as head of the Nevada Gaming Commission, he took on mob bosses in his fight to get organized crime out of the Las Vegas casinos. "The mob bosses I was up against practiced extortion, embezzlement, fraud, public corruption, obstruction of justice, and witness tampering. I faced death threats and constantly worried for the safety of my family. I am here to tell you that polygamous communities in the United States are a form of organized crime."

I could not believe I had heard those words from a practicing Mormon who was also the Senate majority leader. Mainstream Mormons are outraged by much of what happens in polygamous communities, I know, but their silence is deafening. Many are ashamed of groups like the FLDS because of their own polygamous ancestors. Or they refuse to see the problem. Senator Reid's Mormon colleague, Senator Orrin Hatch (R-Utah), once played the organ while visiting an FLDS church in Hildale, Utah, the sister town to Colorado City, where I used to live. According to *The Los Angeles Times*, local reporters asked Hatch about alleged FLDS abuse. "All I can say is I know people in Hildale who are polygamists who are very fine people," Hatch was quoted as saying. "You come and show me the evidence of children being abused there and I'll get involved . . . Bring the evidence to me."

At the hearing Senator Reid was all about the evidence. While he acknowledged that polygamous communities were not exactly the "same thing" as the organized crime syndicate that used to run Las Vegas, he said, "They engage in an ongoing pattern of serious crimes that we must not ignore." Reid talked about child abuse when underage teen and preteen girls are forced to marry older men and have children. Then he said:

> But the criminal activity that goes on in these places is far broader. Witnesses at this hearing will describe a web of criminal conduct that includes welfare fraud, tax evasion, massive corruption, and strong-arm tactics to maintain the status quo. These crimes are systematic, sophisticated, and are frequently carried out across state lines.

This was more than I'd ever dreamed I'd hear from someone with Reid's stature and prestige. He talked about introducing legislation, the Victims of Polygamy Assistance Act of 2008, that would create a task force to coordinate efforts among various agencies to deal with the "broad pattern" of criminal polygamous behavior. "These organizations routinely threaten, harass, and tamper with victims planning on testifying against them," he said, so "it is necessary to provide targeted funds so that law enforcement can protect them and, if necessary, shield their identity. These lawless organizations must be stopped."

These lawless organizations must be stopped. It was stunning. I had rarely heard the crimes of the FLDS confronted so directly—and never before by a ranking member of the Senate. The fact that Reid was himself a devout Mormon only made his remarks more astounding to me.

"In the West, we have a live-and-let-live attitude," Reid continued. "We try not to bother our neighbors, and we expect the same from them. But polygamists have taken advantage of this attitude to form a sophisticated, wealthy, and vast criminal organization that has gone largely unchecked by government agencies."

When Reid concluded, Willie Jessop made his way up the side aisle to sit closer to the front of the room. Plenty of seats were available elsewhere, but Willie made a point of walking to the front of the room, staring at me, and then intentionally going out of his way to brush past me and positioning himself in a seat directly behind me.

I didn't think the FLDS could do much more to surprise me, but I was wrong. Willie sat directly behind me so he'd be in the background of any footage. In reaction to statements he disagreed with, he sighed and groaned obnoxiously, clearly trying to intimidate me. But Willie Jessop didn't intimidate me—he made me mad. Did the FLDS see me as one of its escaped slaves? Did the FLDS think I could be undone by the loud guffaws of someone linked to my former captors?

The Senate security men were watching Willie with the laserlike intensity of Secret Service agents. One of them told me later they considered evicting him. I'm glad they didn't because he'd have played it like a martyr.

Willie hardened my resolve to fight even harder. I was no longer a bird confined to a cage to be tortured. I had found my wings and was determined to soar.

It would spell trouble for the FLDS if the federal government became actively involved in prosecuting its crimes and exposing its abusive behavior. As Attorney General Goddard made clear in his testimony, Arizona welcomed additional federal support and resources in dealing with the FLDS. He emphasized that this was *not* about religious persecution:

> The work being done by my office in Colorado City is not about religion, culture, or lifestyle. Rather, it is about protecting women and children from domestic abuse and sexual violence; combating fraud and public corruption; enforcing civil rights laws; upholding peace officer standards; and ensuring that the rule of law is applied equally and comprehensively throughout our land.

Goddard was blunt with the senators about one of the most outrageous FLDS abuses: education. A child without an education is a child without a future. Why do the Taliban destroy schools and forbid education for girls in Afghanistan? Like the Taliban, the FLDS knows that ignorance and submission depend on each other. I knew Attorney General Goddard's words were true because I was living in Colorado City in 2000 at the time of the events he described next:

> The majority of children in Colorado City–Hildale have not attended school in the Colorado City Unified School District since 2000, when approximately 1,000 children were withdrawn from the District by then FLDS leader Rulon Jeffs. Those children were subsequently enrolled in private schools run by the FLDS in Colorado City or homeschooled, but the FLDS-run private schools have remained closed since September 2006, and it appears that hundreds of children are not receiving an education.

As his testimony continued, Goddard identified the fear that keeps women trapped in the FLDS:

> Under Arizona laws, child abuse complaints cannot be prosecuted unless there is an actual victim who is willing to testify. Most

women and children in Colorado City were, and in large part still are, afraid to testify against their abuser. Child abuse in the FLDS community has included physical and sexual abuse cases and unique situations that involve underage girls forced into plural marriages with much older men. In addition, the FLDS regularly expelled teenage boys from the community to reduce competition for plural wives.

It was enormously gratifying to hear both Senator Reid and Attorney General Goddard condemn such FLDS behavior as crimes. For former FLDS members like Dan Fischer and me, their words provided enormous validation. FLDS supporters often accuse us of making false charges because, they ask, if the FLDS is so terrible, why don't more flee? I know from firsthand experience it's because the women are too traumatized and can't count on any protection if they do escape.

At the hearing I learned more details about the YFZ compound in Texas. Stephen Singular, a best-selling author and journalist who spent two years investigating the FLDS, said the Texas ranch was purchased in 2003 for $700,000 but as of 2008 had an assessed value of $20.5 million. "Where did all the funds come from for these improvements, and for other purchases of land in South Dakota and more recently in Colorado?" he asked the senators. "Has money been laundered or taxes evaded?"

Attorney General Goddard mentioned in his testimony that Texas authorities seized eighty-three computers and four hundred boxes of documents in the raid on the ranch. He added that his office was also still seeking access to four laptops, sixteen cell phones, and the records from the Cadillac Escalade that Warren Jeffs was riding in when he was arrested in Las Vegas on August 29, 2006. Goddard's point to the Judiciary Committee was that criminal information not only has to be shared between states, but that in a situation like the raid in Texas, states need additional resources to process and analyze the material they find.

Dan Fischer's testimony was spellbinding. A Utah dentist and now the CEO of Ultradent, which manufactures dental products, Dan has hard-earned moral authority when it comes to the FLDS. He was born into the cult and raised on its doctrines. As he testified, the FLDS chose his profession and his three wives. He left in 1996 and is in a monogamous marriage with his second wife.

Dan made it clear that there are good, decent, and hardworking people in the FLDS and that he appreciates the need to protect religious freedom. At the same time, he asserted, "The all-encompassing control over mind, person, family, economics and more, exercised under the guise of religion, has moved the FLDS to disturbing cult proportions. Without question, FLDS members will sacrifice self, family, and children if directed to by their leader. Their 'salvation' as taught by their prophet is dependent on them obeying totally what their prophet requests no matter what!"

Dan explained what he knew from his personal experience about tax fraud practices within the FLDS. He said Warren Jeffs (whom Dan knew well) routinely had objectionable schoolbooks destroyed. (I know this is true because my collection of three hundred children's books was seized and destroyed.) Dan said Jeffs encouraged children to spy and report on their parents, siblings, and friends. Dan talked about Jeffs's fascination with Hitler.

I was shocked to learn from Dan's testimony that in 2005 the FLDS police chief in Colorado City received a $600,000 grant for sophisticated surveillance equipment from the Department of Homeland Security. This is mind-boggling. I shudder to think what that equipment was used for, and I am outraged that tax dollars might have gone to help the FLDS improve its ability to spy on its members.

Dan also talked about the Diversity Foundation, which he created to support teenage boys who have been kicked out of the FLDS. But the emotional centerpiece of his testimony was about a problem that cut very close to home: the decimation of families by Warren Jeffs. Fischer characterized this as one of Jeffs's greatest atrocities:

> Since around 1998, about 250 married men of all ages and some with multiple wives, children, and grandchildren (even great-grandchildren) have been expelled. They are instructed to "repent from afar." The men are virtually erased from the history and existence to their families. Wives are remarried, taking their children with them. For the children, their "old father" is no longer their father. This can happen literally overnight with no warning.

"Wives will not object," Dan explained. "They have been taught by their own husband for years that obedience to the prophet must supersede even their love or devotion to him." This is related to the belief that the prophet has the power to determine if a husband is worthy enough to decide where his wife should go in the afterlife.

Dan's own family was destroyed by Warren Jeffs in 1999 when his elderly father was told that he could no longer be a parent to his thirty-six children or a husband to his three wives. The call came at 4:30 a.m. to Dan's brother, Shem, who has since left the FLDS, too. Dan read an emotional account that his brother wrote about the ordeal. In the predawn call from their mother, she said that she had been "released" from their father and that all three wives and dozens of their children were to meet at the hilltop home of the then-prophet, Rulon Jeffs. It was a total shock to everyone.

When the family assembled (minus their father), Rulon, who was in failing health, was slumped in an overstuffed armchair, drooling. An oxygen tank helped him breathe. Rulon's son Warren presided over the gathering, announcing that his father, the prophet, had prayed deeply and that God had told him that Dan and Shem's father was "not worthy" of his three wives and that time was too short to repent. Jeffs said the three wives had to be lifted up before destruction covered the North and South American continents. It was "God's will," he claimed.

Dan, who incredibly had an eight-year-old sister, Lily Ann Fischer, said she interrupted Warren Jeffs with her sobbing, imploring him to show mercy. "Is there no hope at all for my father's salvation?" she begged. "Can't he repent and get his family back?"

Dan continued to choke up as he read Shem's letter. Jeffs, the letter said, replied to Lily Ann in a calm, cold voice, "No, the time is too short—there is no hope for your father to gain the highest degree of salvation." Within five days, all three wives were assigned to three different men, breaking apart a family that had been so close that some children grew up never knowing which mother was actually their biological mother. Even when they did find out, it was a nonissue—until the family was split apart and, in the eyes of the FLDS, these kids were no longer even siblings. Shem's mother (Dan's stepmother) became the fifty-seventh wife of Prophet Rulon Jeffs, sharing him as a husband with two of her own daughters. (Such marriages are not uncommon in the FLDS: I knew a man in Colorado City who married a mother and daughter who were both pregnant with his babies at the same time. And I've heard that currently there's a man in the FLDS who is married to a mother, daughter, and grandmother simultaneously. Cult members don't blink an eye at this sort of thing because the prophet has sanctioned it.)

Dan's father, a devout and dedicated member of the FLDS for decades, was broken, and there was no putting him back together. Even though Dan had already quit the FLDS, he was deeply distressed by the fact that one man, Warren Jeffs, had the power to annihilate families on a whim. "Even I, at age fifty when my family was destroyed," Dan said, "would wake up with nightmares for over a year. I literally felt as if I'd just become an orphan." Dan lost his composure several times as he shared his story. The hearing room fell silent. Dan's anguish and the creepiness and despair of the saga he was relating were hard to hear. The senators, who were about the same age as Dan, seemed aghast.

Dan said that by his estimates one thousand children have gone through the catastrophic trauma he has had to grapple with as an adult:

> Imagine the horror and terror that must occur in their tender minds when they wake up one day to the realization that their father is no longer their father; that they will not be hugging him, talking to him, or even interacting with him ever again. And, then imagine what must be going through their young minds as they discover their mother is married within days to another man who is then kissing and making babies with her. Imagine the scarring that will continue in that young mind for a lifetime.

Dan's father was an old man when his family was shattered. As he advanced in years, he didn't drive anywhere without one of his older children accompanying him because he would sometimes fall asleep at the wheel. But after Jeffs decreed that he was no longer their father, his children cut him off and refused to speak to him or see him. Dan remained in touch, even though he had left the FLDS and he and his father were not particularly close.

One day Dan's father stopped by the house he had built and lived in for thirty years and asked one of his sons to accompany him in the car. His son refused and made it clear he no longer considered himself his father's child. That afternoon, on the road between the towns of Hurricane and St. George, Utah, Dan's father's car plunged into a deep ravine. There were no skid marks. Dan said he does not know if his father fell asleep at the wheel or if he committed suicide. But he has no doubt that in either case, Warren Jeffs is to blame for the misery of his father's last three years and the circumstances of his death.

It was a heartbreaking tale but one the senators needed to hear to fully grasp the evil that consumed the FLDS once Warren Jeffs solidified his power.

Dan's riveting testimony was a tough act to follow, but I was determined to bring my best to this once-in-a-lifetime moment. I wasn't nervous about being the last to testify; what bothered me most, I think, was knowing that what I was about to say would be the launching pad for more FLDS attacks on me personally, on my public credibility, and on my children. The FLDS members sitting in the room were monitoring my every word.

"My name is Carolyn Jessop," I said. "It is both a privilege and honor to be here today." I then spoke for almost nine minutes about my firsthand knowledge of FLDS crimes. I explained how in our FLDS community, the mayor, many city officials, the chief of police, and every police officer were all FLDS members handpicked by church leaders. "If a woman who was beaten by her husband called the police," I testified, "she was typically told by the police officer that she was married to a good man and if she were obedient, there would not be any problems. The police would not interfere with their religious teaching that gave a man the right to discipline his household." This meant, of course, that a woman seeking refuge from an abusive situation had nowhere to turn.

I told the committee members how women drove unlicensed, unregistered, and uninsured cars. This meant that the minute we left the community, we were stopped by police. I was never once stopped for this infraction while I was driving around town.

I spoke about child labor abuse and how my son Arthur, like so many other FLDS boys, was pulled out of school at twelve and forced to work, for no pay, on construction jobs from dawn to dusk. I testified:

I did not know of a safe place where I could go to report this child labor abuse . . . I feared if I went outside the community to Child Protective Services, I would be held accountable because I was his mother. I lived with the fear that my children would be taken from me. This fear was based on reality: I saw women who disobeyed the wishes of the prophet or their husband removed from their homes and their children.

I underscored Dan Fischer's testimony about educational abuse in the FLDS with my personal experience with my children. At the time we fled, they had been out of public schools for five years and were being taught in FLDS schools. When I enrolled them in regular public school, they were so far behind, we could not even establish their grade levels.

In the FLDS-run schools my children attended, listening to tapes of Warren Jeffs was part of the curriculum. Children were indoctrinated with statements like these: "If a man is instructed by the FLDS prophet to take the life of another human being he should do so in humility." Jeffs also told children that no one with a drop of Jewish blood would ever enter the kingdom of God.

I also testified about the practice of underage marriages. With Warren Jeffs in charge, the marital age dropped to fourteen. I said:

While not all men in the FLDS have plural marriages and engage in sex with underage girls, it's considered socially acceptable and religiously desirable behavior, especially under the leadership of Warren Jeffs.

After I escaped from the FLDS, Merril married a sixteen-year-old in Canada, brought her to the United States, and introduced her to my children at lunch as their new mom. Around the same time he married another sixteen-year-old in Utah and moved her into his home in Colorado City. Within months he moved them both to Texas. Legally, this is considered trafficking in minors for sexual abuse.

The dire need for housing for women fleeing polygamy was another issue I was able to tackle head-on. It took two and a half years for me to receive any housing assistance. I had too many children to qualify for low-income housing and spent a month with my family in a homeless shelter. I told the senators that at one point, according to a social worker I spoke to, a woman who was fleeing from a Communist country with her children got more help than I did fleeing from the FLDS.

In conclusion I said:

> I never knew what it meant to feel safe until I was thirty-five years old and we went into hiding on the third day of freedom after our escape. It took me a year before I could think of myself as a person and not an object.

I told the committee specifically what could be done to improve life in the FLDS. There needed to be federal oversight in closed FLDS communities so that if anyone wanted to leave, she would know how to find a safe haven. Educational abuse had to be immediately addressed. In my final remarks I told the senators:

> I stand here today to ask the U.S. government, my government, to show up for children the same as it does with respect to all other citizens, in the form of registrars, census takers, AFDC administrators, social workers, police who enforce law not religion, education administrators, tax collectors and auditors, OSHA and labor regulators, and others whose role is to enforce the law and protect American citizens.
>
> This would not be religious persecution, just equal protection and equal enforcement of the law.

The room was quiet. I exhaled, mentally and emotionally. I felt relieved.

After I finished, Senator Whitehouse (D-R.I.) thanked all three of us who made up the second panel of witnesses. He praised Stephen Singular for his persistence in investigating the crimes of the FLDS, and he thanked Dan for surviving those crimes and then going on to be a force for good in trying to help hundreds of "lost boys."

Senator Whitehouse said I was "most astonishing" because "at such a young age with so many children dependent on you and so little support behind you with a completely unknown future in front of you, nevertheless, you took the courageous step of stepping into an unknown and away from everything that you knew in pursuit of the freedom you knew you and they deserved. It's a very impressive story."

Senator Ben Cardin (D-Md.), who co-chairs a government commission on human rights, said he was shocked by my testimony. "What is happening here is as bad as anything I've seen in the world: children and families who have been denied basic human rights because of the activities of those involved in these polygamous colonies. It is difficult to understand how this can occur in the United States."

When the hearing ended, the FLDS made a mad dash for reporters in the hallway. They reiterated their claim of religious persecution and that they should have been represented at the hearing. In their view, any abuse that might have occurred within the FLDS was an isolated event.

A staffer for Senator Reid offered to take us through another door so we did not have to engage with the FLDS. Dan and I followed him to Senator Reid's office, where we had been invited to a private meeting along with the other members of our panel. Senator Reid was waiting there to greet us.

When it was my turn, I handed him a copy of *Escape*. He thanked me but said he'd read it already. I smiled and said, "But now you have a signed copy."

Senator Reid asked me a few questions and then talked about my handicapped son, Harrison. He said it takes a special person to care for a handicapped child and maybe that was why I carried such beauty in my eyes.

Senator Reid told us that nothing could really happen until after the presidential election in November. But once Congress resumed after the inauguration, the federal government would act. He again drew a comparison between the FLDS and organized crime. He felt that it was scandalous that it had been allowed to flourish for far too long.

At that point Senator Reid led us into his inner office and gave us all signed copies of his autobiography. We looked at the breathtaking view of the city from his veranda.

Dan and I headed to the airport together. He shared my optimism about the future. But we were both realists and knew how easily our hopes could be dashed. We also knew that the FLDS would strike back with a vengeance. We did not know how or when, but we didn't doubt that it would happen.

Indictments and Backlash

Our testimony in Washington was only one aspect of an extraordinary week of FLDS-related news. On July 22, 2008, the first indictments were handed down in Texas. Among those indicted was Warren Jeffs, who'd already been convicted in Utah for being an accomplice to rape and for arranging the marriage of a fourteen-year-old girl to her first cousin.

This news helped temper my ongoing distress about what had happened to the children as a result of the Supreme Court ruling. Perhaps the raid had not been in vain after all. Afterward Texas pursued the FLDS on two fronts, civil and criminal. The custody issue involving the children was a civil matter, and it ended tragically. But the criminal investigation resulted in serious charges of child sexual abuse. Based on evidence obtained in the raid, Jeffs and four other men were charged with first-degree felony child sexual assault—the charge in Texas for engaging in sex with a minor. Another man was also charged with bigamy; the last man was charged with three counts of failing to report child abuse, which is a misdemeanor. (That case ended up being transferred from state court to county court.)

My ex-husband, Merril Jessop, was charged with performing an unlawful marriage of a minor (the marriage of his own twelve-year-old daughter to Warren Jeffs). Merril will be the last of the men to stand trial late in 2010. Also named in the arrest warrants were my stepsons Raymond Merril Jessop and Leroy Jessop. The first of the men to go to trial, Raymond, was convicted in November 2009 on charges of sexually assaulting a sixteen-year-old girl in 2004. On November 10, 2009, he was sentenced to ten years in prison and fined $8,000.

The news that Warren Jeffs would stand trial again came as an enormous relief for me and others who've fled the FLDS. Our hope is that if he's out of power for several years, the FLDS will be unable to continue hurting people. In fact, these trials may well weaken the FLDS to the point where the women and children who have suffered so long may finally get a chance at normal lives.

One of the most shocking indictments to me was that of Dr. Lloyd Barlow. We had been in school together. He was a few years younger, and I remember him as smart, well mannered, and kind. He became a family practitioner. Everybody in the community loved Dr. Barlow. The indictment charged him with three misdemeanor counts of failure to report child abuse. His case will be prosecuted at the county, rather than the state level.

Since the FLDS had its own doctor, a great deal of abuse could have been hidden on the compound. If an FLDS doctor delivered babies of underage girls, set broken bones, and treated other injuries, no suspicions would be raised or questions asked. The fact that the children were rarely seen outside the compound also made it easier for the FLDS to get away with these abuses. Indeed, an aspect of the raid that was mind-boggling to local residents was the revelation that there were hundreds of children on the ranch at all. They had never been seen in town. Why? It's hard, even for me, to imagine the reason they were kept so isolated.

Dan and I were prepared for the FLDS to lash out against us after our Senate testimony, but we didn't know how fast or furious it would be. Within days of returning home, Dan was slammed in *The Salt Lake Tribune*, accused of beating his wives and abusing his children. The ugly smear tactics were submitted as affidavits to the Senate Judiciary Committee and posted online at an FLDS website and blog sites. The FLDS may have been prevented from testifying in the Senate, but it tried to discredit the hearing's star witness nonetheless.

Most of the national media did not pick up the story, but it got big play in Salt Lake City on August 1. Dan was hosting a meeting at Ultradent with about one hundred dentists attending. The timing hardly seemed coincidental. The charges against him were made by family, or former family members, all of whom were still in the FLDS. The sworn statements were made by an ex-wife, three siblings, and three of his children. Others who said they knew Fischer's family filed affidavits as well.

Most people only read *about* the charges in the affidavits. But a close reading of them raises even more questions—about the FLDS. For example, Alvin Fischer, Dan's brother, described a situation he witnessed:

> On one such instance, I watched [Dan's] young son about three years old go behind a bush and use the bathroom. Dan immediately came storming out of his house and began kicking him. He would kick him so hard the child would go up in the air four or five feet. This he repeatedly did up to eight times.

If the beating was as brutal as Alvin claims, why didn't he intervene or call the police? The child could have been killed.

Alvin also accused Dan's wife Leenie of giving Alvin's one-year-old daughter alcohol at a party to make her drunk and then laughing while she made a mess of a chocolate cake. Really? Where were her parents? Why didn't Alvin call the police? Again, the claims Alvin made to discredit Dan's credibility discredited his, too.

The worst accusation was that Dan and Jean, one of his wives, had tortured their seventeen-year-old daughter. Dan's niece, Carla Black Jessop, said in her affidavit:

> I remember the incident of Melinda being whipped for talking on the phone with a boy. The whipping went on for at least three or four hours late into the night. I was in the room across from Dan's bedroom with a couple of his other daughters. Dan and Jean were calling Melinda a whore and a slut and screaming at her. Dan also said that if she wanted [to get] F'd he could get a couple of men in there.

Dan responded to the charges in a measured way. He was quoted in the article as saying:

> We did have spankings on the bottom, we did believe in that, as did most of the FLDS and as many non-FLDS did twenty years ago. I will tell you that I would not punish the same way today. I am not a perfect person nor have I been in the past. I hope I am a better person now [but there is] nothing of the magnitude they are claiming.

I could relate to how Dan felt having his daughter accuse him of vicious abuse. My daughter Betty has attacked me since she returned to the FLDS, and it's painful. Even when you know you've done what you believe is best for them, a piece of you always wonders if you might have tried something else to prevent the estrangement.

For those of us familiar with the viciousness of the FLDS, this attack was entirely predictable. But it was still upsetting. Dan's wife, Leenie, called me, and we talked about it for more than an hour. She said that one of the worst things about the FLDS is that they not only injure people but also make sure they're never allowed to heal.

One reason the anti-Dan affidavits came from faithful FLDS

members was that when non-FLDS were approached and asked to lie about Dan, they refused. Dan's first wife, Jean, was approached by one of her brothers, who insisted that she file an affidavit against Dan. Even though her marriage with Dan was rocky and eventually ended, she was furious that she was asked to lie and refused.

In a way, it was easier for the FLDS to attack Dan than me. It's one thing to take on a millionaire businessman. It's another to attack a single mom with eight kids, one of whom is severely handicapped. Since many in my family had left the FLDS, in order to attack me, the FLDS needed my non-FLDS family members to lie about me. If I was attacked the same way Dan was, with just FLDS faithful, the public might become suspicious of that pattern.

From the time *Escape* was published in October 2007, the FLDS smeared my character. It sent out a religious edict that no faithful member should read my book because it was all lies. It characterized me as a vindictive woman who wanted to spread evil accusations. For the most part, however, the attacks seemed aimed at discrediting me within the cult. It was rare for an FLDS woman to escape with all her children, and I was the first ever to win full custody. But the fact that I was married to Merril Jessop, one of the most powerful men in the FLDS, was enormous. No wife had ever fled from such a prominent FLDS leader.

After the raid on the YFZ Ranch, *Escape* shot back onto *The New York Times* best-seller list for ten weeks and was widely circulated in Texas. Then a smear campaign against me flourished online, whose main line of attack was that I was only interested in making money.

My Senate testimony unleashed a new round of attacks that were even more intense. Some accused me of lying when I said I'd fled during the night—they declared online that they'd helped me pack and move to Salt Lake City. Others said I had never been abused and that I had made up those stories as a justification for leaving my family and faith. Betty denied that the physical abuse I wrote about in

Escape ever happened. She said that I was the only one in the family who was violent with children, and she accused me of blaming others for what I had done myself. Others accused me of selfishness for wanting children to be separated from their parents.

Others who said outrageous things had never met me but claimed they'd gone to school with me and that I had always been a liar; nothing I said could be believed. I didn't even know who these people were.

I felt like hundreds of baby piranhas were all trying to take pieces of my flesh. It was relentless, but I had no intention either of backing down or of engaging in the fray, which would only have escalated the attention around these bogus attacks. I even had calls from the Utah attorney general's office asking me about complaints. I have known Mark Shurtleff, the attorney general, well since I first escaped. He knows my credibility is impeccable. We even spoke together at the Austin, Texas, branch of the Young President's Organization, an elite business group, in March, the month before the raid.

The night I fled from the FLDS, I crossed a line. The day I took Merril to court to fight for full custody of my eight children, I was considered equal to the devil. In *Escape*, I talked about the crimes of the FLDS. Then I testified in the Senate. This makes me one of the worst apostates the FLDS has ever faced.

Shortly after the attack on Dan Fischer, my mother, Nurylon Blackmore, called me. She was born into the FLDS and left when she was fifty-five, after Warren took over because she felt he was too dangerous. Our relationship has had its ups and downs, but she stood by me when Harrison was so desperately ill, and she helped me fight to get him medical care. She was appalled by Merril's callous disregard for his son and his cruelty toward me.

My mother sounded urgent and exasperated. "Carolyn, I have to know what's going on. I'm getting calls nonstop from your sisters in the FLDS. I'm being told I have to write up an affidavit against you and publish it. Elisa was the first to call. She tried to persuade me that lying about you was not only the right thing to do but it was something that had to be done. I continually refused."

Mom continued, her frustration rising. "Then I started getting phone calls from your half-sister Shirley. She wasn't asking politely or trying to persuade. She was telling me what I was going to do and demanding that I do it. She came after me like a bulldog. Well, her approach didn't work with me either."

After what the FLDS had done to Dan, none of this surprised me, though I was relieved that my mother had stood up for me and refused to be recruited by one daughter to lie about another. Her refusal to lie was a setback for the FLDS, but there was no turning back the tide of vitriol and lies unleashed against me.

Mom said my full sister Lydia also called begging her to lie about me. Mom asked her outright why it was so important. Lydia told her if she didn't lie, Merril was going to lose all of his kids. My mom said that might not be such a bad idea. That's when the phone call ended.

Mom and I talked a little longer, and I told her what I had been involved with, and we both discussed why the FLDS was coming after me in a furor. Mom sounded exhausted. We have had a complicated relationship. But while it was hard during my childhood, she saw my marriage to Merril for what it was and supported me as much as she could. I think the FLDS wanted to take me down even more than it did Dan because I had such a compelling story. Not only was I Merril's ex-wife, but I was related by marriage to many of the women and children in the YFZ compound. I knew the FLDS for the criminal organization it was, and I had no qualms about telling what I knew after seventeen years as an eyewitness.

Several family members attacked my credibility online. The FLDS used Betty to attack me, which I find despicable. The week after the hearing, in a polygamy blog in *The Salt Lake Tribune*, Betty talked about how unhappy she had been in her life outside the FLDS. "There were a million reasons to come back and not one reason to stay," she said.

Betty was PR gold for the FLDS. A few months later I heard that she was writing her own book, although I don't know if that's actually happening. "It's time for the other side of the story to be told," she said. She accused me of trying to keep her from her faith and of seeing her as a representation of everything I hate. Not true. Betty is representative to me only of my children, whom I love more than anything else in my life.

The harassing phone calls to my children from their half-siblings escalated. Some days there were as many as twenty. My kids were hammered with questions about why I had testified in Congress and were told that everything I said was a lie. My children defended me. The older ones knew the truth because they remembered it.

The hostility intensified between my kids and their half-siblings. I knew how close they had once been and how hard this was for them. But I stayed out of it. I didn't want them to have to choose, although eventually they did. They became so disgusted by Merril's other children that they finally cut them off. Even though they knew their half-siblings were being told what to do and say, the calls made them too uncomfortable. My kids love me. We all know that the bonds we've forged as a family are closer than anything we could have experienced in the FLDS.

The FLDS wasn't having any real success in damaging my credibility on the Internet, so it began a new campaign: Why was I the only one complaining? If the environment was really as abusive as I claimed, why weren't more women speaking out? That line of attack went nowhere and proved nothing. Most of my peers in the FLDS would have had little hope of surviving in the outside world without tremendous support. Most had not been to college, and some hadn't completed high school. They knew how hard the FLDS would fight to take their children away from them—even if they managed to get out with all their kids.

Some FLDS women get shipped off to mental hospitals when they try to stand up for themselves or their children. I recently met a woman who works for the Dove Center, a domestic violence shelter in St. George, near Colorado City, where I used to live. She told me that they see young women who are diagnosed by FLDS doctors as bipolar when they are not. These women were put on powerful psychotropic medication and labeled "mentally ill" when they tried to assert some control over their lives.

Women in the FLDS all knew of situations when Warren Jeffs had taken children from one mother and given them to other wives. For us, losing our children was a real and terrifying fear. When women were separated from their children, often no one knew where the children were sent. Sometimes these mothers were under the watchful eyes of "spies" who would report back to Jeffs on what they were doing while they were "repenting." When Jeffs severed a man or woman from their children or spouse, it was supposedly because the person had sinned. His or her task was to go and repent. Jeffs would ask the person to write out his or her sins to see if they matched what Jeffs knew already.

There were so many reasons why it was terrifying to take on the FLDS. I had a strong sense of myself and had spent several years preparing to flee. But even with all of that, I almost didn't make it. Without Dan's help, I'd have ultimately failed. He got us into hiding when we first fled and a posse of men was hunting us down.

A Face-off with a Former Enemy

Testifying in Congress was one thing, but testifying against one of the most powerful women in the FLDS was another one altogether. Shortly after I got home from Washington, Jeff Schmidt, a CPS attorney in Texas, called me to say that the state was building a case to remove several children from mothers who were refusing to comply with court-ordered parenting classes. Barbara, Merril's wife, was one of them. Texas was seeking custody of two of her children, including the fourteen-year-old who was married to Warren Jeffs at twelve.

Even after the Supreme Court ruled that the FLDS children in state custody had to be returned to their parents, CPS continued to pursue its case against Barbara Jessop because she was refusing to work with it and would not take parenting classes. The only compromise was that CPS decided not to try to win custody of her oldest son, who was seventeen. So the custody case centered on her fourteen-year-old daughter and eleven-year-old son.

Jeff asked me if I would be willing to testify about abusive behavior I had witnessed during my seventeen-year marriage to Merril. This gave me pause. I was already under attack by the FLDS for publishing *Escape*. My congressional testimony had intensified the pressure.

What would happen if I told the truth about Barbara and Merril's abusive behavior in court and under oath?

No doubt I would be accused of seeking revenge or trying to sell books. The pressure on my mother to write an affidavit full of lies underscored the hostile environment I'd be entering. But what scared me most was confronting someone who had made my life hell for seventeen years. We all feared Barbara more than Merril because she was crueler than he was. Not only was she abusive to nearly everyone's children in the family, but we were forbidden ever to speak about it. Barbara determined the severity of the punishments we received and what we could and couldn't do with our children. She controlled the family finances and had the power to obliterate anyone who got in her way. Merril protected her and came down hard on anyone who upset her.

I told Jeff I wanted to help but shared my concerns about how I would be attacked on the stand. Could I end up actually hurting his case?

But I never had any real doubts. My outrage about a child being given to a man more than four times her age for sex trumped my own fear of standing up to Barbara.

Barbara had never been held accountable in her life. Texas was now going to try. I knew she would willingly give up all of her fourteen children before she would answer to someone she felt had no right to question her—even a judge in a court of law.

Three days before I went to Texas my father, Arthur Blackmore, called and urged me not to go without some sort of protection. Dad knew full well how dangerous it was to stand up to the FLDS. He had been kicked out of the cult three years earlier after a confrontation with Merril over the sale of a motel they jointly owned. Dad had sold the motel and paid off the balance of the mortgage. He gave Merril two-thirds of what remained, but Merril wanted all of it. He told my dad he should contribute his profits to the construction of the FLDS compound in Texas. Dad refused.

By that point my parents were divorced. Under the terms of their settlement, Dad was to provide an adequate home for Mom. To fulfill his legal obligation, he used his profits from the motel to buy Mom a house. Merril claimed Dad had no such obligation. He said that as long as he was fulfilling the will of the prophet, God would protect Dad from any legal consequences of disobeying the court. My father held firm against Merril and told him the money was already gone.

Several weeks later Warren Jeffs sent several men to Dad's house to inform him he was no longer a member of the FLDS. They told him he'd have to relinquish the home he was living in—one he'd spent his life building—and leave his two wives and nine children. They also demanded that he turn over all of his retirement savings to Jeffs. Once again Dad refused.

"Talking about Merril and his personal family issues in court is one thing," Dad warned. "But if you're going up against Barbara, there's more of a chance they'll do something." Dad said the FLDS community was especially riled up right now and very antagonistic toward anyone they saw as a troublemaker. Jeff agreed with my father; he'd encountered plenty of hostility himself and said he would make sure I had protection.

Brian agreed that he should come with me to Texas. I can face almost anything if Brian is by my side. He knew how important it was for me to stand up to Barbara in court and kept giving me pep talks. I was pretty sure I had the strength to go through with my testimony, but Brian's confidence shored up my own.

We flew to Texas on Friday, August 15, and I worked on my testimony with Jeff all day Saturday and part of Sunday. Despite the strenuous preparation, I was still petrified. In Merril's family, criticizing Barbara's behavior was suicidal. Sure, I was now in a strong place in my life, but seventeen years of learned and reflexive behavior kept barging in. I was absolutely convinced of the rightness of facing down Barbara in court, but how did I translate that certainty to the cellular level? I kept telling myself that Barbara no longer had power to harm me or my children.

Compounding my anxiety was the news that Betty might be called to testify against me. At this point she and I had lost all contact. The last time we had spoken was a few days before the raid, and it was a peaceful conversation. She talked to her siblings off and on throughout the crisis, but she refused to speak with me. One of the kids tried to get her to talk to me, but Betty adamantly refused even to consider it. Now that she was completely under FLDS control, they'd use her to try to undercut me.

In Washington, I had been nervous because I felt the enormity of my responsibility. But testifying against Barbara Jessop was personal. Theoretically I knew I was safe, but part of me still felt like I had bought a one-way ticket back to hell. I had worked hard to make a new life and had been enormously supported in therapy, but seventeen years of fear and terror don't exactly evaporate overnight. Undeniably she was one of the masterminds behind the engine of evil that had controlled our lives. Also, the FLDS had hit back after Dan and I testified in Washington. If it lost this case, I didn't want to think about the fury that would be unleashed on me.

In the courtroom, Barbara was sworn in and was asked for basic information. She stated that she was living in an apartment with three of her children and maintained that she and they were the only ones who lived at that address. After the raid she had agreed to keep her children away from the adult males on the YFZ Ranch. Jeff Schmidt then asked her to name everyone who lived at the home. She named herself and her three children.

Jeff asked Barbara if anyone else stayed in her home during the day or spent the night there. She said no one ever did, although

she acknowledged that there were nights when she was not in the
house.

Jeff asked if there were times when her fourteen-year-old daughter
and eleven-year-old son were ever left alone in her home overnight.

"I don't want to answer any more questions," she answered. "I
stand on the Fifth."

The court, presided over again by Judge Barbara Walther, then had
to decide if Barbara could take a blanket Fifth Amendment exemption
for herself. (The Fifth Amendment protects against self-incrimination.)
The court decided she could not and would have to answer each question individually.

JEFF SCHMIDT: Can you please name your offspring, in
    order, the natural children that you've given birth to?
BARBARA JESSOP: I stand on the Fifth.

Jeff then tried to get Barbara to identify her daughter in a photo.
She took the Fifth. Jeff objected because he couldn't see how this
could be incriminating since she'd already admitted that they were
mother and daughter. Barbara's attorney countered that she needed
to take the Fifth because of the ongoing criminal investigation. Judge
Walther ruled in his favor because she said he had the right to object
if he felt his client might be incriminating herself in another case.
Barbara's attorney also claimed the photo of Barbara's twelve-year-old
kissing Warren Jeffs was irrelevant to the case.

After taking the Fifth more than twenty-five times, Barbara finally got a question she agreed to answer.

JEFF SCHMIDT: Would you also agree with me that it is in a
    child's best interest that a parent protect their children
    from anything that may cause them physical or emotional
    or psychological harm?

BARBARA JESSOP: Yes.

JEFF SCHMIDT: You agree with that?

BARBARA JESSOP: Yes.

JEFF SCHMIDT: Would you also agree with me that a parent
has a duty to provide financial support for their children?

BARBARA JESSOP: I stand on the Fifth.

Barbara took the Fifth to more than fifty questions before her testimony ended! This was a mother who risked losing custody of two of her children. It was hard to comprehend why she and her attorney thought that taking the Fifth over and over again would help her case.

What casual observers couldn't appreciate was the line Jeff had crossed in asking Barbara who was in her house at night. She and Merril were together nearly every night and always had been. Merril Jessop, despite his twenty-plus wives that I'm aware of, was essentially monogamous. Yes, he slept with other women, but he often returned that same night to the bed of his third and favorite wife. Merril did not practice plural marriage in the traditional way. For a man as powerful in the FLDS as he is, that was a potential embarrassment.

Barbara could not testify that he was there every night because she and the other mothers had signed agreements that adult males from the ranch would not be allowed around their children. Nor could she say that she was leaving her children alone every night to go off with Merril, as had been her pattern for years. The fact that they were together every night was a problem any way you sliced it.

When I came into the courtroom to testify, Barbara and I looked at each other. She was sitting next to her attorney, Gonzalo Rios, and had to lean over a little to see me. She was smiling and had a friendly demeanor that I found unsettling. She was trying to pretend that we were friends, but it was a lie. Abusers often use this tactic in public to intimidate their victims. I just stared back at her.

I was shaky as I took the stand. My body remembered what my mind tried to forget. This was the first time I had seen Barbara since I escaped. My face felt pale. Life seemed to rush out of me.

I scanned the courtroom and saw friendly faces of strangers. Brian was sitting in the back of the room so he could see me and I could see him. If my strength faltered, I knew I could draw on his. I was forty years old and safe.

Jeff asked the first question.

JEFF SCHMIDT: Can you tell the court why you're here today? Why you agreed to testify in this case?

CAROLYN JESSOP: I agreed to testify in this case because I was involved with the FLDS for thirty-five years. I was able, or I feel like I was able, when I left the group, to protect my children. It took a lot. But most of them, I believe, are in a safe place now. However, I was also involved with around twenty children, eight of them being mine, during the course of my marriage. And just because I was not in a position to legally protect all twenty, does not mean that I don't have some pretty strong emotions and protective feelings toward the children I left behind.

Jeff asked more questions about my involvement with Merril and Barbara and then about abuses I had seen in the family. I described several, including one that happened at Sunday school in 1988, when my son Arthur was about six months old.

"I was nursing him," I said, "and so I wanted to be able to dart to the kitchen quickly if he began to fuss during Sunday school. I was standing between the living room and the kitchen, and I noticed Barbara, who was sitting at the front of the Sunday school room with her baby. At the time, Barbara Joy Jessop was probably a year, around a year in age. She wanted to—it appeared to me that she wanted to sit on her mother's lap. Barbara was trying to get Barbie to sit on this little chair in front of her.

"But when Barbie started fussing, her mother went into the kitchen and got a broom and took her daughter out onto the deck. It was chilling to witness. I could see—through the glass windows—I could see her hitting Barbie with the broom. She was holding her hand with one arm and then hitting her with the broom with the other arm. And then she took Barbie into the kitchen to get her to stop crying.

"The beating quieted Barbie for about ten minutes, but then she started fussing again. Barbara took her out on the deck again and beat her with the broom. Then she took her into the kitchen to try to calm her down. Sunday school was almost over."

But the beating continued, as I told the court. "And I don't know what Barbie did the third time. I didn't see it. I just saw Barbara get up, take Barbie. And this time Barbie collapsed on the floor. She refused to walk. Her mother took her arm and dragged her out of the room, out on the deck, and once again began hitting her with the broom.

"And the picture that I remember in my mind is we all stood to sing the final song or closing song of Sunday school. We were singing 'When There's Love at Home.' And I remember seeing the broom hitting Barbie and her little feet flying off the floor—off the ground."

When the questioning continued, Jeff asked me if there was ever a time when Barbara would have medically neglected my children. I told the court about an incident with my son Andrew. I was on a trip with Merril and Tammy, one of his other wives, when I learned that Andrew, who was about a year, had fallen from his high chair and had broken his arm. I told Merril he had to go to the emergency room. Here is what I said in testimony:

Merril called Barbara and told her to take him to the hospital. She told Merril that when I got home, I could take care of it. We were planning on being gone for two more days. I immediately told

Merril, "We have to go home now." Merril refused and told me that I didn't need to worry about it, he was in good hands and being taken care of, and that there was nothing to be concerned about, and that my concern should—needed to be whether or not I was in harmony with my husband.

I became sick. I began vomiting, had a severe headache. Merril had to pull the car over every ten minutes, sometimes every five. It became an annoyance. Then he agreed that we should go get something to eat. I told him I did not want to eat. I wanted to go home. Merril at that point picked up his phone, called home, and told Ruth [another of his wives] to take Andrew to the hospital.

Ruth took Andrew to the hospital, and we did return that night, but very, very late. The doctor had been unable to set his arm because it was still too swollen.

By the time the swelling went down, I took him back. The arm had come out of place again. The doctor had to mold the arm into place and then put a cast on it, which was excruciatingly painful for my son.

I was also asked to describe an incident with my disabled son, Harrison. Merril wanted me to go on another trip, but I was terrified of leaving Harrison in Barbara's care. Merril insisted I had nothing to worry about. Before I left, I made sure that Audrey, Merril's daughter, who had medical training, would check on Harrison every two hours. I was asked to tell the court about Harrison's needs at the time.

CAROLYN JESSOP: He was on a pulse oximeter. He needed oxygen. He was on a feeding pump, where I could only put so much high-calorie formula into his stomach during a period of time or he would begin to vomit. He was very critical.

JEFF SCHMIDT: Go ahead with your story.

CAROLYN JESSOP: I came back the next day. Harrison was at Audrey's house. I went over to Audrey's to pick Harrison up. And Audrey was very angry about the condition she had found Harrison in when she had gone to check on him.

Jeff asked me to tell the court what had happened to Harrison under Barbara's watch.

"He was screaming," I said. "He was covered with feces. The feeding tube had come—was—it was not connected. Formula was all over. His bedding was saturated with formula, and his pulse oximeter was off."

During my cross-examination, Barbara's lawyer asked me several questions about my profits from *Escape*. The book had been on the *New York Times* best-seller list for two weeks after it was released in October 2007. The public firestorm over the raid put the book back on the list for an additional ten weeks. But that hadn't made me wealthy.

I spent almost a year writing *Escape* and then several months promoting it after it was published. When the advance is subtracted from the royalties, what I earned amounted to a decent salary for an equivalent full-time job. I had no other income during those years since Merril never paid a dime in child support. If he ever had, I might not have written *Escape*. Writing from home was one way I could work and still be a full-time mom, especially to my handicapped son Harrison. But Barbara's attorney pressed on.

GONZALO RIOS: Would it be safe to say you made a lot of money from your book, is that correct?

CAROLYN JESSOP: It would be safe to say I have made some.

GONZALO RIOS: And it would certainly be in your best interest to show up here today to testify and continue this crusade of—of doing the publicity deal, correct?

I told the court that I had not even notified my publicist at Doubleday that I was testifying in the trial and that I preferred not to speak publicly about it. It was painful to be accused of testifying only because I wanted to make money on my book. He asked me if I was being paid to testify, and I said I was not.

He also questioned me about the fact that I had cared for Barbara when she was very ill. The assumption was that I wouldn't have done that if we weren't close. We weren't close, but I had always tried to be decent to her. Nothing really changed after she was diagnosed with a nonmalignant brain tumor.

He made a point about Merril's paying for my education, which was true. He did let me go to college and paid the tuition. But I didn't feel guilty about that. My tuition was less than $1,200 a year for three years. I turned over my teacher's salary to Merril for years. If we ever did the math, he would come out way ahead.

I think Barbara was angered by my ability to answer questions and remain calm. She had not been as successful in maintaining her composure. When Jeff was asking me questions about her abusive behavior, she had almost looked proud, as if I were complimenting her strength. She later told reporters that she had been a strict mother. I think Barbara saw abuse as power and validation of her strength as a righteous mother.

The next morning Brian and I awoke to a newspaper story quoting Willie Jessop to the effect that Betty was going to take the stand and testify about me. I hated the fact that she was being so crudely manipulated by the FLDS.

I called Jeff. He said he hadn't been informed that Betty was going to be put on the stand but that I should be in court just in case.

Our two police escorts came by the hotel to take us to court. They turned out to be fantastic. Their spirited humor was an enormous boost to my morale at a time when I really, really needed it. I was feeling discouraged. The state might be winning its case—which was good news—but that meant that the FLDS might sink to more desperate tactics in court. I couldn't protect my daughter from being cannon fodder for the FLDS, and I hated that. Being unable to protect your child is the most helpless feeling a mother can have.

In the end Barbara's attorney didn't put Betty on the stand. That was a smart strategy: if she had testified, then I would have been cross-examined about what Betty had alleged. My testimony had been damaging to their case because I had firsthand knowledge of many instances of abuse.

I saw Betty once but only from behind. She was about twenty feet away from me, and it would have been so easy and natural to run up and throw my arms around her. I couldn't because it would have made her angry. But my heart ran to her anyway, even if my feet stayed fixed.

Judge Walther's verdict was a split decision. She ruled that Barbara's eleven-year-old son could remain in her custody, but that the state would take custody of her daughter, the twelve-year-old bride. The girl went into foster care for about nine months and reportedly did very well. But then for reasons that are unclear, she was given to a permanent guardian, Naomi Carlisle, a member of the FLDS who lives on the YFZ Ranch. For all intents and purposes, that handed her directly back to Barbara and Merril.

When Barbara learned she was going to lose custody of her daughter, she did something shocking: she asked if she could substitute someone else's daughter for her own so she would not have to relinquish custody of the daughter at the center of the trial! Barbara proposed swapping a random child who belonged to another FLDS mother whom the state had never suspected of being sexually abused.

Barbara's request came in a meeting with CPS after the verdict. It was indicative of the arbitrary power Barbara still felt she had. One of the CASA workers who described this incident to me said Barbara was told, "This isn't about us wanting your child or that we want a child from you. This is about protecting your daughter from you."

I don't think there was any way that Barbara could have known how ugly her child-swap offer—which was immediately rejected— would appear to those who had been working for weeks with the 439 children from the YFZ Ranch. I wasn't shocked because I knew how readily the FLDS trades people around. We were all objects, movable, disposable, and replaceable. When a marriage is being arranged, it is not at all uncommon for one girl to get swapped for another if someone more powerful wants to protect his daughter. I learned after my marriage that Merril had intended to marry my sister as part of a business deal but had mixed up our names and asked for me instead.

Shortly after I returned to Salt Lake City, the *Tribune* published an article on August 23, 2008, in its online polygamy blog by Brooke Adams: "Barbara, Carolyn, and their two daughters."

There was a picture of Barbara and Betty, my daughter. The point of the blog was that I had testified in a trial that would sever Barbara from her daughter while my daughter, nineteen-year-old Betty, had returned to the FLDS. The reporter saw these as two parallel stories. Adams wrote, "Barbara is Betty's other mother, the one to whom she has returned."

Barbara told Adams that her memory of our past differed from my own and that she preferred "to remember the Carolyn I once knew." She said, "I've never known her as anything less than a friend. I don't have bad memories of her, I really don't."

The blog mentioned a photograph in which all of Merril's wives wore identical dresses, as if that meant anything at all. There were many times when we had to dress alike and sing to each other. In one photo we have our hands on our hearts because we are pledging our allegiance to Merril.

A lot of the blog entry was nonsense. Betty returned to her father. Period. She adored Merril. None of my children ever liked Barbara. They feared her cruelty.

I never wanted to see Barbara's daughter taken from her because my daughter chose to return to her father. I want to see FLDS children protected and have the freedom to make choices as Betty did—at eighteen. I am disappointed by Betty's choice, but it was absolutely her right to make it. Forcing a twelve-year-old girl to marry, on the other hand, is an outrage and a crime.

But I never expected that the last time I'd ever see Barbara was that day in a Texas courtroom. I was finishing up the dinner dishes and getting Harrison's medications ready when the phone call came on December 8, 2009, at about eight o'clock. Barbara was dead.

She'd complained of being tired in the early evening and went to rest. She died soon after from an apparent seizure or stroke. Barbara had a seizure disorder but when I knew her, she wasn't consistent in taking the medication that would have kept her stable. She was fifty-six when she died and had fourteen children with Merril. I was stunned by the news. I'd always assumed Merril would die first because he's much older and has serious heart problems. Part of me feels relieved, deeply relieved, that the anger, viciousness, and cruelty that were such a part of her would never hurt anyone again.

My children and I have all moved on in so many ways, yet this news was still a bombshell. Betty called us several times wondering if she would see any of her siblings at Barbara's funeral, which was held five days after she died in Colorado City. None of my children had any interest in attending. Merril called and tried to talk Arthur into going but he explained that he was in the middle of finals at college.

I wonder what will happen now in Merril's family. Barbara was the center of gravity. I think the family will spin into its own version of nuclear war. She was Merril's enforcer; now that era is over. They were married almost forty years and I think he will be lost without her in many ways. Her death is a seismic shift in his world.

I will never rejoice in the death of another person, not even Barbara. I hope she is now at peace.

Cut and Run

After the hearing about my stepdaughter was held, CPS quietly began dropping or "nonsuiting" FLDS cases. As the Department of Family and Protective Services (DFPS) explained in its final report on the FLDS raid, "DFPS nonsuits a case when CPS staff believes the parents of family members have taken appropriate action to protect the children from future abuse or neglect." By the time the DFPS issued that final report on December 22, 2008, 96 percent of the children removed from the ranch, it said, were "now determined to be safe in their households to the point that there is not a need for court oversight."

Most observers didn't realize that some key lawyers were opposed to nonsuiting cases so rapidly. Jeff Schmidt, the CPS attorney prosecuting the case against Barbara, felt that FLDS children weren't being adequately protected because the cases were being resolved too quickly. He refused to drop cases involving children he believed were still at risk or who had been injured. He protested as vociferously as he could, and when he would not back down, CPS took him off the cases and transferred him.

Jeff told me he was unable to sleep at night because so many cases were being dropped. Everyone at CASA wholeheartedly supported Jeff and Charles Childress, the lead attorney for CPS. "They were really fighting for these kids," Debra Brown told me. "They knew what they were doing, saw the problems immediately, and were just shut down."

After the Texas Supreme Court ruling came down, Childress was asked to represent CPS while the cases were being litigated. An expert in family law and legal issues impacting children, Childress was on the faculty at the University of Texas Law School. His background is impressive, his reputation impeccable.

Childress began work on July 23, 2008, about two months after the Supreme Court issued its ruling. His first task was to get the cases legally organized in a way that would allow him and his team to deal with each family situation on its own merits. He also, as he explained to me, began reviewing with the local staff the huge amount of documentary evidence removed from the YFZ Ranch. It struck him from the outset that the number of adolescent boys on the ranch (25) was out of balance with the number of adolescent girls (45). The documents he studied indicated that 37 men who'd been living at the ranch the year before had had 132 wives and 332 children. Records of the "spiritual marriages" performed at the ranch showed that most of the women and young girls came from within the thirteen-to-eighteen age group. For the senior FLDS men who claimed adolescent girls as their "spiritual wives," the presence of large numbers of adolescent boys would obviously have been a threat. The solution was to cast out these boys.

In fact, the FLDS routinely kicks adolescent boys out of the cult by the dozens. These naïve and unworldly young men are simply dumped on highways and told never to return because they have been rejected by God. It's a matter of numbers. In a polygamous culture where older men marry many young girls, boys are expendable. Over the years, the boys who've been expelled from the FLDS—severed from everything they have ever known and lacking the skills necessary to adapt to the outside world—have become known as the "lost boys." (The names of at least one thousand "lost boys" have been collected by the Diversity Foundation, one of the few nonprofits trying to help them.)

"I have been involved in this field for too long to be outraged by much," Childress told me. "The way I see it, most of these parents loved their daughters as much as, or perhaps more than, the average parent. They probably genuinely believed they were guaranteeing celestial glory to these girls by 'sealing' them to the prophet or other senior men in the cult. They also no doubt believed that the boys who were cast out had to be in order to protect the prospects of the rest to get to glory." Childress came up with an interesting analogy: "What comes to mind is the story of the Inca mummies that were given to the priests by their parents to be sacrificed to the sun god. By all accounts, these children were subjected to a hard march into the mountains, but otherwise showed no signs of abuse. I suspect they were loved by their parents in much the same way these FLDS children are."

Childress was particularly concerned with the emotional health of the children and how polygamy affected it. "Warren Jeffs freely 'reassigned' women and their children to men he deemed more worthy than their original husbands and fathers," Childress explained. "One young mother had been reassigned to three different men in the course of a little over two years—and she had children by two of her three 'spiritual husbands.'"

Also complicating matters, he said, was the appellate court's out-of-hand rejection of DFPS's argument that the YFZ Ranch should be treated as a single "household" under the law, so that the pattern of sexual abuse could be attributed to the entire group and justify the intervention. "But the records reflected," Childress pointed out, "that there was, indeed, only one person, Warren Jeffs, making all important decisions at YFZ Ranch, and that person was 'sealing' girls as young as twelve to himself or his favorites, and 'reassigning' both the women and children as he deemed the circumstances to warrant."

Childress also noted that some FLDS parents seemed genuinely bonded to their children and sad to reject the extreme practices that put their children at risk. Accordingly, Childress created a litigation strategy that would include the development of specific tasks and goals for those parents willing to change. This in turn would free him to concentrate his efforts on those, including Jeffs, who in the name of their religion orchestrated and carried out the sexual and emotional abuse that DFPS's investigators had uncovered.

Childress told me he worked with caseworkers to help develop "service plans" with specific tasks and timelines for those families who were concerned for their children and cooperative with the department. The goal was to dismiss the suits involving those parents as soon as necessary therapy or educational services had been completed. He'd then focus on the biggest offenders—Warren Jeffs and his inner circle of followers who were shown to have actively engaged in the underage "marriages" and other extreme practices that placed their own children and other YFZ children at risk. He believed that the evidence, presented at a final trial, would justify termination of their parental rights.

But Childress never got a chance to pursue his plan. The reason? The DFPS had not filed the necessary legal pleadings to ask a court or jury to terminate the parental rights of any parents involved in the YFZ cases. Since that paperwork had not been filed, Childress had to amend the pleadings to ask for termination of parental rights in the few cases he thought should go to trial. Sadly, despite his best intentions, he could not proceed with his comprehensive plan. The permission Childress needed to file the necessary pleadings never came, and he has no idea why. The upshot? "Ultimately, I decided that I could not in good conscience continue to represent the department under the circumstances." He resigned on October 23, 2008, just three months after he started.

"He quit when he was told he couldn't do what he wanted to do,"

Debra Brown told me. "It was a moral decision. He had too much evidence to say, 'Okay, we'll do it your way.' He came by our office and told me how sorry he was that he couldn't help the children. It makes me mad all over again when I think about it. CPS would not even terminate the parental rights of Warren Jeffs.

"I think a point came when CPS decided to cut and run, just get out," Debra continued. "My feeling is that in its final report, CPS massively underestimated the level of abuse that took place at the ranch—even though CPS had access to the documents that were seized from the ranch as part of the criminal investigation. I honestly believe that CPS nonsuited children too rapidly and never adequately determined if they were genuinely safe from the threat of forced underage marriages."

Childress remains convinced that the state's intentions were good. But he also believes Texas overreached by taking all the FLDS children from the ranch. "If it were possible to rewind to the initial raid," he explained, "the state should have realized that it was not prepared to handle the volume of work they took on by removing all the children at the same time. The situation would have been quite different if Ms. Voss [the state's lead child-abuse investigator] had stuck with her initial inclination to remove the eighteen young women who appeared to be underage brides, and attempted to continue the investigation with some orders from the trial court requiring cooperation by the FLDS members as the family situations were being sorted out and the facts determined. The concern at that time was that some parents would flee and possibly take children with them in spite of any orders. For this group, the only law is the command of their prophet. I think that risk would have been worth taking."

More than a year after the children were sent back to the YFZ Ranch, in a courtroom in Eldorado, Debra Brown bumped into one of the FLDS mothers she'd worked with during the raid whose family had no abuse issues. "She came up to me and asked, 'The families that may have had problems, why did they nonsuit them just like they did me?' I told her that was a really good question and I'd been asking myself that a lot but didn't have an answer. Her question just blew my hair back."

A Sea of Pastel Hostility

Once the Texas courts ruled in favor of the FLDS, the cult felt a fresh jolt of invincibility. One dramatic example was its emboldened stance toward the United Effort Plan trust. The UEP was created in 1942 by the fundamentalist Mormons who eventually became known as the FLDS but at that point called their sect "The Work." The goal of the trust was to facilitate communal living in plural marriage by pooling members' assets.

At the time Utah seized the UEP in 2005 and put it under court oversight, its net worth was estimated to be $110 million. Subsequent estimates have placed its value at $180 million. A large portion of that total is UEP-owned homes. FLDS members don't own their own homes; all property is owned by the UEP.

For four years the FLDS was completely unresponsive to its legal obligations regarding the trust, ignoring court papers, tax notices, and direct pleas from the judge. But after its win in Texas, the FLDS came out swinging and started to ramp up its legal push to regain control of the UEP. Because of the substantial amount of money involved, it's a crucial battle. Bruce Wisan, the court-appointed fiduciary for the trust, said an FLDS representative told him, "We're going to be fighting from now on." An FLDS attorney, Peter Stirba, echoed that view when he said, "The days of the FLDS people not defending themselves in court are over."

So on July 29, 2009, I was once again preparing to testify, this time at the Salt Lake City courthouse. The occasion was another battle in the ongoing war over the UEP trust. Judge Denise Lindberg was hearing motions about a multimillion-dollar land sale that the FLDS was trying to block. I was one of the witnesses called to testify about my knowledge of the FLDS, based on my marriage to one of its ruling elite and my membership on the UEP advisory board.

As I headed into court that morning, the contrast between the woman I'd been and the one I had become could not have been more stark. I was wearing a black pantsuit and a pale blue blouse. My hair was short and stylish, my makeup simple. I wore low heels and carried a black Dolce & Gabbana handbag that Brian had given me as a birthday present. (I'd never heard of the designers until Brian decided to replace the ratty and overstuffed bag I'd carried for years.) I felt proud of how I'd survived and grown, proud that my children were safe, and proud that a man as fine as Brian was by my side helping me navigate the crowds.

We took an elevator up from the parking garage, and when the doors opened, all I could see were the pastel dresses. Hundreds of FLDS women had dutifully turned out in their long, shapeless attire to take part in the massive protest that the FLDS was staging. Judge Lindberg had issued a court order prohibiting the FLDS from protesting within the courthouse. In a show of defiance the cult members had ignored that order.

I had not been in such a large crowd of FLDS women since my escape. It took my breath away to be face to face with my past. I knew many of the older women in the crowd, but most of the younger girls had only heard the stories about me. They looked confused. Clearly I didn't fit their image of an apostate doing the devil's work. FLDS members were taught that anyone who left the work of God could never find happiness. We were conditioned to believe that any woman who left the FLDS would lose not only her health but her beauty.

Most of these girls had had very little exposure to the outside world. I'm sure they expected me to be ugly. Seeing me look strong, confident, and feminine with a handsome man I loved at my side undercut everything they'd been indoctrinated to believe. Hostility spat from the eyes of most of the older women, but not all. One reached out to hug me and asked if her mother would be in court. The two of them had been estranged since her mother was kicked out of the FLDS a few years earlier for refusing to obey her abusive husband. Several of the woman's older children, including this girl, had remained in the FLDS. Her warm embrace made me instantly think of Betty and gave me hope that one day she and I might reconcile.

But even more surprising was hearing my cousin Lucy call out "Carolyn!" Looking exhausted and pale, Lucy jostled her way through the crowd and smiled when she hugged me. I was incredulous that she dared to hug me in front of an FLDS mob. Lucy and I had had some serious disagreements about the FLDS when she and I were part of a group that secretly went to Curves to exercise. We remained close during some of my worst times in the FLDS, and she was one of the few people who would give me the time of day after I left. But I hadn't seen her for a while and was startled that she dared call out to me so publicly. My heart ached to see how worn and lost this once-spirited woman looked. We were close in age, but she looked much older now. If she dared to hug me, it meant she almost certainly was on the margins of the FLDS and felt she had nothing to lose.

Brian and I had to get to the fourth floor of the courthouse, but there was no way we could make our way through the crowd to the next bank of elevators. Our only option was the stairs. But the mob had jammed into the stairwells as well.

By flooding the courthouse with people and clogging the security, the FLDS seemed confident it could disrupt the proceedings. Hundreds of kids had come with their parents. Most of the boys carried pocketknives, which brought everything to a standstill as they went through the metal detectors. The FLDS had alerted the media to its protest, and TV crews were there. Willie Jessop bragged that four thousand FLDS were there, but I think the true number was closer to a thousand.

The FLDS leadership was probably hoping that Judge Lindberg would bar them from the building, giving them a way to turn public opinion against her. But the judge was savvy enough not to take the bait. She knew that finding the FLDS in contempt for ignoring her order would have played right into its hands.

The immediate issue for Judge Lindberg was whether to allow the UEP trust to sell a large parcel of land—Berry Knoll Farm—and use the proceeds from the estimated $3 million sale to pay trust debts and generate income to keep functioning. Ultimately, of course, the FLDS was fighting to regain control of the trust altogether because of the tens of millions of dollars at stake.

The trust controlled virtually all of the land and homes in the FLDS community along the Arizona-Utah border. But non-FLDS lived in this area, too, and for them, conditions were becoming less and less safe. The FLDS was determined to assert its power, whether it had legal control of the trust and its assets or not. And the FLDS-controlled police force collaborated in the harassment of nonmembers. Criminal trespassing warrants were issued to people who had every right to be in the area. A young non-FLDS mother was arrested several times for working in her yard and for putting a lock on her power box. Another man was arrested for working on his farm. These people had signed agreements acknowledging that they had the right to live where they did.

This kind of harassment rarely held up in court, but it created immediate and enormous problems for its targets. My father, Arthur Blackmore, was one of the witnesses called to testify about the crimes he'd seen the group commit. I was proud of him for standing up for himself. He had been deeply opposed to my escape and had been a staunch defender of the FLDS until he was kicked out and his family was stripped from him.

An attorney from the Arizona attorney general's office finally helped Brian and me maneuver our way through the crowd. I wasn't afraid, but I had never been in an atmosphere of such rampant hostility. People who had once been my friends glared at me with cruel disgust. A cousin I'd worked with as a teacher shot me a look of such loathing that it almost burned. There was no shouting, just venomous stares. At one point Brian whispered in my ear, "It doesn't matter how many of them there are. The law is the law."

The sadness I felt moving through that sea of pastel dresses outweighed the hostility directed at me. The women were doing what they had to do to survive in their world. They had been told to show up, and they did.

When we finally made it to the fourth floor, I turned in my cell phone and gave Brian a quick kiss good-bye before walking into the courtroom. The young girls in that crowd had probably never seen an affectionate couple. I'm Brian's lover, not his slave, and I hoped the young girls in the pastel dresses would begin to consider the difference between the two.

In many of their eyes, I had run from power into a shallow, gentile life. As Merril Jessop's wife, I had been at the pinnacle of FLDS society. But I didn't run to experience love; I knew virtually nothing about true intimacy. I ran to free myself—and my children—from a world where abuse, degradation, and exploitation masquerade as faith and love.

I stood for everything a woman in the FLDS believed would take her to hell. It was painful to see hostility in the eyes of women who'd once been my friends. But what really hurt was seeing how many were still trapped in a hopeless cycle of abuse.

For the millionth time, I thanked God that I had found the strength to get out and stay out.

Triumph?

Thinking again about the reality of the raid and its implications has been painful, exhausting, and often disappointing. Where is the triumph in a tale that reeks of betrayal? How do those children who were promised security and protection feel now about their lives, their worlds, and their futures?

When some FLDS children were staying in a San Antonio shelter, they asked if they could see a dog. Patsy Swendson, who runs the Penny's from Heaven Foundation, a therapy dog program, brought in two of her dogs—Zoe, a big Irish wolfhound, and Gracie, a little blind French hound dog. "It was the most heartbreaking thing I have ever done," said Swendson, who has worked with therapy dogs for twenty years. "Children and dogs go together, they belong together. These children had never seen a dog, touched a dog, read a book about a dog, or ever looked into a dog's eyes and felt a dog's unconditional love."

Swendson had been warned that the children might be abusive toward the dogs. No one knew how they would respond. But the kids were mesmerized, gentle, and curious. "Within ten minutes they went from fear of the dogs biting them to lying on the floor beside them, petting and loving them and begging us to bring them back again 'real soon,'" she recalled. "They turned from little robots into children laughing and playing with a dog.

"The boys were all over the dogs and the girls, more standoffish," Swendson said. "But one little girl had a tiny pink slipper, like a shoe from a Barbie. She picked up Gracie's little foot and put it on one of her toenails." Swendson remembers a handsome young boy who was about twelve. "He just melted on the floor. It was like Christmas Day for him to see a dog. Seeing him react was reward enough for me. But the sad part was when we were getting ready to leave. He came to the door, and the feeling I had in my gut was that he wanted to run away with us. It was eerie. I will never forget the sadness in his face. It broke my heart knowing what these children were going back to, but it did help somewhat knowing that at least for a moment, they were able to experience nonthreatening, nonjudgmental devotion that we find at our feet every day."

The absence of dogs in the children's lives stems from a day in the late 1990s that I remember well. On orders from Warren Jeffs, all the dogs in the community where rounded up and killed or taken to the pound. This was in response to the death of a small boy who had been attacked by his stepfather's pit bull. People in the community had dogs as pets, although it was generally frowned upon, and sometimes people would kill each other's dogs in retaliation for something. I think Jeffs's motivation in ordering the elimination of dogs was an attempt to see how far he could get the community to go. It was chilling to me that no one—*no one*—challenged him.

So it wasn't a surprise to me that none of the FLDS children had seen a dog. It's a small but telling detail about how different their world is from ours. Similarly, some of the kids held in state custody after the raid had never seen crayons before and tried to unwrap and eat them.

Dogs and crayons: small signs of big problems. But ultimately it's facts—not signs, impressions, assumptions, or opinions—that speak the loudest. Here are some facts that appeared in the report (available online) on the official investigation of the raid on the YFZ Ranch published by the Texas Department of Family and Protective Services. The DFPS report is dated December 22, 2008, seven months after the children were returned to the YFZ Ranch on orders from the Texas Supreme Court.

Investigation Results

- **12 girls** were victims of sexual abuse and neglect at the YFZ Ranch with the knowledge of their parents. The 12 girls were "spiritually" married at ages ranging from 12 to 15, and seven of those girls had one or more children. The 12 confirmed victims of sexual abuse were among 43 girls removed from the ranch from the ages of 12 to 17, which means that more than one out of every four pubescent girls on the ranch was in an underage marriage.

- **262 other** children (in addition to the 12 girls) were subjected to neglect under Texas law. In these instances, the parents failed to remove their child from a situation in which the child would be exposed to sexual abuse committed against another child within their families or households.

- **124 designated perpetrators:** Designated perpetrators included men who engaged in underage marriages; parents who failed to take reasonable steps to prevent an underage daughter from marrying an older adult male; and parents who placed their child in, or refused to remove their child from, a situation in which the child would be exposed to sexual abuse committed against another child.

- **Of the 146** families investigated, 62 percent had a confirmed finding of abuse or neglect, including one or more children in the family. The final disposition of the 146 CPS cases involving families at the YFZ Ranch is listed below:

- **91 families: Reason to believe** CPS determined that is was reasonable to believe that one or both parents in the family sexually abused or neglected a child in the family by entering into an illegal underage marriage with a child; failing to take reasonable steps to prevent the illegal underage marriage of a child; or failing to remove one or more children in the family from a situation in which they would be exposed to an ongoing underage marriage in their family or household.

- **12 families: Ruled out** CPS determined that it was reasonable to conclude that no child in the family was abused or neglected.

- **39 families: Unable to determine** There is not a preponderance of the available evidence to find that abuse or neglect did occur, or to rule it out.

- **1 family: Unable to complete** CPS was unable to complete the investigation due to an inability to locate the subjects of the allegations.

- **3 families: Administratively closed** After reviewing the information received, CPS determined that an investigation was not received.

How can anyone look at those numbers and not be outraged? The state of Texas removed 439 children from the YFZ Ranch and found that in only twelve families could those children be considered completely safe from abuse or neglect. Of the 145 families investigated, 62 percent had a confirmed finding of abuse. Yet parenting classes were somehow supposed to straighten all of that out and establish an environment where children are safe and protected? The raid and investigation cost $12,436,310.

It's fair to ask where the triumph is in all those numbers.

I could have been one of those mothers because for seventeen years I was. My own life bears witness to the possibility of change and transformation. The lives of my children show the power of human resilience. My life feels like a triumph because with love, support, and persistent determination I was able to forge a life of joy from one of desperation.

Whenever I feel depressed about the outcome of the raid in Texas, I remind myself that losing the battle is not the end of the war until we give up hope. That is as true in epic struggles as it is in each of our lives. The raid on the YFZ Ranch did yield mountains of evidence that are the basis for state trials against eleven FLDS men. If those trials continue to result in convictions, as did the first against Raymond Jessop, it could end up loosening the grip of abuse, degradation, and exploitation that FLDS women and children have endured for years. That is a dream I will never abandon.

On September 15, 1963, a bomb placed by a white man went off in the Sixteenth Street Baptist Church in Birmingham, Alabama, killing four African American girls who were in their Sunday school class. The week before, George Wallace, the governor of Alabama, had told the *New York Times* that his state needed a "few first-class funerals" to stop integration.

On November 4, 2008, forty-five years later, hundreds of thousands of people filled Chicago's Grant Park to celebrate Barack Obama's election as president of the United States. I voted for the first time in my life on that day when I cast my ballot for Obama. I, who had been taught in an American public school that Abraham Lincoln was evil for freeing the slaves, helped elect the first African American president.

It was a moment of transformation that would have been unimaginable just a few years earlier. When I think of the FLDS in Texas, I force myself to remember that the horizon is never the end, but only as far as the eye can see. I remind myself that my life today affirms the astonishing, mysterious, and often miraculous power in the human potential for change.

The Tools of My Transformation

My Personal Power Source

Whenever I contemplate how I summoned up the power to leave the FLDS, my thoughts inevitably drift to my maternal grandmother, Jenny Bistlane. Although she lived in a culture dominated by men and worshiped a faith controlled by men, Grandma Jenny never sacrificed herself to any man. She never needed a man's validation to feel valued or accepted, and she enjoyed being feminine and powerful. "Women are the footstools men use to get into the kingdom of heaven," she once said.

Grandma Jenny was a paradox in the FLDS. She made her own decisions and was always guided by what was best for herself and her family. When I was growing up, she was the only woman I saw who had genuine respect for herself. I didn't realize at the time what an impact she would have on me. She adored me, and I loved her spunk and her blunt sense of humor.

I don't think I ever heard Grandma Jenny talk about marriage as good for women. One day she was complaining about her husband to my mother who, still a child, asked, "If marriage is so bad, why don't the married women warn the unmarried ones not to do it?" Grandma looked right at her and said, "Misery loves company!"

Yet Grandma had married a man she loved, and they had ten

children together. Both were Mormons who believed in plural marriage, but they didn't join the FLDS until much later. When my grandfather died, Grandma began receiving a small Social Security pension. She ended up marrying Merril's father and, for a time, turned over her pension and everything she had to him.

Grandma learned that she could survive on her own after the raid on Short Creek in 1953. The raid was a pivotal moment in FLDS history and is routinely cited as an example of the religious persecution of the cult. On July 26, 1953, Arizona police invaded the FLDS community in Short Creek (now Colorado City) and began arresting men and women for practicing polygamy. In all, 122 men and women were arrested and 263 children seized from their families. Public opinion quickly turned against the state when newspapers published photographs showing law enforcement officers taking children from their mothers' arms.

Grandma's brother pressured authorities to release her children to live with her at his house in Phoenix until the issue was resolved. The new independence she had in this life changed her. When she eventually came back to the FLDS, she continued in her marriage to Merril's father. But when he wanted to marry one of her teenage daughters (a girl he helped raise), she went ballistic and blocked it. Grandma stood up for herself and was an example of a woman who would not be subjugated to her man.

She died several years before I was assigned to marry Merril Jessop, but I know she would have been appalled. At the time I still believed that God had told the prophet whom I should marry. I also still believed that I needed to pray harder to accept God's will for my life. My future depended, at eighteen, on finding a way to be accepted by Merril and his other wives. I wasn't thinking about what my grandmother's life could teach me.

Like most FLDS girls, I would do anything to fit in and feel valued by my husband. I was resigned to being the youngest wife of a complete stranger. If I had balked at my marriage, I would have brought enormous disgrace to my family, and I did not want to let them down. I had to find a way to succeed as wife number four.

I wholeheartedly embraced the work of acceptance. I had always turned to God when I didn't understand aspects of my life. I prayed and prayed for understanding when it came to my marriage. I had tried to avoid Merril's daughters in high school because they were shallow and petty. I was the same age as two of them, and younger than several others. Now I was one of their mothers. How could I win their acceptance? We were competing for the same man, except that I was sleeping with him.

On my first morning in Merril's gargantuan house, I went to take a shower in one of the four bathrooms shared by thirty children. (There were three additional bathrooms that were private.) I managed to slip in before anyone else. When I finished, I ran into two children who were scampering down the stairs. I felt like an intruder. They had no idea why a strange woman in a bathrobe was coming out of their bathroom.

Bewildered by my sudden new reality, I went into the kitchen and made myself a cup of coffee. Two of Merril's daughters whispered to each other. I took my coffee back to my room. After two sips there was a knock on the door. It was one of the daughters from the kitchen.

"Father wants you to bring him a cup of coffee," she said. "He's waiting for you in his office."

"There's coffee in the kitchen," I said, genuinely perplexed. "Why don't you take him a cup?"

She looked at me with disbelief. How dare I reject an order from her father!

"He wants to talk to you," she said, turning away in disgust.

I took the coffee to Merril. He said nothing. He took one sip, then another. The silence felt deliberately calculated to make me feel uncomfortable. Finally he spoke. "I appreciate my ladies asking me before they make themselves coffee." (Men in polygamous groups commonly refer to their wives as "my ladies.") Was this for real? I had to ask him if I could make myself coffee in the morning?

"I also am very disappointed in you for wearing a sweater top," he added. "I don't allow that kind of clothing in my family." Two of his wives, Barbara and Ruth, were in his office as he humiliated me. Barbara seemed to be enjoying it. He cited her clothing—she was wearing a dress with puffy sleeves that were gathered in at the elbow, a fitted bodice, and a skirt with ruffles—as an example of how I should dress. It was the last thing on the planet I wanted to wear. But Merril didn't stop there. He went on to complain about the inappropriate clothes he'd seen my mother wear.

Little goes unnoticed in a community as closed as the FLDS. The intense level of competition among women means that they keep each other under a close watch. Even the "sins" of a woman's mother can be held against her. Over and over I'd hear people say, "After all, you know who her mother is. She's going to be just like her." Moreover, FLDS families intermarried for generations, so most of us were related in one way or the other. My grandmother Jenny had married Merril's father when my mother was two years old, so she was Merril's stepmother. She used to say that Merril was "the worst little shit that ever lived in the community."

That morning in his office I saw exactly what Grandma meant. When I finally left, it was abundantly clear that his other wives, like Barbara and Ruth, would never accept me. I was their competition, and neither had any interest in friendship. They were also old enough to be my mother. Figuring out a way to be accepted in this bizarre family was a huge challenge. Even so, I continued to pursue acceptance as my salvation. Acceptance would guarantee my survival, if not my success, in this weird world that was now my home.

No one in Merril's family was loved for who they were. Love and worth had to be earned, and Merril enjoyed pitting us against each other. This was obvious from the first week. Barbara completely dominated Merril and his entire family. I knew the only way to avoid being controlled by Barbara was to win acceptance from Merril and so be able to influence him.

Audrey, one of Merril's daughters, told me she had once asked her father why he spent all of his time with Barbara. She was nineteen and knew she could be assigned to a husband at any time, so she was trying to understand the dynamics of a plural marriage. She knew she didn't want to end up like her mother, Foneta, Merril's first wife, whom Merril had shut out in the cold. Ruth was another poor advertisement for polygamy because she did most of the work in the family and got none of the credit. Audrey knew Barbara was controlling and narcissistic. She wanted Merril to explain why it was all right for one wife to bully everyone else and keep them in subservient positions.

If Merril had been remotely capable of being truthful, his answer might have gone something like this: *When I was young, I was passionately in love with a non-FLDS woman. I was not allowed to marry her. When Barbara came along and took control of me, I didn't protest. Over the years we've both enjoyed hurting those we control.*

That sort of honesty, of course, was way beyond him. Merril denied that he had a favorite wife and told Audrey that because he was a man who was inspired and instructed by God, there was a divine hand in everything he did.

Poor Audrey paid dearly for her blunt questioning. Everyone knew the family was unfair, but talking about it was taboo. Barbara became very abusive toward Audrey. Audrey's other sisters ridiculed her and felt she got what she deserved. Audrey became an example of what can happen to anyone who dares offend Merril or Barbara. So I worked from the beginning to stay out of Barbara's line of fire.

It was obvious that I did not have a friend in the family, but I kept studying its social structure to see if there was a place to fit in. I persisted in my efforts to find acceptance, but I felt as though I had been sentenced to a life of isolation. During the first seven months of my marriage, I felt stranded in an unbelievable world that was becoming ever more disturbing and bizarre. My well-being was totally in the hands of others. My self had been outsourced.

While he was on a business trip around this same time, Merril married two more wives, Tammy and Cathleen. They were the youngest wives of Leroy Johnson, the FLDS prophet who had died three weeks earlier. Tammy was ten years older than I, and Cathleen, two. I was still the youngest of Merril's six wives, but it was a relief that neither of them was old enough to be my mother. I naïvely hoped we could be friends.

Tammy was not only confident of Merril's love but bragged about her ability to win his acceptance. She had been married to the prophet when he was in his late eighties and she was eighteen. She had a decade's worth of practice in catering to wives who were old enough to be her grandmothers.

Cathleen was upset by Tammy's cavalier attitude because she believed Tammy's prior marriage to the prophet was sacred. Cathleen scrubbed floors endlessly, without complaint. She received no recognition for the work she did. She often reminisced about how perfect her past life in the prophet's family had been. She would correct Merril's daughters and explain how a job or chore had been carried out in the prophet's family. They looked at her with disdain and began avoiding her.

Cathleen had been married to Leroy Johnson, the so-called prophet of God, when he was ninety-six and she was seventeen. The seventy-nine years between them mocked the very idea of a genuine marriage. But Cathleen still reveled in having been the prophet's wife. She cried constantly about being married to Merril. But because she had once been married to the prophet of God, she felt superior to me.

When Cathleen and I did the joint interview with Anderson

Cooper on CNN during the Texas raid, I felt heartbroken when I saw the wreckage of what she'd become. Cathleen was not evil; she was a true believer. Now she exemplified what the FLDS lifestyle can do to a woman. She had worked herself into the ground, desperate for the approval of Merril's family. But it never came. Merril didn't really care about her, and over the years that pushed her to try even harder. When I saw Cathleen on CNN, I felt a rush of sadness.

I too slammed into so many dead ends trying to find acceptance that for a time I started to believe there was something wrong with me. I kept seeking acceptance because a lifetime with no connection to the people I lived with seemed unbearable. But Tammy's and Cathleen's difficulties made me realize that we were three women in a bad environment, not three bad women. I concluded that I had to disengage my self-esteem and value as a person from Merril and his family. It was futile to wait and hope for something they could not give.

Years later, when I moved through that sea of pastel dresses, I knew that every woman there was trapped by her need for approval from her husband, her sister wives, her children, and most of all the FLDS leadership. I doubt many of them even knew what the court case was about. They were just doing what they'd been told to do, because they craved acceptance, as I once had.

This craving is like an addiction; you always want and need more. But it is insatiable. As long as my sense of self was defined externally, not internally, my needs were never going to be met, because in Merril's family power depended on the exploitation of others. Valuing anyone else threatened the power structure.

When I thought about my grandmother Jenny, I realized she had never made a decision based on how it would appear to others. Merril remembered that his father liked to spar with my grandmother. I think that was because she knew what she thought about things and would always hold her ground. She would not have walked across the street to get approval from a man or anyone else. She wanted to feel good about her life and the choices she made. Grandma Jenny accepted herself, and her own sense of self was nonnegotiable. The more I understood how much personal power this gave her, the more I wondered if I could ever find any of my own.

This knowledge kept me going, both consciously and unconsciously. Even when I wasn't thinking about my grandma Jenny, her spirit was strong inside me. I'd always been more self-reliant than most. But now my survival depended on my self-reliance because in Merril's family I could depend on no one else. In a sense, that made me very free. Painfully free.

I was nineteen years old and pregnant with my first child. Like my grandmother, I had concluded that the only real acceptance I would ever have was my acceptance of myself.

Strength in Silence

New life was growing in me, but so far it was only making me sick. The thought of my baby triggered emotions bigger and deeper than any I'd ever known. Along with the love came worry: how would my child be accepted in a family that refused to accept me?

My first wedding anniversary was approaching. Morning sickness made everything surreal. As I looked through the dining room window marveling at the softness of the spring sunlight hitting the pink peach blossoms, waves of nausea would wash through me. Except when I was asleep, I felt dizzy and weak all the time. I was trapped in a marriage and family I never wanted, having been forced to abandon my dream of becoming a pediatrician.

But as sick as I was, I was desperately in love with the child I was carrying. But I also felt panicked because my first year of college was almost over and I would be losing the only part of life that was mine and mine alone. In college I was taken seriously, and my potential for achievement was unlimited.

Summer school was not an option because my morning sickness was too severe. While I was in college and commuting home on weekends, I knew I could survive two days of craziness and head back to campus on Sunday night. But now, as a full-time member of Merril's hateful family, I needed a survival strategy.

One morning, as I approached the kitchen, I suddenly heard loud voices.

"You should tell father!" the first one said.

"You know how he feels about keeping secrets from him!" said the other.

"I will be the one to report what happened," retorted the second. "You stay silent!"

Merril's daughters were startled when I walked into the kitchen. Instantly the room fell silent. I wondered what would be reported to Merril. Family members routinely informed on each other. A daughter who brought an offense to her father's attention would be rewarded by him with more power and status.

Merril insisted that no secrets be kept from him. Every time he and I spoke, he'd ask, "Is there anything I need to know? Anything you want to tell me?" In the first months of my marriage this confused me. Was he asking me to confess something? Had someone reported something about me that I needed to defend? I finally gathered the courage to ask Merril what he meant.

"I feel strongly that every member of my family understand the seriousness of bringing a report to me of behavior that isn't in line with my wishes," he said. "Reporting can be seen as trying to get another person into trouble by being a snitch. But in reality if someone is straying from the work of God, reporting to me is one of the most merciful things that can be done for them."

Merril then told me one of the family's cherished stories. As an adolescent, his daughter, Merrilyn, began to fall away from the teachings of the prophet. Her friends were disreputable, and she started to associate with boys and skip school. This wild and uncontrollable streak had been evident since Merrilyn was small. When she was a year old, Merril took her from her mother, Ruth, and gave her to Foneta, his other wife, to raise. When Merrilyn started ditching school, no one noticed except her sisters, who caught her in lies and other unacceptable behavior. They reported her to Merril.

Merril looked at me proudly when he said, "I was only able to pull Merrilyn away from the black hole of hell because I was made aware of her problems before it was too late." He told me he got "very harsh" with her. When that didn't work, he made his wife Barbara shadow Merrilyn for months until she finished the eighth grade. At that point Merril decided she no longer needed to go to school, and he kept her home for a year.

Merril was proud of this story. His daughters also recounted it as one that promoted faith. They felt virtuous because they had pulled their sister back to the way of God. Merrilyn was never again taken seriously by her sisters. She eventually graduated from high school and tried college for a short time. When she was in her early twenties, she was married to the prophet Rulon Jeffs, who was decades older. When I left, she was up for blood atonement—in other words, death—because she'd allegedly had other relationships after her "marriage." I don't know if blood atonement was ever practiced by the FLDS, but I do know that Warren Jeffs told Merrilyn that this was the only way she could ever be forgiven for the sin she had committed.

As far as I know, he told her that unless she was granted the mercy of that ordinance—blood atonement—she would have to live the rest of her life at the mercy of Satan and work as a slave for the family she was assigned to serve. At the moment of her death, the devil would be there to claim her, and no one would be able to save her. Her only chance for any form of salvation was to die now via the gift of blood atonement. She would never receive this gift unless she proved worthy. In other words, Merrilyn had to prove herself "worthy" of being murdered by the FLDS for the "sin" of having a relationship outside of her "marriage," before this perverse "gift" could be granted. I don't think blood atonement was ever used on Merrilyn or anyone else, thankfully, but I heard Warren Jeffs preach about it.

I had no interest in reporting on my sister wives or Merril's daughters; it was a line I did not want to cross. Even though I had always lived in an exceedingly controlled society, I could see that Merril was trying to keep all of us off guard. He was suspicious and dominated the family through fear. He felt that forcing people to do good—as he saw it—meant he was a righteous man. I knew better and quietly took a vow never to engage in these tactics.

I have always been a keen observer. It was a skill I honed in childhood to help predict the violent outbursts of the adults in my world. I learned and studied power. During my first year of marriage Merril's daughters tried to force me to submit to them. I ignored their mandates, which drove them crazy. They'd manipulate situations to control me. I didn't fight back, nor did I ever report them to their father. I refused to play their games.

The day after I interrupted my stepdaughters' argument and they left, Cathleen came into the kitchen to get some coffee. As she stirred milk and sugar into her mug, I smiled and said, "Good morning. It's such a beautiful morning."

"How are you feeling? Any better?" she asked.

"No, I'm still fighting to keep something down," I said. "Plus, I feel sicker after overhearing our daughters and realizing someone has committed a crime that will be reported to Merril as soon as he gets home."

Cathleen shook her head. "When Tammy and I lived in the home of the prophet, he would not allow his wives to report on each other. If we had a conflict with each other, we were required to work it out. Uncle Roy [the wives' nickname for Leroy Johnson] didn't like to get in the middle of our conflicts."

I sat down next to Cathleen. "The kind of reporting Merril encourages isn't just about him getting in the middle of a conflict. It's more about using this spy system to force all of us into a corner."

The power games in the family were not centered on genuine or moral power. No one submitted to Merril's daughters unless we'd run out of other options. Merril's daughters had created enemies out of those of us who could have been their friends.

Tammy prided herself on her ability to get along with people. But she mistook being popular in the family for having real personal power. I was learning that the two qualities had nothing to do with each other. Real personal power is the ability to influence, lead, and inspire. Real power is when people follow your lead because they choose to, not because they're forced to. Real power has a moral basis. A true leader understands that if you build people up instead of tearing them down, they are more likely to respect and follow you. Merril controlled his family through the abusive power of fear and manipulation.

The family was a hierarchy, and Merril was at the top of the ladder. I opted not to get on the ladder at all. I'd learned that if I didn't provoke or challenge him, I could basically manage to avoid most conflict. It worked as long as I was in college. The summer was more of a challenge. On top of that, becoming a mother would change everything. Before my baby was born, I could disengage from the family dynamic. But I couldn't ignore or rebel against authority if it put my child at risk. The stakes would become higher once I had my baby.

As spring gave way to summer, the climate in the family heated up. Tammy was outraged with the treatment she was receiving. She became masterful at the game of "reporting to Father first." She also courted favor with Barbara. This was dangerous terrain to navigate. Barbara held an unchallenged monopoly on Merril's time. She controlled the family finances and was deeply involved in Merril's business. She spent unlimited time with Merril and understood his business dealings as well as he did.

Barbara was as dangerous as a wild animal. I decided in the first few weeks of my marriage that I would be insane to give her information about myself. Seeing what happened to Tammy early in my marriage reinforced this decision. I remember sitting with her in her bedroom while she wept, rocking in pain and gasping for breath. "I only wanted to explain," she cried between sobs. "I thought if he understood me better he would forgive."

While Tammy had been courting Barbara, she'd made the fatal error of telling her that she was jealous of the amount of time Barbara and Merril spent together. Tammy used the influence she thought she'd gained to insist that if Barbara was serious about living the gospel, she would have to accept Merril's other wives. Merril had made a covenant to five women other than Barbara, Tammy pointed out, and he had obligations to them.

Tammy would tell anyone who would listen—guests, children, and Merril's employees—that she felt she wasn't being treated as a wife. I tried to stop her. "Tammy, you shouldn't make those statements publicly," I said. "Image means everything to Merril. Crossing that line and embarrassing him is totally unforgivable to him."

The amount of time Tammy was getting with Merril decreased even more. He essentially stopped having sex with her, upsetting her even more.

Tammy continued to sob. "I decided to come clean with Merril," she said. "He's a good man who possesses the spirit of God. I thought if he understood my inner feelings about some of the things I've been through, he'd understand why I acted so badly."

Tammy had chosen a rare occasion when Merril came to have sex with her to show him the journal that contained her most intimate thoughts. If he understood the depth of her feelings, she thought, maybe, just maybe, he would accept her for who she truly was. "I knew I was risking everything," she admitted. "I felt like I couldn't breathe, but I was hoping I would earn his understanding for what I have suffered."

For ten years Tammy had been married to "Uncle Roy," seventy years her senior and the ruler of the FLDS. The vast age difference between them complicated some aspects of their marriage. She wrote about it in her journal. Even though being married to the prophet put her on center stage in the FLDS, she still felt alone and trapped. Her writing also detailed the insecurity she felt toward Merril's other wives. "I know I'm a beautiful writer, but I watched Merril's face," she continued. "None of what he was reading was religiously acceptable, which is why I never allowed anyone to read my writing before."

Merril read in silence, then stood up and told Tammy to follow him. He took Tammy's journal to a coal-burning boiler and ripped out each page and threw it into the fire. He said that she should never have allowed herself to feel the terrible things that she'd expressed in words and that his actions would put an end to her unholy emotions.

Tammy stopped talking and continued wiping tears from her face. She seemed scared. In the weeks ahead she began spending more time away from the family. She seemed to be giving up on having any kind of a life with Merril. However, one month later, when she poured out her heart to me, she was clearly worried about offending Merril. "He is upset with me because Barbara is complaining that I am not spending any time with her on weekends," Tammy said.

"Why would you even consider spending time with her after all the trouble she got you into?" I asked.

"I got myself into that trouble by keeping secrets from my husband and not reporting things I should have," Tammy said, looking serious. "I will only have the place in this family that I earn and deserve."

I believed that if Merril, who never went beyond the eighth grade, had lacked power to wield over her, Tammy would have ignored and despised him. Twenty-two years younger than Merril, Tammy was a college graduate trapped in a world where her only status and recognition came from submitting to Merril and Barbara. I could see she was determined to claw her way up as far as possible on the ladder of power. Watching her desperation opened my eyes to how a woman acts when she's trapped and powerless to leave.

When I gave birth to Arthur on December 20, 1987, he was so beautiful, I felt that anything I'd given up was worth it to have him in my life to love. I was lonely in the family, but between a new baby and returning to college, I was sure I would be happy and stimulated.

Once Merril and Barbara realized I was not going to talk about the way I felt or rat out other family members, they felt more threatened. Slowly I began to understand that I had the power of silence and the power that comes when you choose *not* to talk. No one knew what I was thinking, and no one was close enough to me to make me do what Barbara wanted.

Unlike Tammy, who blabbed her feelings to anyone and everyone, I never volunteered a single scrap of information. My unwillingness to report on other family members was seen as outright mutiny. No one could figure out why, if I loved and cared about the people in my life, I wouldn't report on them to Merril so he could help them live the rule of God. He told me I was offending him by choosing to ignore what he had asked me to do. He continued to insist that the most loyal thing a person could do for someone she cared about was protect the person by keeping him informed of his or her behavior. I held firm. I didn't want anyone spying on me, and I had no intention of spying on anyone else. At nineteen, I was entitled to make my own choices.

Merril preached about this endlessly at family prayer and at dinnertime, but I still couldn't see a religious justification for intentionally hurting someone. This practice had created a life where family members constantly watched their backs. We were always on the defensive. No one acted out of respect for Merril. Fear and coercion determined our choices.

I couldn't understand how God could be used to justify force and domination. This view directly conflicted with what I had been taught about my fundamentalist Mormon faith as a child. I was raised to believe that there had been a war in the heavenly realm that defined who we, as Mormons, were. The logic went like this: God created a planet so his children would have somewhere to go to work out their salvation. But he needed a savior who would experience an earthly existence and point the way for human salvation.

Satan stepped up to the plate. He said he would save everyone by taking away their free will. No one could possibly make a choice that would compromise their salvation so everyone would automatically go to heaven after dying. The only thing Satan wanted in return was credit for what he had done.

Jesus Christ also offered himself to God as a savior. Growing up, I was taught that Jesus promised to teach correct principles and that all who *chose* to follow his teachings would be saved. Jesus wanted no credit; all the glory would go to God.

Satan's offer was rejected. Jesus *wanted* individuals to retain free will; he was offering a power that aligned with God's plan. This was how I knew what Merril was doing was wrong. I'd been taught that power, sanctioned by God, involved free will. God did not want robots as followers; he wanted people who chose to serve him.

This conflict provoked a war in heaven. Satan was cast out and chose to come to earth. By now I truly believed that someone like Merril, who used the power of force, was aligned with the dark power of Satan. Within days of my marriage I realized I no longer had the right to choose; total obedience was expected. Yet I knew this was wrong. Not everyone was like this, even in the FLDS. Six generations in my family had been polygamists; I had strong feelings about my faith. My father had had two wives while I was growing up. He eventually gained a third and had thirty-six children. He was strict, but not a dictator. His wives did not fear and compete with each other, nor did he want family members spying on each other. There was relative harmony in our family—unlike Merril's, where only the most cunning, cruel, and manipulative thrived. I had been raised to believe in the power of Jesus Christ and not Satan, so the power I wanted in my life was based on free will. As the months passed, I learned that, for me, finding the source of real power is something as simple as honoring a principle and staying true to what you believe.

After my first child, Arthur, was born, I knew that I needed power over my own life in order to empower my son. Refusing to be subjugated to the abusive powers in the family would place me among the least powerful in Merril's family. Even so, this course seemed less destructive than the complete surrender that Tammy and Cathleen had embraced. I might become a target or a threat because I was challenging the established way. But if I could find the strength not to bow to an evil system, I could at least hold on to my self-respect.

There were many times in the years ahead when I would have to defer to Merril's power. But by the time I gave birth to Arthur, I understood what I was up against. Even today I apply the same rule of thumb I learned back then when I'm backed into a corner: I ask myself, what's the worst thing that could happen if I resist? If resisting Merril was too dangerous, I gave in. But, importantly, the decision had been mine. I might not have wanted to make the choice I did, but I still had the power to decide whether to resist or comply. This limited Merril's power over me. If *you* understand what you're doing and why, an abuser can never wholly control you.

Besides, those who rule by fear and abusive power have less control than it might appear. Those under their control rarely respect them. Yes, Tammy and Cathleen caved in completely to Merril and Barbara, but I believe they harbored enormous hostility toward them. If Merril's status in the FLDS were ever compromised or diminished, I wouldn't be surprised if his influence collapses. (That's one of the reasons, among many, that I am so hopeful his trial in Texas in October

2010 will result in a conviction.) Merril has a lot of enemies among FLDS men.

Within that first year of my marriage, the family saw me as an out-of-control member because I refused to submit totally to its power elite. While this was often an uncomfortable position, I possessed something no one else in the family had: the real power that flows from self-respect.

Staying True to My Bedrock Beliefs

I struggled to make sense of a world that made no sense. When I married Merril, I had little to hold on to because rules in the family changed on his whim. What was true one day might be false the next. I never knew what to believe, and that was unsettling.

Compounding my confusion was the way Merril reversed values that I'd been taught to hold dear. My father had insisted on equality in our family; it was the principle that governed our family. Dad divided his time equally between his two wives, made sure each had the same number of trips with him, and practiced fairness in small matters as well as large. Money and privileges were always equitably distributed. Dad also made a point of generosity. Hunger was prevalent in many FLDS families, and some kids would show up at our house at dinnertime because they wanted to be fed. They always were.

Merril was his polar opposite. He used inequality and favoritism to engineer instability in his family. He discarded the values that I had grown up with in my own family and faith. I could not question his behavior because he was the God of his family and, as God, over-

ruled us all. If Merril said day was night and night day, I was supposed to believe him.

This was madness. I was cut adrift from my moorings at a time
when I needed and wanted to put down anchors in my life. In time I
realized that even if my world did not make sense, I could *make* sense
of it. I began to articulate (to myself, of course) the values that would
define and support me. My core values became my guiding principles.
What made sense for me might not work for someone else, but figuring out what works for you is what's important. Core values can be like
the GPS system in an automobile that guides you to where you are
going. When my journey was rough, knowing who I was and what I
stood for became essential.

Here are the five values that are most important to me:

1. Claim the power of *no.* When I first joined Merril's family, filth and
chaos reigned. By seven o'clock every night, the smallest children were
famished and whining. No one was even making dinner. Dishes were
piled high in the sink, the cupboards were stained with food, and
the countertops were coated with grimy residue. I was disgusted by
the mess. Little did I realize that attacking it and getting a meal
on the table for the children in our family every night at six would teach
me something invaluable about life: the enormous power that comes
from saying no.

One night after I'd been married a couple of years, I asked one of
Merril's daughters who was in the kitchen, "Monica, who is supposed
to be fixing dinner?"

"I don't know," she said sullenly.

"Let's look at the job chart," I said. "We'll figure it out."

"The job chart has changed, and the new assignments aren't up
yet." She had no interest in helping me sort out the situation.

I was sick of the daughters' put-downs and hostility. It was also revolting to live in such squalor. When I spoke again, it was with determination. "It's too bad you don't know who's in charge tonight," I said. "We'll just have to do it together."

"I can't. I have to do Mother's laundry," she replied.

I wasn't about to let Monica skate out of the room with an excuse. I guided her toward the kitchen sink, removed the dirty dishes, and filled the sink with hot water. Monica looked hostile, but she knew I was serious and started washing dishes.

I began peeling potatoes and making my game plan. Once I got dinner under way, I would clean. Monica made some excuse and slipped out of the kitchen after a few minutes. I was furious. She and her sisters rarely kept their commitments, nor were they ever accountable for anything. Merril's daughters would sing to their father on weekends as part of a family tradition. When they serenaded him, they acted like hardworking saints, but I knew they were anything but.

As I scrubbed dishes while potatoes boiled and corn cooked, I fantasized about a concert by Merril's daughters singing songs about who they *really* were:

> We are slobs, great big slobs,
> Never expect us to greet you
> We only understand how to mistreat you,
> If you don't like being corrected, realize you have been rejected
> And stay out of OUR way!

I did not want my son to grow up in such a disgusting environment. I was in no mood for extending any compassion. I barked at the first child who wandered into the kitchen: "Go tell everyone to get into the kitchen right now! We should have eaten hours ago!"

The smiling bright eyes of this famished little boy touched me. He was thrilled to see the table piled high with a simple meal of potatoes, gravy, corn, salad, and bread. Running out of the kitchen, he began yelling excitedly, "Mother Carolyn has made dinner! Come and see!"

Within two minutes a flood of children surrounded the table. I began pouring milk for the smallest ones as some of Merril's daughters bounced into the kitchen. They were all smiles and very hungry. "This looks so good!" "I love it when Mother Carolyn fixes a meal!" Even the belligerent daughters were grateful to be fed. I felt some pangs of compassion toward them. Maybe I would tone down my slob song—a bit.

After the meal several of the daughters stayed behind and helped me clean up. I did not quit until everything was shining. It was eleven o'clock, and I was exhausted from a grueling second pregnancy, caring for Arthur, and finishing my final quarter of college. But I was proud of what I'd just accomplished.

Tammy couldn't sleep and came into the kitchen just after I finished. "How do you live with this every night?" I asked her. "It's worse than living in a zoo."

Tammy shrugged. "If you find the evenings repulsive, they're nothing compared to the mornings," she said. "Each daughter is supposed to get one child up and ready for school. Two others are supposed to get breakfast on the table. But no one ever does what she's supposed to do. Breakfast is never organized. Ruth makes a last-minute dash to do something before the kids head out the door. They're late for school every morning. At lunchtime someone tries to throw something together, but the kitchen is a total heap from breakfast. When the kids come home from school, they make some kind of snack, but it just adds to the mess from breakfast and lunch."

I was suddenly thankful that my school schedule had me out of the house on weekday mornings. "I won't raise my children in conditions like this," I said.

"Then do what you did tonight," Tammy said. "Do everything yourself. The daughters will promise to do almost anything, but they never follow through."

I knew Tammy was right. "Do you think the reason they can't keep commitments is because no one ever has?" I asked.

Merril was a prime example. He was never on time for anything. He constantly broke promises. He told people what they wanted to hear, then did whatever he felt like doing. Barbara just barked orders. She never promised anything, so there were no commitments to keep. But Tammy, Cathleen, and I had all been either working or in school before marrying Merril and so were used to discipline and structure. I had an idea.

"Tammy," I said, "there's no way we can keep up with everything that needs to get done. But we could tackle the things that make us craziest and make a commitment to do those every day. If we really follow through, there would be at least two examples in the family of what keeping a commitment means."

Tammy was quiet for a moment, then said, "Since I don't sleep well, I'm always up early. I could wake up the kids and make breakfast even though I hate to cook."

I was surprised by her generous offer. My back hurt from all the bending and cleaning. The last thing I wanted to do was spend the rest of this pregnancy doing what I had just done. But I couldn't stand the thought of my children growing up in such a slovenly household. I took a few deep breaths. If I made this commitment, I had to keep it.

"All right, Tammy," I said. "As soon as I graduate, I will fix dinner every night. If I'm not up to cleaning, I'll at least mop the floor." We had a plan.

Tammy made an announcement to the family that she would be waking the kids and making breakfast. It sent shock waves throughout the household. After I graduated a month later, I started making dinner, as promised. It soon became an issue. Merril was angry because his sons were working for his construction company, and he wanted them on the job until after dark.

I knew the boys needed to eat before then and kept putting dinner on the table at six o'clock. They started sneaking home to eat. I thought they would probably work more efficiently if they weren't starved. It was also cruel to expect the littlest children to wait until after dark to eat. The tension escalated. Merril was not happy with me: people acting under their own power were a threat. I saw how much power there was in something as simple as keeping a commitment. I vowed never again to back down once I gave my word to do something. I often agreed to things because I was forced into a corner. This new vow meant I'd be saying no a lot more often.

Most of us fear rejection and, as a result, continually seek approval and find it hard to say no. It seems selfish. We give in to our fears of what might happen if we stand up for ourselves. But it's impossible to say yes to everything. When I made that pledge always to keep my word, I found the power in saying no.

And ultimately I discovered that exercising this power gave me real protection. I kept doing what I believed was right and served dinner every night at six o'clock. I would not back down and said no to every attempt by Merril and Barbara to force me to change. I had accidentally hit upon a new way to maneuver in the oppressive and claustrophobic world I was trapped in. Barbara and Merril were bullies. But their control depended on the rest of us ceding our own power to them.

2. Set your own standards. We were taught that everything in the family belonged to Merril. He worked as God's project manager and made sure we did God's will daily. Not owning things ourselves generated another level of chaos. We lived under very cramped conditions. I now had two small children, with whom I shared a room with a queen-size bed. Five of Merril's teenage daughters lived in a room next to mine that wasn't much bigger and that was ready to explode with their mess. No one was responsible for anything: if a daughter couldn't find a clean dress to wear, she took one of her sister's. Since no one owned anything, you had no right to protest when someone took something of yours.

Tammy and I did the family shopping. There was barely enough money for food and no extra money for personal items. We all had to buy our own. I scrimped to be able to buy shampoo, deodorant, and toothpaste. I kept them in a basket in my room, but items would disappear even when I tried to hide them, and often I couldn't afford to replace them. Betty was a newborn, and Arthur a toddler. I had more responsibilities, and less money, than ever before. I hated that my room was being searched and my privacy invaded.

One day I was walking by Ruth's room and noticed a bottle of shampoo that looked like the one that had disappeared from my room that morning. I decided to take it back and confront her. As I turned to leave, I noticed several other items of mine. In the end I left the shampoo on the sink. Ruth could keep her stolen loot, but not without getting a piece of my mind. I found her in the kitchen fixing lunch.

"Ruth, I find it interesting that most of the personal items I've asked you about lately are in your bathroom," I said. "Do you have any idea how they got there?"

Ruth turned away from her work. "Everything in our home belongs to Father," she said unapologetically. "Nothing belongs to anyone. I answered truthfully when I said I hadn't seen your shampoo. I haven't seen any shampoo that belongs to you because nothing belongs to you."

"You took the shampoo from the place where I'd hidden it," I said, scarcely able to believe what I was hearing. "This isn't a quarrel over whether the shampoo belongs to Father. Why is treating someone like that all right?"

"The bedroom I sleep in doesn't belong to me, and where you sleep doesn't belong to you," she said. "I have no problem if you need something and take it from the bedroom I sleep in. We all belong to Father, and if you were in harmony with him, you would be 'keeping sweet,' and we wouldn't be talking to each other like this."

"Keeping sweet" was just another club used to beat us into submission. I was having none of it. "Ruth," I persisted, "have I ever invaded your bedroom, searched every square inch of it, and taken what I wanted?"

Ruth did not stray off message. In a pious voice she said, "My room is always open. Everything I have belongs to Father, and you are welcome to anything you need. I don't begrudge any members of Father's family from using something they need."

"Did you ever consider that perhaps Father in his infinite mercy allows me to use and keep personal items in the area I sleep in for his benefit?" I stared straight at Ruth. "Maybe he'd prefer that I not smell like a stinking pig. Perhaps he allows me to buy shampoo so that the odor of unwashed hair will not offend his nose."

Ruth looked caught off guard by my assertiveness, but she kept repeating the same excuses over and over. She was incapable of responding in any meaningful way.

"I am not begrudging you something you need," I said finally. "I am asking you to consider my feelings and ask before you take something."

But it was pointless. My personal items kept disappearing. As more and more of them went missing, it became obvious that my strong reactions invited more abuse. The more I reacted, the worse it became. The angrier I got, the more the saintly Ruth tried to "keep sweet" while stealing me blind. By "keeping sweet," she could think of herself as doing the will of God, while I was selfish and out of control.

My attempt to establish standards had failed miserably. I was tempted to take Ruth up on her offer of swiping things from her room. I *wanted* to strike back at her. It felt fair. But if I did, Ruth would flip. When I had time to really think it through, I saw that there was nothing to be gained by stooping to her level. Why should I demean myself? Ruth was trying to provoke me into a confrontation, but I decided I wasn't going to play her nasty little games. I'd do what I could to protect myself and never leave my bedroom door unlocked.

I once heard a story of a town built on a floodplain. Periodically the town would be wiped out by rising waters, but it was always rebuilt in the same place. The residents were trapped in a constant cycle of flooding and rebuilding. The cycle wasn't broken until the town was built on higher ground.

I could not change the family dynamic or the established patterns of behavior. Trying to teach someone how her abuse felt by doing the same thing to her was like rebuilding the town in the same old place. I had to move to higher ground.

I decided I would treat everyone in the family with respect. It was my version of the Golden Rule, except I had few expectations that people would do unto me the way I tried to do unto them. But I did free myself from the vicious cycle of reacting to every crazy thing that was done to me. My privacy in the family was never going to be respected. But by setting my own standards and refusing to engage, I opted out of a lot of the madness. Even though I couldn't control the others in Merril's family, I could control the way I reacted, and that was a far more meaningful power.

In his memoir, *Man's Search for Meaning,* the psychiatrist and Holocaust survivor Viktor Frankl wrote about how even in the concentration camp, he understood that he still had choice. While he couldn't control what happened to him, he could control his response. This gave him a power that the Nazis could not destroy. Even amid the most acute suffering, Frankl was always able to find meaning.

Following Frankl's inspiring example, I decided that whenever I felt powerless, I would remember that I always had some choice. By controlling my response to my circumstances, I could avoid being their victim, no matter how ghastly they might become.

3. Hold on to whatever power you do have. I vividly remember the relief I felt when the sixth graders streamed out of my classroom and I was finally alone after my first full day as a schoolteacher. Once again my fate had arrived unexpectedly. I had been substitute-teaching for weeks, but suddenly, with only a day's notice, I was permanently assigned to the sixth grade because the regular teacher got sick and abruptly quit.

The south wall of my classroom was lined with bookcases that held months of uncorrected work stacked up in piles that were covered with dust. It was a special-needs class with just under thirty children, about a third of whom had learning disabilities. The school year was half over. My head was spinning. How could I possibly get this class caught up and ready for the seventh grade?

It didn't help that I was twenty-two with two small children of my own, yet constantly mistaken for a sixth grader. Every time another adult walked into my classroom the first question was, "Where's the teacher?" Still, I reminded myself that it wasn't the students' fault that they weren't being taught.

I tried to sort through the stacks of work, but none of it made sense to me. Clearly, I wasn't going to be able to pick up the pieces. I reached for the wastebasket and began dumping in pile after pile of papers. We were going to start fresh.

The next day I announced to my students that all of them were starting with an A. The work they would do in the coming weeks would determine whether they kept it as their final grade. We were going to go all out and give the semester our best shot.

While I was tossing all the papers into the trash, I'd come across a pile that looked like more than just busywork. It was a basket filled with student journals. As I read through one journal after another, I discovered that the voices of my students were filled with the wealth of their personalities. Some of them might have had learning challenges, but that did not prevent the power of their personalities from flowing onto the page.

Even though I was a decade older than my students, nearly all of whom were FLDS, I had a lot in common with them. One student wrote about the conflict in her father's family and the confusion she felt every day. Many wrote about how insecure they felt because their teacher's illness made him absent so much. In an entry written after I'd substituted in the classroom for a day, one student said that she hoped I would become her teacher because she wanted to learn something. It was poignant to see how much she wanted to learn; I felt an even greater responsibility to her and the rest of the class.

One student had written a poem. I began reading about a perfectly sunny day and a ride in the back of a truck to a picnic. I shuddered. I realized I was reading about the death of my youngest sister, Nurylon, who'd been thrown from the back of a truck and killed four years earlier, when she was two years old. I felt my hand tremble as it gripped the pages. My student had shared the experience of one of the worst days of my life. The poem described the joy of being in the truck with the rush of wind and laughter. Then in an instant, screaming bodies were hurled into the air.

I put the journal down. Flashbacks to that awful day exploded in my mind, and I felt overcome with grief. It wasn't just the loss of my sister; it was the loss of my dream of becoming a doctor. It was feeling beaten down by having two children in less than three years and being trapped in a marriage based on degradation instead of love. I was grasping for a moment of clarity, something real, something I could physically feel because I was completely numb. I needed someone to trust. For too long, I'd shoved my feelings down and pushed grief away whenever it hit me. I was living in a constant state of grief but simultaneously denying it.

My world was out of control. There was so little in my life that I could control. Every important decision in my life up to that moment had been made by someone else. I had to turn over all the money I earned to Merril and had no say in whether I even wanted to teach this class of unruly, woefully behind sixth graders.

The fact that I had never been allowed to make any important decisions in my life had convinced me I was powerless in every area. But that was untrue. What *was* true was that I wasn't taking control over the areas where I did have genuine power.

The fact that I couldn't become a doctor did not mean that I couldn't be a superb teacher. No one would hold me accountable for the job I did with my class since many were learning-disabled. I had a built-in excuse to fail. But my students deserved my best. If I didn't act, every one of them would be going into the seventh grade completely unprepared. There wasn't much time left in the academic year, but I could still teach them skills to take to seventh grade. I would give them as much as I could. I saw that teaching, like pediatrics, was about protecting the ultimate well-being of a child.

I got my class on a routine and soon had everyone working at a level that was appropriate. Some students were almost up to grade level, and others were way behind. I tried to work out individual plans so students could move at their own pace. Each day that a student mastered a new skill was thrilling. It was a moment of pure power for me.

I had arrived unexpectedly at a core value for myself: I would hold on to the power I did have. Just because I couldn't control some things—even if those things were huge and important—it didn't mean I couldn't control others. Victimhood requires our acquiescence, and I was opting out.

4. Forget about perfection, and do the best you can. Good was never good enough in the FLDS. Life was based on perfection. It didn't matter how much of the spirit of God a person had, how hard she worked, how much she "kept sweet" and complied, she could always do better. Regardless of how much she accomplished, she needed to do better because the work of God was about being in a constant state of progression.

I soon found that working full time and having a baby every other year put me in a constant state of failure. I was always dropping the ball and felt torn between my teaching career and my children, never able to give enough to either. Then I realized that perfection was one enemy I could conquer. I banished it.

The concept of perfection was so ingrained in our culture and such an integral part of my upbringing that letting go of it made me feel acutely disoriented for a time. I was not alone in this respect. Working with the mothers of my students was eye-opening. Many of them told me how hard it was to find the courage to face each day because of the staggering workload they shouldered in such large families. They were up against impossible expectations and never got credit for the work they did. Every small setback was always their fault: if they only had more faith, God would give them the strength to achieve the necessary level of perfection.

I found myself telling them the same thing I told myself: do the best you can today, and know you can face the rest tomorrow. Take credit for all the good you're doing and keep your expectations realistic.

I could see in my own life that by aiming for perfection, I accomplished less, not more. Life wasn't perfect or fair. I faced this reality every day. Why was I supposed to be perfect as a person? Merril and Barbara, who constantly advocated perfection, were about as imperfect as two people could be.

I was reexamining religious values I'd accepted unquestioningly since childhood. To stop striving for perfection was quietly liberating for me. I determined to give a task my all, take my best shot, and then let it go. I wouldn't win all of the time. But sometimes I would, and whatever happened in between would be just fine.

A member of the FLDS is supposed to strive to become more like God, who is perfect. Embracing your imperfect humanity is thus, in the twisted logic of FLDS dogma, a rejection of God. I realized that to totally accept the FLDS view of perfection, I had to totally reject myself. If I did that, then I'd have nothing left to hold on to. Many women in the FLDS were on antidepressants. I didn't want to wake up in the morning and swallow a handful of pills just so I could stumble through the day.

I'd already found an enormous power in realizing that if I wanted acceptance, I'd have to get it from myself. I decided I would accept myself just as I am—imperfect, struggling, and very human. This became another weapon in my arsenal of personal power.

Abandoning perfection, of course, can easily be used as an excuse. But I wasn't letting myself off the hook—I was pushing myself to achieve more. In areas that are not my strong suit, however, I've learned to let go and not beat myself up with unrealistic expectations.

5. Do whatever it takes to protect those you love. One night Merril sat in his living-room chair as if it were a throne. His six wives and children were kneeling before him in a wide circle. It was late and our fatigue was apparent.

Merril was making pronouncements:

> Our prophet has, in his infinite mercy, given us principles of what it will take to become like him. "Where much is given, much is required." It is a serious thing for God to reveal one of his principles to his people. He will never reveal something they are not capable

of living and he will always grant them enough time to come to an understanding before he will reveal a higher law. What is one of the most recent teachings of our prophet?

Hands shot up in every direction. Merril called on one of his sons, who shouted out, "Perfect obedience produces perfect faith!" Merril smiled approvingly and then got to the heart of the matter:

This morning at Monday meeting I was asked a question by dear old Uncle Fred. He put his hand on my shoulder and said, "Brother Merril, why is it that our ladies always look so sad and miserable? Why is it that I don't see smiling, happy women?" How do you think that kind of a question from our bishop made me feel?

The silence was heavy with our collective guilt. We knew this was terrible for Merril. Miserable-looking wives exposed his life for the lie that it was. None of us spoke, so Merril continued:

When a person finds themselves in harmony with their husband and in obedience to his wishes, they also find peace. If my ladies were united with me they would wear an expression that demonstrated that unity. Any woman in my family who wants my will in her life is at peace. If she is at peace with her life she will also be happy and always have a pleasant and sweet smile.

Merril asked for comments. Barbara asked permission to speak first:

Father, we all know the serious effect a mother has on her children. Our prophet, Uncle Roy, has said, "Show me a rebellious child, and I will show you a rebellious mother." It is critical that all the mothers in this family are in harmony with you for the sake of their children's eternal salvation. If a woman in your home finds herself in a condition where she is not happy it is a clear condition of selfishness. For we all know that any woman living in harmony with the teachings of the prophet and her husband raises faithful children.

From then on we manufactured plastic smiles whenever we were in public.

In the FLDS, everything that goes wrong is a woman's fault. If children grow up and leave the work of God, it's the mother's fault. A woman whose child has problems must be guilty of something; otherwise God would not be punishing her. When my son Harrison was fifteen months old, he was diagnosed with cancer in his spine. Merril told me it was God's punishment for my rebellion to my husband. He insisted that Harrison did not need to go to the doctor. According to Merril, if I became more obedient to him, God would heal my son.

My goal was to be invisible. This was the status I craved above all else. Invisibility was my oasis and my reward. If somehow I managed to raise faithful children—and early in my marriage my faith still mattered to me—then in my later years I could be invisible.

My invisibility would be a great gift for my children, especially my daughters, because it meant that nothing I'd ever done could be held against them. (Men see women as a threat if they have a frisky grandmother or rebellious mother.) That dream died the day I came home from school and found my son Arthur standing in a corner of the kitchen, sobbing.

Esther, one of Merril's daughters, was berating him. "If you get out of that corner, Arthur, I will spank you!"

I was outraged. "Esther, what's going on?"

She flipped her long braid to the back of her head. In a snotty voice she said, "He's Father's child, not yours. I don't have to answer you when I'm doing what Father wants."

Fire shot from my eyes. "What did you do to him, and why did you do it?" I yelled. "You'd better tell me right now!"

"You need to get in harmony with your husband," Esther said, a big smirk on her face. "You know how Father feels about interfering in the discipline of his children."

Interfering would cost me my invisibility. If I didn't back down fast, talk of my being a protective mother would roil through the community. Esther did not realize the power she had over me in that moment. But the fear of those consequences ended when I heard one more sob coming from my son. I was never going to be beaten down to the point where I would fail to intervene when someone was hurting my child.

"Esther, Arthur is *my* son," I said. "I want to know everything you have done to him. Right now."

Esther stiffened with defiance. "I will not answer to you," she said. "You have no right to interfere with my discipline."

I shook my finger at her. "You will never hurt one of my children again!"

I walked over to the corner, grabbed Arthur, and carried him out of the room. I had crossed a line in the family that I now knew would have explosive and permanent repercussions.

They began immediately. I was instantly branded an interfering mother who would not allow her child to be disciplined to conform to his father's will. Every time I intervened, I was in conflict with my husband's wishes. If I faced down people who hurt my children, it could backfire by making them angrier and thus encouraging more abuse. But I also noticed that when I came down hard on them for hurting one of my children, people in the family began to realize that, even though they tattled to Merril, there was no escaping my wrath. I didn't care if they reported me to Merril. I was not backing down.

No one in the family had ever dealt with this kind of force before. One of the most consistent weapons family members deployed was to say "I'm doing what Father wants and you are not." I neutralized that weapon. I told my opponent that the issue was between the two of us and had nothing to do with Merril.

I made it so uncomfortable for people who hurt my kids that eventually many realized it wasn't worth it. I couldn't always protect my children, but I always tried. Fearful of getting pregnant for the eighth time, I'd stopped having sex with Merril. When the word got out that I was in rebellion, the other wives started abusing my children to get at me. So I started sleeping with Merril again just to protect them. But at least it was a strategic choice.

Trying to protect my children put me in constant conflict with Merril. He retaliated by cutting me off financially. When I asked for something, he would tell me that only people who did what he wanted could get the basic necessities they needed. The message was that if I protected our children, he would hurt them in every other area that he could. I ignored him and became determined never again to get myself into a position where I actually depended on him financially.

One effective way I found to counter Merril's manipulation with money was to create a hidden savings account. When I was teaching, I dutifully turned over every paycheck to Merril. But I didn't include the stub that itemized my deductions. What he didn't realize was that I was having a tiny percentage of my salary automatically deducted and deposited directly into an account at the credit union. So when the children needed shoes or clothes that Merril refused to provide, I had a way to take care of them myself.

Merril's next step was to inform me that others in the family needed to discipline my children because I didn't do it properly. My inadequacy made it necessary for others to step in and do the job the way Merril wanted it done. It was my fault, as always.

I was so angry with Merril and the rest of the family that I decided that if I had to give up my religion, my culture, and my heritage to protect my children, I would. It made no sense to me that I had to allow my children to be abused in order to become like God. I knew I would never be accepted as a respected member of Merril's family. At the same time my dream of being an invisible woman was gone.

But that dream was less appealing than it once had been anyway. It had slowly begun to dawn on me that an invisible woman is one who lives in the shadows among the living dead. In place of that dream, another was being born—that of a woman who had self-worth and values she was willing to die for. I had no guarantee of success, but the cost of doing nothing was too high. I wanted my children to know that they had a mother who would always fight to protect them. This became my most important core value—albeit one that put me in constant conflict with my husband, my faith, and my community. Merril repeatedly told me that if I continued to insist on protecting my children, it could cost me my salvation. Yet he was making my life on earth such hell that spending eternity with him in heaven held absolutely no appeal. This tension was never reconciled until I fled the FLDS on April 21, 2003.

Over time, finding and sticking to my core values transformed my life, giving me the ability to understand and cope with bullying, stay out of vicious power games, and advocate for myself and my children. By changing the way I reacted to my environment, my values provided structure in a chaotic world. Each of them shifted my attitude to the world around me, not the world itself. But each tiny internal shift in my reactions—a percent here, a percent there—kept accumulating and compounding until my life was headed in a completely new direction. If you hold fast to your core values, whatever they are, I guarantee your life will improve. In my case, they ultimately gained all of us our freedom.

A Place for Peace

I may have been speechless, but the 120 names carved into the granite memorial spoke loudly and clearly to me. They were of the men, women, and children known as the Fancher party who were butchered by Mormons as they crossed Utah by wagon train in 1857.

Growing up, I'd been steeped in the lore of the Mountain Meadows massacre and listened to romanticized stories of John D. Lee, one of the masterminds of the slaughter, which was taught to children as a heroic tale. The massacre was always spun as a mandate from God carried out by the Mormon faithful. As children we were told that the Arkansas migrants who were headed to California were poisoning our well water to kill our livestock. According to the story, after settling in California the Arkansans planned to return and kill all the Mormons. This was why God gave the prophet, Brigham Young, a revelation to destroy all whose intent was to sabotage the work of God.

The names of the women and children screamed at me. By now I had three children under five. They were the sole source of love in my life, and the thought of their coming to harm was unbearable.

Merril had taken me on one of his business trips and made a detour so we could visit the massacre memorial and learn more about our Mormon heritage. He could never have known what a radicalizing effect this brief stopover would have on me.

How could children be killed in the name of God? Struggling to regain my composure, I turned to Merril and said, "I can't believe there are so many names of young children. Why were they killed?" It was unsettling to confront what had actually happened instead of what we'd been taught to believe.

Merril was matter of fact. "They were all over the age of eight, the age where they are accountable in the eyes of God. They were helping their parents poison wells. They would have all grown up to be the people who came back to Utah to destroy the Mormons."

I was incredulous. "How can such evil be of God?"

"You're taking this too seriously," Merril said, looking puzzled. "Don't trouble yourself with something if you can't understand it. Put it in God's hands, and when you have become close enough to Him and His will, then and only then can He give you the answer."

I wasn't sure I wanted an answer from a God who could do something like this. There was no excuse for murdering so many people. None of those massacred in the five-day attack had been proven guilty of any crimes. How could John D. Lee know what lay in the hearts of the people he murdered? The story I'd grown up on was a childish fairy tale compared to the gruesome reality I read about at the memorial. Mormons disguised as Indians first attacked the wagon train. Then a second group of Mormons came to their rescue, telling the terrified survivors they'd negotiated a ceasefire on their behalf with the Indians.

Believing they were being led to safety, the survivors of the initial attack, many of them gravely injured, gave up their weapons, wagons, and cattle and began a thirty-five-mile trek back to Cedar City, Utah. The most seriously injured rode along with the youngest children in two wagons. Everyone else walked. When the command was given, "Halt! Do your duty!" each of the armed escorts turned and shot the man walking by his side. A second order went out, and the women and children, who were farther along up the hill, were slaughtered.

Nancy Huff, one of the seventeen survivors (spared because they were under eight), was four years old at the time and later wrote about what she remembered: "I saw my mother shot in the forehead and fall dead. The women and children screamed and clung together. Some of the young women begged the assassins after they ran out on us not to kill them, but they had no mercy on them, clubbing [them with] their guns and beating out their brains."

The 120 bodies were left on the ground and never buried. The vultures and the elements soon stripped their rotting corpses to bare bones that were bleached by the scorching sun.

Growing up, I'd always heard stories about why the Mountain Meadows massacre was necessary. The tale of John D. Lee was larger than life. He was the only man tried for the attack and sentenced to death. But the firing squad shot blanks, and he pretended to fall over as if he were hit. He was carted away and disappeared into hiding, never to be seen again. The Hollywood ending has never been confirmed by historians, but we children swallowed it hook, line, and sinker.

The FLDS believes that a man doing God's will would never have had to pay with his life. God had inspired a godly man to do what was necessary. Lee massacred a wagon train full of people, not because he was bloodthirsty. No, he went with a humble heart to do what God needed him to do. That, at least, was the version we were taught.

Historical debate rages about whether Brigham Young actually ordered the massacre. But to most of the faithful, it didn't really matter. The members of the Fancher party were evil; if God didn't want the massacre to happen, he would have stopped it. The flawless way the massacre was carried out was proof that it had been divinely sanctioned.

The names told a different story. I was blindsided by a rush of emotion that day. The seventeen children who survived were raised by foster families. I was reeling at the thought of all the trauma those small children endured.

Were the heroic stories of my youth only heroic lies? How much else of what I'd been told contained partial truth and outright fabrications? A belief system governed every waking moment of my day. I was not supposed to think, only obey. But I was thinking now, and my religion did not feel safe. What if I was told to do something I couldn't live with? I was starting to have serious concerns about blind obedience "in the name of God."

I'd been raised to believe that if God gave me a commandment I couldn't understand, like marrying Merril Jessop, I should shelve all my doubts and do what I was told. But my overloaded shelf was ready to collapse. I was going to have to find some serious support, or it would come tumbling down.

I had two identities, my FLDS cult identity and my authentic self. No matter how domineering the mind control of a group or cult is, the authentic self can only be suppressed, never totally erased. And suppress it I did. There was no way that a person's authentic self could surface and survive in the FLDS. It was dangerous to let any aspect of one's true self be visible.

So I wasn't really prepared for the truth that rushed out at me when I faced that granite wall of names. At the core of our faith was the belief that God's judgment on the last day would kill all the wicked and that only the righteous would be protected and saved. It was impossible for me to stare at those 120 names on the Mountain Meadows Massacre Memorial and think of them as evil. A shift was beginning to take place in me that was deeper than I could possibly understand at the time: much of what I had been taught about my history and my faith was a lie.

Merril and I arrived home as the sun was setting on El Cap, the mountain plateau that shadows Colorado City. The sun's disappearing rays sprayed the red sandstone with a brilliant blaze of color. The cliffs burned like a bonfire. But I couldn't enjoy the beauty. My heart was drowning in the evil I'd witnessed that day.

As I put my three children to bed that night, even my complete love for them wasn't enough to overcome my sense of loss and futility. My life felt as if it had no purpose. My sister Annette had recently remarked that others were noticing my sadness. "Carolyn, what's happening to you? One of your old classmates went over to your house to talk to Merril about something and couldn't believe his eyes when he saw you again. He said you looked like a shell of who you used to be." I couldn't tell her how miserable I was. She'd never understand.

Was the bottomless emptiness I felt on the inside visible on the outside? My terror was that the emptiness would be all-consuming. Beliefs that had once grounded my life were gone. I was facing another night of tossing and turning over too many things that felt evil and wrong. If living the will of God's laws was so great, then why did my life feel so meaningless? I was lost.

A few weeks later, after fixing dinner and mopping the kitchen floor, I noticed the setting sun as I was dumping out the dirty water. I went outside and stood on the deck searching for answers. Why, when this was just another dismal day, did the sun set in celebration? For me, there was nothing to celebrate on that day or any other. I feared that the harshness and brutality of life would eventually consume me. I would become as evil and ugly as all the things I hated. My fight not to surrender, not to be consumed, was constant and exhausting. I was holding on to the edge of a cliff with no sign of anyone coming to pull me to safety.

The sunset was brilliant, but I couldn't appreciate it. I was buried in grief for my life. I couldn't relate to beauty at any level. It was impossible for me even to imagine seeing the wonder in each day. It was spring, and the world was shedding the bitter brown of winter for the green of new life. The alfalfa field near our house was a brilliant emerald and alive with new leaves. Sprays of water from the sprinklers were splashing in the light of the sunset and casting off mini-rainbows. The field was calling to me, and for once, I wanted to answer.

I quickly left the breathtaking scene and found my three children. I got them ready for bed, and after giving them several books to look at, I told them to stay put—I'd be back soon.

I left the house and fled to the field. It was getting dark, so I knew I was safe and no one would see me. Everything I did was watched, critiqued, and reported. I was desperate for a moment of freedom from my oppressive life. All the grief and unpleasant moments were over for that day, and I wanted to release them by running through the alfalfa.

I made my way to the field. The sprinklers were turned off, and the only sound was the quiet whoosh of the willows blowing in the breeze. I sat on the soft sandy earth and removed my shoes, which kept filling with sand. I wanted to run completely unencumbered.

I took a few fast steps. My feet felt as light as the tender new alfalfa leaves felt soft. The sand sifting between my toes was pure pleasure. The heat of the day was gone, the air crisp. Each deep breath of air filled my lungs and centered my soul like a spiritual CPR, breathing life back into an empty heart.

I ran the length of the field several times. Alone after the sun had fully set, I began to come alive. My anguish and despair were released for the day. I'd face them again tomorrow. I felt at peace. I felt like me.

This was my first run in the alfalfa field but far from my last. Whenever I felt like I was drowning in a day, I waited for sunset, then returned to my alfalfa field. There were no rules in the soft sand, and in the evening twilight no one was waiting to trap me or to catch me in a crime. With every breath of fresh night air I connected with my authentic self. It was the only way I knew to feel centered and grounded. Waiting until it was dark enough to run in the field became my secret rendezvous. It was like going to meet my lover amid the splendor of the natural world.

As the summer heat hit, the alfalfa grew tall and was ready for cutting. The first time I ran after it was cut, the field was a sea of sharp shoots. The harsh stubble stung the heels of my feet the way my inner conflict sliced at my soul. There seemed no way for me to reconcile my own self with a faith that condoned murdering those who were perceived as a threat. My children were my life's only purpose. I could not continue to live in a way that obliterated all hope.

As I was sitting alone after my run, nursing the scratches on my feet and listening to a choir of crickets, a new thought came to me. Maybe it was my resistance to the difficulties in my life that was destroying me. Maybe it wasn't the pain of being injured, or the shock of the next method of torture. Maybe I was being consumed by my constant searching for a way around the reality that I faced.

What if I accepted that my circumstances were not likely to change? Maybe I needed to let go of the idea that there was a better way and concentrate on finding a path through the systematic abuse in the family. I knew that each time I was emotionally smashed into the ground, I hated myself that much more. I hated my weakness. I hated the fact that I was powerless to protect myself. I hated the fact that I felt broken inside.

But maybe I was wounded and suffering but not broken. Maybe I was more than trash that should be discarded. For me, the fear of being hurt is often worse than actually enduring the injury. I walked back toward my shoes, and the sharpness of the field merely pricked my feet. Maybe running in the field had conditioned them to be less sensitive. I picked up my shoes and decided to walk the field that evening. It was cool and clear. Maybe my reality would be less harsh if I could accept it for what it was and, like walking on the stubble, learn to deal with it.

I'd spent so much time cleaning the kitchen, hoping somehow it would lead to more. If I polished one more counter, if I mopped the floor more often, if, if, if, I might be rewarded with some personal power for doing something religiously acceptable. I kept trying. Every night I'd get into bed, exhausted and beaten. But I had no personal power. I realized now that no matter what I did or how well I did it, I'd never get any.

At that point I was still years from even thinking of escape. My three children were too young. I desperately wanted a voice, some form of personal expression, but that too was unthinkable for a woman in the FLDS. What would happen if I put my effort into what I believed in my heart was right instead of reacting to and recoiling from the continual abuse and cruelty in Merril's family? I would reclaim some small sense of decision making in my own life.

Constantly trying to avoid the next attack in Merril's family kept me in a defensive posture and took me out of the moment. If I paid close enough attention, I thought, I could ward off an attack before it happened. But I was so focused on what *might* happen down the line that I wasn't as able to protect myself in the actual day-to-day. I was always on guard, controlled by my fear, and mortgaged to the future. My strategy was to outmaneuver Barbara and Merril by figuring out what would come next. As a result, I was missing the possibilities in the present. I was surrendering my power in the now.

I decided I was going to seize the moment. No matter what it took, I would confront every humiliation, abuse, injury, and hurt that came my way. Maybe I would have *more* power if I successfully faced down everything I detested. It was a terrifying prospect in a terrifying world. What if I wasn't strong enough? What if I succumbed? I would find out who I truly was, and that made me vulnerable.

The alfalfa field became my place of solace. The best time for running was a few days after the field had been cut, so that the shoots would be covered by tender new leaves. Running in bare feet made me feel like I was breaking every taboo. I could dare to disobey. I felt more alive than I had in years. If I could feel, I could stay alive.

The Kindness of a Stranger

Growing up in the FLDS, I was indoctrinated with a variety of religious beliefs. One I heard again and again was from the prophet Leroy Johnson, who talked about the importance of "religious education." He would say, "Those early teachings and trainings that we give our children stay with them throughout their entire lives. It's no wonder that the Lord said that we should raise our children as calves in the stall."

I'd been raised in a stall all right, and I was aching to break out of it. I was caged in by a strict set of beliefs that dictated who I was and what I could become. The principle at work was mind control, pure and simple.

I started studying mind control after I escaped. I truly had had no idea that I'd been in a dangerous cult. I'd seen the FLDS referred to online as "the largest polygamous cult" in the United States and dismissed that as ridiculous. But as I read and studied more, I realized that's exactly what I was born into.

One of the books I encountered early on was Robert Jay Lifton's *Thought Reform and the Psychology of Totalitarianism: A Study of Brainwashing in China*. It was a revelation. Lifton articulated the most common criteria of mind control. When I considered them in the context of the FLDS, I knew all of them applied. Just as in a totalitarian system, the FLDS took steps to control our environment, demand purity, claim scientific and moral truth for the cult dogma, destroy personal boundaries, require confession, and insist on the supremacy of group belief over individual thought. Language was manipulated to keep everything in black and white. We were to follow the teachings of our leader and no one else—least of all women, whose submission was essential for polygamy to thrive.

Arbitrary limits are the horizons beyond which we cannot see. Sometimes they are self-imposed, but in my life the FLDS controlled everything. For years I accepted these limits and assumptions without question.

The prophet always reminded us that the stakes could not be higher.

> KEEP SWEET! It is a matter of life or death. You have had the teaching regarding what is required in order for us to survive the judgments, sufficient of the Holy Spirit of God that we can be lifted up and then set down after it is over. That will be the remnant which will go to redeem Zion. The wicked will be swept off the face of this land. The wicked are they who come not unto Christ. There is only one people who comes unto Christ, and that is this people under His servant.
>
> *FLDS Prophet Rulon Jeffs, Sandy, Utah, December 4, 1992*

This religious doctrine created and enforced the arbitrary limits that defined who I was. With no genuine and sustained exposure to the outside world, I had no way to challenge my indoctrination, which is how mind control thrives. I believed I was being protected from the destruction of God and a dangerous, frightening world. It never occurred to me that this "protection" was in fact destroying me.

I had been conditioned in the FLDS to believe that my husband had the right to treat me any way he wanted because he was a man of God. If I argued or protested, he had the right to turn me over to what the prophet called the "buffetings," or blows, of Satan. To be a woman who is cast out from her husband and no longer under the protection of his priesthood is one of the worst fates imaginable in the FLDS. I never liked the way Merril treated me, but in the beginning I felt it must be my fault because my religion said that a husband treats a wife the way she deserves to be treated.

A turning point came for me on a three-day trip to Phoenix with Merril and Tammy. Patrick, my fourth child, was with me and about six months old.

Just before we left home, there was an outbreak of viral pneumonia in the community. It was almost an epidemic. In more than one case a baby or small child had nearly died in the ambulance while being rushed to the hospital.

Patrick had been fine for the entire trip, but as we were leaving Phoenix, he started fussing. Two hours later he spiked a high fever. I gave him Tylenol, but his fever got worse and he began vomiting. He had all the symptoms of viral pneumonia. We needed help as soon as possible.

Merril could have stopped at an ER on our way home, but I would never have dared ask him to do that. I knew as soon as I got home, I could call the ambulance. If the paramedics told Merril how serious Patrick's condition was, Merril *might* allow him to go to the hospital. In the FLDS a mother needs her husband's permission to take her child to the hospital.

The more Patrick vomited and cried, the more annoyed Merril became with both of us. "Merril, he keeps throwing up, and I can't keep his fever down," I explained. "I have got to get him home."

"He's all right," Merril replied. "Maybe not feeling his best, but there's no need to make more out of this than it really is. Maybe he'd be a little better behaved if his mother was interested and concerned about the comfort of others."

"He's crying because he has such a high fever!" I was getting more and more upset. "He's so hot and miserable."

Merril stared at me. "Maybe he is miserable because his mother's actions are making her a miserable person to be with."

There was no point in trying to reason with him. He decided to stop in Flagstaff for dinner. I insisted that I needed to get Pat home and begged him to eat at a fast-food restaurant. Merril scolded me again and again, insisting that Patrick would be all right if his mother would get herself in harmony with his father. Merril also warned that I would be in trouble if I kept insisting on having my own way.

Tammy was elated by my distress, even though she knew how serious viral pneumonia was. My degradation made her feel righteous and gave her a chance to score points with Merril. She began ridiculing my efforts to help Patrick and said I needed to learn to listen to my husband.

We entered the restaurant. By now Patrick was so listless that he could only whimper; he had no strength to cry. Tammy and Merril took their seats in the restaurant, and I went straight to the back of the room to find a quiet place to walk back and forth with Patrick. I thought if I could get him to sleep, he might fight the infection better. I was furious with Merril.

Tammy and Merril ordered and tried to ignore me. I was still within earshot and could tell from Tammy's voice that she was annoyed that I had tried to tell Merril what to do and that I thought Patrick's health was more important than dining with them. "Father, why would a woman refuse to listen to her husband and put both of us in an awkward position publicly?" Tammy asked. "Carolyn understands what you have asked of her."

"She will have to learn a hard lesson if that is what she wishes to invite into her life," Merril said. "It isn't wisdom for any woman to get on the wrong side of her husband. She is doing no good for her baby by allowing herself to get out of control with anger."

I was terrified. Patrick's life was at stake. My religion had taught me that my husband was a man of God and that he would make all the right decisions; all I had to do was obey. But obedience could cost my baby his life. In pure desperation I had started thinking for myself. I knew what was right but was being prevented from doing it.

I looked up and saw an attractive African American man at a nearby table listening to what was being said. The look in his eye said he couldn't stand watching a woman being treated this way. The two white guys who were eating with him couldn't have cared less. But every time the other man looked at me, it was clear he was disgusted with Merril's behavior. Even though we were not sitting together, our FLDS clothing gave away the fact that we were related.

Merril and Tammy spent over an hour having a leisurely dinner. While Merril paid the bill, she and I went out to the truck. The man who had been observing me in the restaurant approached Merril and threatened to pound him into the ground for the way he was treating me.

All I heard was Merril's side of the conversation, but it shook him up. As far as I know, it's the only time he was ever confronted about abusing his wives. It was the first time in my life that any man had ever stood up and defended me.

Of course, no one within the FLDS would have confronted Merril—he was one of the most prominent and influential men in our community. And when we were out, in the outside world, most people ignored us and never intervened. But this moment altered the very foundations of my world. When this man stood up for me, I felt like a human being who was worthy of dignity and respect for the first time in my marriage and my life. His simple actions in my defense opened up an alternative universe in which I had rights, where I was not Merril's possession.

In fact, it was mind-blowing to see that men in the outside world valued women at all. I was twenty-six years old and still believed the FLDS propaganda that men outside the cult treated women very badly. Although I'd been to college and had been exposed to other people and ideas in a limited way, I didn't develop many relationships there, and those I did confirmed my view of outsiders. One of my classmates, a woman in her forties, had cried one day because she had just found out her husband had been having an affair. Another woman told me about the violent relationships she'd been involved in. I kept to myself most of the time because I didn't understand how things worked in this strange new world. I was afraid of outsiders and knew they did not accept or understand my way of life.

What happened in the restaurant was a moment that cracked the mind control I'd been under my entire life. If women outside the FLDS were treated so much worse than we were, why had this man stood up for me? Could I have been fed lies? The experience was disconcerting; it was outside my frame of reference, and I really didn't know what to feel.

I took advantage of Merril's being somewhat shaken to buy some ibuprofen at the gas station next door. I took Patrick into the bathroom, changed his diaper, and secretly gave him the medicine to bring his fever down. When I got back in the truck, I didn't say a thing. Patrick's fever dropped, he stopped vomiting, and he fell into a deep sleep. When we got back, he was diagnosed with viral pneumonia at the local clinic.

Most FLDS women do not perceive themselves as victims. Few among them even know that, as Americans, they have rights. Not until a year after I fled did I understand that as an American citizen, I have constitutionally guaranteed rights that my government is pledged to protect. The actions of a total stranger were my first small glimpse of that world outside the cult, and I felt empowered by it. Merril did not stop being abusive, of course, but I did start to think of myself in a radical new way. The perpetrator didn't change, but I changed my relationship to him.

"Perfect obedience produces perfect faith." The FLDS mantra had been an organizing principle of my life and governed many of the assumptions I operated under. My new way of thinking made me a rebellious wife, and that in turn gave Merril the right to turn me over to "the buffetings of Satan." Most women were terrified by that prospect, but I was no longer so sure. Merril's cruelty when Patrick's life was on the line seemed diabolical to me. How much worse could being "buffeted" by Satan really be than my present reality?

I was not yet willing to give up every aspect of my religion, but I'd already begun questioning its inexplicable dogma. What was true and what was false? What needed to be tested by reality? What if I sailed over the horizon?

One FLDS tenet I still believed was that life is a proving ground and if we pass our tests here, we'll reap the benefits in heaven. But if we're rewarded too much in our earthly existences, we'll pay for that in the afterlife. The more we suffer here, the better we do there. Tests in this life are sent from God.

All that was well and good, but I just wasn't buying the idea that Patrick's suffering was some short-answer quiz from God that I had to ace in order for him to survive.

I'm living proof that mind control can be overcome, but the process is a long one, and it occurs in stages. It would be years before I would be completely free. But those first heady moments of thinking for myself were essential to my ultimate triumph over the FLDS. A stranger who stood up for what was right transformed my life in ways he will never know. All I can do is express my gratitude to him and try to do for others what he did for me.

The Freedom of Forgiveness

Forgiveness did more to free me from the FLDS than almost any other quality and liberated me years before I fled. But it was a slow and deliberate journey.

One summer day in the early 1990s, I walked into Dan Barlow's Sunday school building. I had no idea what I was getting into. I had several small children by then and was excited to be on my own and learning something, anything. A group of us had gathered for a class in acupressure. We were all eager to learn new things, especially since FLDS members were no longer allowed to attend the local community college. (Before the ban nearly all of us at one time or another had taken classes. It was stimulating and a refreshing change from the daily grind.) This was also an unusual occasion because the teacher of the acupressure class was a woman from another polygamous community. It was extremely rare for FLDS women to be allowed to interact with women from non-FLDS polygamous groups. This class had been approved by the prophet Rulon Jeffs, and several members of his family were there.

I honestly don't think that most of us knew enough about acupressure even to say why we wanted to study it. We were just hungry to learn. Several of Merril's other wives and daughters came. We entered the building as a large crowd.

The teacher and several other ladies hosting the class were all dressed in normal street clothes and didn't look like polygamists at all. They followed a different prophet in Salt Lake City and were not associated with the FLDS. All we had in common was the belief in plural marriage. The most dramatic difference between us was that these women were allowed to choose their own husbands. Love and desire could be part of their marriages, which was rarely, if ever, true in our world because our husbands were chosen for us. Being able to dress normally and marry for love gave them a level of independence and self-expression that was almost unimaginable to us.

The teacher began the class by introducing herself and explaining that she was in a polygamous relationship. She ran a health food store in addition to teaching acupressure. She was tall and had a gentle manner. Her poise, grace, and beauty were assets we could all admire, but it was her hair that we downright coveted. She had a beautiful dark braid. We all grew our hair long, but few of us had hair as naturally thick and lush as hers. She had several children and a lot of experience, yet she also seemed really comfortable in herself as a woman.

After lunch she told all of us from the FLDS how she'd become involved with acupressure. We all knew that eating properly, taking vitamins, and using herbal remedies could have a tremendous impact on healing our bodies. But natural methods are not always enough. We didn't understand that thoughts, persistent bad attitudes, and depression could make us sick. We'd never considered the mind-body link seriously. We didn't dare. We had all become such masters in stuffing and shoving our feelings inside that we had good reason not to think about the consequences. For us, the unexamined life was not only worth living, it was the key to surviving the oppression that defined us. We learned in class that day that sometimes a body cannot recover physically until emotional issues are healed. This was a radical idea for us. Our religion required us to be divorced from our emotional lives.

Our teacher expanded on the mind-body link by telling us about a time when her health had crashed. She did all the right things but still did not heal. Then someone working with her asked if there were any emotional issues she hadn't dealt with. She told us that her father had sexually assaulted her as a child. As she talked about the abuse, she held up a book, *Feelings Buried Alive Never Die,* and told us that it changed her life by giving her a way to deal with her trauma. She said she not only improved physically but she became a far better mother and far more functional in general. The women with her looked on proudly as she described how hard she'd worked to heal.

The reaction among the FLDS women could not have been more different. The FLDS considered it unacceptable to talk about abuse of any kind, but especially sexual abuse. We spoke openly among ourselves about sex with our husbands, but talking about abuse was off limits, especially if the abuser was a father or husband, because they were what we called our priesthood heads—the men we had to answer to. (Boys, at twelve, are given the priesthood by the prophet. When a man is assigned a wife and has a family, he is known as their "priesthood head." FLDS women always have a man who rules over them.)

A silence fell over the room as our teacher talked about her abuse. Everything shifted. Women stared at the floor. Our teacher explained that we had to deal with our emotional lives if we wanted to be truly well. The room became even quieter, and even more women stared at the floor.

The woman had touched a nerve because in the FLDS dealing with emotions was taboo. "Keeping sweet" was shorthand for "staying silent." We never dared admit we had negative feelings. In fact, I began to worry that when people told the prophet what the class was about, the rest might be canceled. I would have hated that—I was riveted. Secretly I'd always wished that women in our community could open up and confront the abuses we'd endured. But we had no tools to deal with crimes committed against us. I didn't have a lot of experience with psychology, but I knew hanging your head in shame was never a solution.

I felt protective toward our teacher. She'd taken a risk in opening up to us, and I wished we could support her like friends and offer more than strained silence. During the break she took questions and mentioned that she'd brought several boxes of the book for purchase. A long line of people wanted to talk to her about their personal health concerns, but few inquired about the book. I noticed one woman quietly asking to buy a copy. I was eager to read the book and decided to buy one, too. I remember walking from the front of the class to the back proudly holding the book in my hands as several women stared at me in disbelief.

After the class ended, complaints flew through the community about what had been taught. They were not about anything specific; they centered on the class not being in harmony with the priesthood. I knew exactly why people were critical; the teacher had opened the door to talking about abuse, and that was a line too perilous to cross.

While the drama was playing out over the controversial class, I was looking through the book and finding it fascinating. I'd read only a few chapters before I became concerned that the book would disappear from my bedroom if I didn't find a place to hide it. So I locked it in a cabinet in my bedroom, where it stayed for several years. Something inside me knew this book could change my life, but I wasn't ready. I was more interested in protecting the book than in actually reading it. It remained hidden—until my son Harrison nearly died of cancer in his spine.

The first winter of Harrison's illness was the toughest period of my life. He was eighteen months old and in and out of the hospital. Every morning began the same way: Do I take Harrison to the hospital, or is he well enough to make it through the day at home? After several surgeries and treatments to keep his immune system suppressed (so it wouldn't attack his nervous system), Harrison had seemingly endless staph infections. It became rare for him to finish an antibiotic before we were treating a different strain of infection.

In the middle of it all, I found out I was pregnant with my eighth child. This was catastrophic news. I soon began hemorrhaging—it was my third high-risk pregnancy. How could I manage Harrison's life, my own, and my unborn baby's? I suffered such severe fatigue that my situation seemed even bleaker and more frightening than before. I felt myself spiraling into an out-of-control rage that kept building.

I was constantly told that Harrison's cancer was my fault because I was a rebellious wife. This chorus of condemnation came at me from all directions: I heard it from Merril, his daughters, and most of the other wives. All insisted that until I repented, nothing could be done for Harrison. Not only did I hate them, and my life, but I grew frantic because my weakened condition put all my children at risk. What would happen to them if I died?

Then, to make matters worse, my doctor prescribed bed rest for the remainder of my pregnancy. Audrey, one of Merril's daughters, was a nurse practitioner. She understood that Harrison and I had life-threatening conditions that were not being taken seriously by anyone in the family, least of all Merril. Audrey, who was kind, competent, and smart, agreed to help me with Harrison's care so I could stay in bed. She also promised that if I had to be hospitalized during the pregnancy, she would keep Harrison alive. This was a huge relief. But it was only a stopgap solution.

I was plummeting into a deep depression. Nothing I did and nothing anyone said gave me any comfort at all from the anguish. But if I continued to spiral downward, I wouldn't be able to make the decisions necessary to protect Harrison and my unborn baby, let alone my six other children. Being confined to bed gave me a lot of time to think, but that only made things worse.

So much in my life filled me with resentment; so much should have turned out differently. Instead, I was trapped in an endless cycle of pain. I craved stillness and peace and wondered if I'd ever find them. From the moment I married Merril, peace had felt distant and remote, like a far-off country I'd heard of but knew I would never visit.

Then I remembered the acupressure teacher from several years before. She had had an aura of perfect peace. Even when she talked about her sexual trauma and then a later bout with cancer, she radiated calm. She had faced betrayal and the threat of her own death, yet she still knew peace. Why couldn't I?

I remembered her holding up that book. I couldn't remember the title. I had a vague memory that it had to do with forgiveness and healing. Maybe I could learn something from her saga.

The anger, hatred, and rage that I felt were completely justified. I believed that then and still do now. But my rage was propelling me into such a downward spiral that my survival was on the line. Something had to change, and it had to be me.

I had never before considered changing my relationship to my rage. I didn't think it was possible. But I had to face reality. Merril wasn't going to suddenly see the light and own up to his abusive behavior. My sister wives were not going to morph into different people.

The pain I felt was real. Terrible things had happened to me that I knew were not my fault. But I learned that I didn't have to hang on to the pain anymore. I could stop nurturing it and feeding it like a stray kitten.

I scoured my bookshelves desperately searching for that book. When Warren Jeffs banned outside material, nearly all of my books had been destroyed, but I still had a few left. This book wasn't among them. I collapsed next to my bookcase in defeat. But then an image came to mind: I saw myself taking the book off my nightstand and putting it in the locked cabinet in my room.

Even though the cabinet was locked, family members could find the key and get into it. The cabinet had been searched many times. I took the key from its hiding place and opened the cabinet. I slowly removed one item after another. No book. I kept going until I reached the bottom, and there it was: *Feelings Buried Alive Never Die*. I was shocked. Maybe I'd intentionally hidden it at the very bottom in the hope that anyone searching the cabinet might not look that far.

I was confined to bed, but I held salvation in my hands. I devoured the book in one sitting. Its impact was profound. The author outlined a series of steps that I could follow to "re-script" my relationships to those who'd harmed me. Step by step I faced what each person had done to me. I had to remember it, feel all the harm and ugliness it triggered, and then consciously replace that negativity with other feelings. At the end I had to let all the painful emotions go and forgive. Sometimes I would dredge up emotions with Merril and Barbara that were so powerful, I could barely breathe. But I kept at it throughout my bed rest and continued for months after I gave birth to Bryson, my eighth child. The process was incredibly liberating.

I no longer wanted to fix the people who had hurt me. I released them all to their miserable and mean-spirited worlds. I worked with the book for months, "re-scripting" my relationships with everyone in the family, even Merril's daughters. I also worked through my complicated relationship with my mother.

I didn't have to forget. I couldn't and shouldn't. I will always remember what happened to me. But by forgiving the people who mistreated me, I took myself out of any relationship with them and pulled all of that energy back into myself. At times the emotions I experienced felt like they were going to tear me apart. But I kept going. After working through the script several times with different people and feelings, I began to feel emotional relief. I was setting myself free, and the effort was empowering.

By letting such volatile emotions go, I wasn't letting anyone off the hook; I was taking their hooks out of me. I wasn't justifying what they'd done; nor did I think I had a religious duty to forgive. It was simply that those negative feelings were sapping my power, and I wanted it back.

As I progressed, I could see that I needn't take things so personally. What Merril and his wives did to me, they did to everyone else, too. That was just the cruel way they wielded power in their nasty lives. It wasn't because they hated me or wanted to hurt me. What was revealed in their abuse was their character, not mine. I had done nothing to "deserve" their harsh treatment and hence had no reason to feel shame.

In the "keep sweet no matter what" world of the FLDS, forgiveness meant you accepted what had been done to you, you weren't angry, and you trusted the perpetrator not to do it again. I'd had no idea there was another way to forgive. But now I was learning it: by letting go of anger, never trusting my abusers again, and by seeing them for who they truly were, I achieved genuine forgiveness.

In the FLDS, if someone harmed you and you refused to have anything further to do with that person, you were the one committing a crime by holding on to bad feelings. If you ever complained again, you were the offender. This twisted logic created a kingdom of sociopaths, because no one was ever held responsible for harm except the victims. The FLDS notion of forgiveness had been used in such hurtful and damaging ways that it became a way for an abuser to maximize the damage he or she could inflict without any consequence. It certainly guaranteed that a victim would remain powerless. To forgive in the FLDS seemed completely masochistic. Now I was wrapping my mind around a new reality: forgiveness had nothing to do with trusting a person who'd injured you. It involved letting go of the anger you felt and making space for new emotional growth.

But knowing all this was one thing; putting it into practice was another. Despite the huge impact the book had on me, it was excruciatingly hard for me to forgive Merril and my sister wives. Still, I was determined to do it. I had to free myself from the storm of rage that was churning inside me. I remained furious at what had been done to me and my children. I wanted vengeance and vindication, which are driven by a craving for justice. But that craving had trapped me in an out-of-control cycle: I wouldn't let go of my victim status until justice was done.

I wanted Merril to stop rationalizing cruelty as "necessary." I wanted him and the other wives, especially Barbara, to understand that there was absolutely no justification for their treating me, or anyone else, the way they did. I wasn't naïve enough to think that Merril Jessop would ever apologize to me. But I wanted some acknowledgment that what had happened to me was not my fault. The fact that this was never, ever going to happen didn't make me stop wanting it.

In truth, my insistence on justice in an unjust world was really holding me hostage. *Forgive? Me?* I thought forgiveness might make me more vulnerable to my abusers because it might make me appear more pliant.

I was beginning to grasp that forgiveness was about breaking the chains that bind you to your captor. Being in a relationship with someone dangerous is self-destructive. Holding on to your anger at someone dangerous is self-destructive. The only way to break free is to sever all the emotions you have toward that person. For so long, I thought that unless justice was done, I could never heal. But sometimes justice is impossible, so the choice becomes to remain unhealed or to let go of the anger that the lack of justice has aroused. It came back to exercising the power I had: I couldn't control whether justice would be done, but I could control my attitude toward the injustice.

It's been said that desiring revenge is like swallowing poison and waiting for someone else to die. I believe that. It took discipline and work for me to release all the anger I felt toward Merril. But nothing I'd ever felt compared to the relief of dumping one bad emotion after another. *Go. Goodbye. Gone.* I had no more expectations. I no longer had to fix anything. Once I forgave Merril, his power over me evaporated.

Nothing externally had changed in my world; we were still married, but internally everything had been transformed. Forgiveness was the key that freed me from years of psychic imprisonment.

Forgiving Merril and the others did not mean that they "won." What is winning, anyway? What I gave up was nothing in comparison to what I gained. The liberation I felt was exhilarating.

Let me be clear about the kind of forgiveness I'm talking about. Sometimes one forgives in order to remain in a relationship with someone she cares about, even if the person has caused her pain and anguish. It's not a blanket pardon; it's the trade-off one is willing to make when preserving the relationship is more important than correcting the injustice. Allowing people to be human and make mistakes, even though those mistakes have hurt you, is important. You don't want to eliminate the person from your life simply for hurting or disappointing you. This kind of forgiveness is far more common than the kind I used to change my life.

The forgiveness I practiced enabled me to move ahead and start making my life more about me. It renewed and deepened the strength I needed to deal with the challenges facing me. Most dramatically, it changed my need to remain in Merril's family. From that point on, I was no longer emotionally or psychologically engaged with them. Justice was up to a higher power; my job was to discover a way to protect myself and my children. This meant, of course, that I'd eventually have to leave the FLDS. In the meantime I continued to appear as a relatively obedient wife. But my decision was made. I escaped psychologically long before I fled physically.

During my book tour for the paperback edition of *Escape*, I made an appearance in Salt Lake City. After my reading, a man asked me to name the single most important factor in my getting away, and staying away, from the FLDS.

I talked about the liberation of forgiveness. I explained that letting go of my anger did not mean that what had happened to me was okay. It will never be okay, but I refuse to let the past sabotage my life or curtail my energy, purpose, and joy. I wanted no ties to my perpetrators; forgiveness cut them all.

That same night in Salt Lake City as I was signing books, an older woman came through the line. When she got to me, she started to cry. "I have been involved in an abusive marriage for more than thirty years. I have tried and tried to leave but never could stay away from him," she said. "The piece that has been missing all these years is what you talked about tonight—how through forgiveness, you can break the link between you and your abuser."

I like to think that the woman went home that night and began packing her bags.

An Education in Education

When I reflect on what made it possible for me to survive—and eventually flee—the FLDS, one word always comes to mind: *education*. When I think about the damage currently being done to FLDS children, the same word says it all. By pulling FLDS children out of public schools and forcing them to be homeschooled, Warren Jeffs effectively guaranteed that these young people would remain hostages of the cult. Academically abysmal, the FLDS "schools" fail to teach the basic knowledge and skills that people need to get by in the outside world.

I attended public primary and secondary schools, then married Merril at eighteen. That was the price I had to pay for going to college. Still, I managed to get my degree; the day I was handed my diploma was one of the proudest of my life. I majored in elementary school education with a minor in teaching reading. Although I did not get to fulfill my original dream of being a pediatrician, I found deeply rewarding work as a teacher and have strong feelings on educational issues, especially homeschooling.

My college education transformed me in profound ways. I took classes in psychology and child development that enabled me to see my life in the FLDS in a dramatically different way. In my psychology class, for example, I learned that mental illness is often hereditary but, even more important, treatable. Merril's second wife, Ruth, was mentally ill. (Years later she was so out of control that then-prophet Rulon Jeffs ordered her to be taken to a hospital, where she was diagnosed as bipolar.) The FLDS believed that Ruth's illness was her fault because she had invited false and delusional spirits into her life. Merril accused her of feeling sorry for herself. When he slapped her mercilessly, it was understood in the family that he was trying to bring her under control. That was what passed for treatment.

I hated seeing not only Ruth's mental distress but also how frequently Merril lashed out at her. Until I went to college, I had no idea that even the most severely mentally ill could be treated with therapy and medication. It was revelatory to me that something so harsh and ugly in my life didn't have to be that way. If medical help was available, why wasn't Ruth getting it? Why was she left to languish in her suffering? The religion I had been steeped in said she was bad for being sick, and that Merril was the good martyr for trying to discipline and control her "bad" behavior. It was widely known in the community that Ruth's mother had similar problems. When I learned that mental illness can have a genetic component, I really understood that there was no way that what was happening to Ruth was her fault. This was one of my first steps toward seeing the FLDS in a new light.

My courses in child development were also eye-opening. I studied the impact of violence on children, recognizing behaviors that I saw being played out on an almost daily basis in Merril's family. My classes introduced me to the masses of research detailing how detrimental abuse is to children and how abused children can become angry and shut down and sometimes act out in violent ways themselves. Both physical and sexual violence have a lifelong impact on children. This was something I did not appreciate in a major way before I went to college. Every fiber in my being said it was wrong to hit a child. But now I had hard evidence for the truth I knew in my heart. Mothers who beat their children to make them obey were "righteous" in the eyes of the FLDS. Studying child development and psychology, I saw that they were anything but.

College was also transformative in teaching me life skills that I otherwise might have missed. Not only did I learn how to drive, I mastered city driving. I figured out how to budget the little money I had to make it through the week, and how to make daily decisions on my own. Activities that might seem routine to anyone else, like registering for classes and talking to professors about my coursework, gave me a real-world competence that many FLDS women never get a chance to acquire. If nothing else, I knew how to fill out paperwork. That was an enormous advantage after I escaped. Navigating the benefit systems and applying for welfare and Medicaid took a monumental effort, but governmental bureaucracies did not intimidate me. Without the life skills, self-respect, and confidence I gained at college, I am not sure I could have succeeded on my own as well as I did. Imagine if I'd never gone beyond junior high, was functionally illiterate, and had never had any contact with a world beyond the FLDS. Tragically, that's a common reality for many FLDS women today. Even if they do escape, they lack the tools they need to make it on their own. I did make it, and for that I am eternally grateful for my education.

When I was married to Merril, I taught for seven years in the public schools of Colorado City, Arizona. During my six years as a second-grade teacher, I developed a reputation for being able to teach almost any child to read. I did so by combining a variety of approaches. A child who is a visual learner is going to master reading differently than a child who's an auditory learner. The trick is to understand each student and to find a way to reach and teach that child. The only children who *can't* read, in my experience, are those with severe learning disabilities or similar challenges.

One of my strategies was to invite the parents of my students to come in and read a story to the class. Several came each week. They'd show up after recess, and the kids were always excited to come back in and see whose parent was there. They were thrilled to have their parents in the classroom. It was one of my greatest successes as a teacher because that kind of individual attention is so rare in the FLDS, where families are so large. The moms—and sometimes dads—felt proud to be in the classroom. I did have a few parents who were illiterate, but I invited them to come in anyway and tell a story. The more involvement parents have, the better their children's education.

When I was a teacher in Arizona, parents who chose to homeschool had to pass a basic competency test—essentially, the same one given to teachers—before they could legally homeschool. If they weren't literate and didn't have basic skills in math, they were not allowed to teach. How could anyone argue with that?

But as the homeschooling movement became more sophisticated and better funded, it was able to successfully fight to remove regulations in many states. I saw this happen in Arizona, which went from having well-regulated standards for homeschooling to having almost none. The same thing happened in Utah. Politically, homeschooling became the third rail here in the West. Politicians who wanted to stay in office learned to leave homeschooling alone because its supporters were a substantial voting bloc.

I have never understood why homeschoolers are so defensive. If you are educating your children well, why fear accountability?

Texas has barely any standards for homeschooling. The Texas Home School Coalition requires homeschoolers to use a curriculum, but it doesn't have to be approved by the state. Homeschools in Texas are classified as private schools and not subject to state regulation. Public schools in Texas must be in session 180 days a year, and students cannot miss more than ten of those days. Students in Texas private schools, by contrast, do not need to register with their local school district, and there are no requirements for attendance or minimum length of the school day. Texas also does not require private school students to pass any mandatory or standardized tests to ensure that they're learning. It's hard to see how that protects the caliber of the education that Texas children receive.

Public schools operate with a myriad of checks and balances; these are absent when homeschools don't have to be accountable. Only when a child goes into the job market or tries to go to college does an inadequate preparation become apparent.

Homeschooling parents love their children and undoubtedly want the best for them. But as a teacher, I know that parents aren't always the best judges of how their children are learning. Teaching is both a skill and an art. Not everyone can teach, and certainly not everyone should. Great teachers have not just knowledge but passion and commitment. Highly accomplished and talented people can be terrible teachers. And experience matters. The longer I taught, the better a teacher I became. My college degree provided a foundation, but my students kept me learning, growing, and inspired.

One of my friends in the FLDS was also a certified teacher with a college degree. She had three handicapped children and tried to care for them and homeschool her other five kids. She soon realized this was too much and let her children join other FLDS homeschoolers. It was a disaster. The teachers were so unskilled that the woman's children didn't learn. So she went back to teaching them herself. Even with fewer hours of "school," her kids learned more from her because she was a trained teacher.

I also know from my teaching experience that not everyone can handle every subject. Homeschoolers are often taught all subjects by the same person. This aspect of homeschooling deeply concerns me. I was a superb reading teacher and did well in math and science, but I felt less proficient in subjects like social studies and music. Part of what I think is invaluable in public education is that children learn from a variety of individuals.

In addition, homeschooling parents often teach three or four of their children at once. It's extremely demanding, even for a trained teacher, to teach different ages simultaneously. My colleagues and I all brought additional material into our classrooms. But we were doing it for a single grade level. It's an enormous undertaking to put several lesson plans together every day for several subject areas *and* several grades.

Children also learn a tremendous amount from the social interaction that takes place in school. Children who behave inappropriately are usually called on it by their peers, and the interaction among the kids helps them regulate themselves. Children also learn from school how to navigate around difficult personalities. Since these types inevitably show up in the adult world, why not get kids acclimated earlier?

Parents often are in denial about the academic problems or learning issues their children have, which compromises their ability as teachers. The sooner kids get help in areas in which they struggle, the more quickly they turn around. Public schools, while far from perfect, have resources to draw on that help children succeed, including learning specialists, tutors, classroom aides for kids with special needs, individualized learning plans for children with challenges, and sometimes even medication for kids with serious hyperactivity or attention issues.

The public school system can seem unresponsive and inadequate, but I firmly believe it succeeds more often than it fails. I watched my second graders learn social skills they'll use for the rest of their lives. Also, it's a rare child who does not know how to manipulate his or her parents in some way. Homeschooled children are no exception; they're equally capable of trying to "work the system" to get what they want.

It's also easier to hide cruelty or neglect when children are kept out of public schools. When a child comes to school every day, a teacher can pick up on the physical or behavioral changes that signal abuse and can take appropriate action.

For some children, homeschooling unquestionably has value, and many, many homeschooling parents are extremely conscientious. My greatest concern is with individuals and groups like the FLDS that use homeschooling to indoctrinate and control their members.

There is another, sometimes overlooked, factor in the public-versus-homeschool debate: public schools prepare children to get up every day, get dressed, and get somewhere on time. Since discipline is crucial to any kind of success, children need to acquire this life skill. Homeschoolers can sleep in if they're up late the night before or if their parents have other things to do. Lunchtime can be whenever. Children also need to learn to separate from their parents and see themselves as distinct individuals. This transition, I think, is harder to make in the homeschooling environment.

As for homeschoolers' complaints about public school curricula, I have long felt that if parents are concerned about controversial ideas or a damaging environment at school, the best way to cope is by becoming involved in their child's education. I always encourage parents to volunteer at their children's school and to help out in the classroom. Children love it when parents engage with their education. Some of the children I taught, especially those from big polygamous families, felt like king or queen for the day when their moms came to the classroom.

I remember a group of mothers who were concerned both about their children's behavior and about what the kids were being exposed to at the school where I taught. They took turns babysitting for one another's younger children so that they could volunteer in their kids' classrooms. These moms stayed actively involved until their sons and daughters were in junior high school. That's when kids typically become too embarrassed to have their moms in the classroom, so these women sought out ways to help in other areas of the school. It was win-win. The children understood that they had moms who were on top of their behavior at school, yet they had the latitude to be who they were and get a good education. And for me, having parents in the classroom supporting my work was a godsend. It meant I could focus more on the children who needed extra attention. The children knew that and were proud that their moms' help enabled me to help someone else.

Homeschooled kids tend to be isolated from different ideas and ways of seeing the world. Their views can become extremely limited as a result. Children who never set foot in a classroom miss out on so much. They rarely meet children from homes with a different culture or perspective on life. Exposure to those differences can plant seeds that nurture intellectual growth. Curiosity and an open mind are essential if a child is to reach full potential.

Homeschooling is on the rise. In the past eight years, by one estimate, the number of homeschooling parents has jumped 44 percent nationwide. In 2007 homeschooled children numbered approximately 1.5 million, according to the National Center for Education Statistics. According to the center's research, there are three main reasons for homeschooling: in 36 percent of the families, religious reasons drive the decision; in 21 percent, it's concerns about the school environment; in 17 percent, it's unhappiness with the academic instruction their children are receiving.

I believe the homeschooling movement should stop being short-sighted and should encourage more government oversight. But that is unlikely to happen because religious fundamentalism drives so many of the decisions to homeschool. Responsible homeschoolers have nothing to fear from being held accountable.

Many of the "lost boys" who were kicked out of the FLDS are unable to read much beyond a first-grade level. They are victims of educational abuse. Many argue that the public school system produces children who can't read, and sadly that is sometimes true. But in my experience, severe learning disabilities are almost always the underlying problem.

In 1998 the three of my six children who attended public schools were forced to leave them and enroll in FLDS "schools." This development seriously alarmed me. I was powerless to protect my children even from an action or philosophy that I was adamantly opposed to. As a teacher, I knew that the education they'd be receiving would be a joke. I wanted my children taught by accredited teachers, like myself, who were dedicated and committed to education, not to religious indoctrination. My children's futures were on the line. How could I acquiesce to a change that would have an enormous and defining impact on them every day for the rest of their lives? I wanted my children to be educated to their fullest potentials, and they were about to be robbed of this legally protected right.

The *only* way to guarantee this right for FLDS children is to regulate homescooling more closely. Ultimately, I think, this issue will attract enough heat that stricter regulations will have to be implemented. We need laws that contain reasonable checks and balances to protect children from abuse not only in the homeschooling environment but in all educational venues. And the homeschooling movement itself should take a leadership role in insisting that the privilege of homeschooling not be undermined or abused by cults and sects whose agenda is to indoctrinate and brainwash believers' children.

Tuning In to Self-Respect

By the summer of 2000 all FLDS children had been taken out of public schools, and our access to the outside world through media and newspapers was essentially shut down. Children were sent to "religious" schools, and only Warren Jeffs could approve the curriculum. (Although Rulon Jeffs was still alive, his son was effectively running the FLDS.) Parents were not allowed to have any other educational material in their homes. It was around this time that the large collection of children's books I'd been amassing for years was destroyed.

But I had a radio. It had been a gift from Merril on our first wedding anniversary, the only one he ever gave me. Little did he know that it would become my source for a radical and liberating view of my role as a woman, mother, and wife.

I became hooked on the *Dr. Laura* show. I first heard her on my car radio. Then I started listening to her in secret after I came home from the hospital with Bryson, my eighth child, having nearly died in childbirth. I kept the volume low and locked my bedroom door so no one in the family would walk in unexpectedly and catch me listening. Her show was on in the afternoon, when the young children were napping, the older ones were in school, and Merril was usually out. The house was quiet. The family rarely helped me with Harrison, so

I could count on uninterrupted time when I was in my bedroom caring for him.

Dr. Laura Schlessinger eventually became quite controversial for her incendiary comments about homosexuality, with which I disagreed. But I learned important lessons from her about setting boundaries and holding myself accountable. I also learned that my passivity helped make Merril's crimes possible. This idea was new to me.

Dr. Laura affirmed unequivocally that I had rights as a woman and value as a human being. No one had ever told me that before. Nor had anyone ever challenged my religious beliefs as she did. She urged women to think and be responsible for themselves. It began to dawn on me that one of the rights I had was the right to protect my children. This view put me in direct opposition to Merril. I was walking a fine line that led straight to hell. Hell was a bedrock belief in the FLDS and terrifying to contemplate. That was the point: the greater the chokehold of fear over our lives, the more easily we were controlled. And even though I hated the FLDS and the tyranny of Merril Jessop, the threat of hell was still all too real for me.

Dr. Laura made me question that, too. I began asking myself, How much worse could hell be than the life I was actually living? I concluded that I must have already been handed over to the devil when I was forced to marry Merril. In the FLDS we believed our husbands determined where we went in the afterlife. If Merril was abusive on earth, why would he stop in heaven? Being stuck with Merril for eternity—now that would be pure hell.

Even so, the thought of cutting myself off from the faith that was my one connection to God was terrifying. I had no alternative vision. My beliefs were like walls inside me. Now I know that these beliefs severed me from reality, but I couldn't see that then. The mind control I'd been raised with made me believe that anyone who left the work of God would be punished forever. The cost of sinning might be AIDS, rape, addiction, or prostitution. If God's spirit was removed from my life, according to the FLDS, I could go insane, commit suicide, and would never be happy again. Without any chance of salvation, my soul was condemned to rot in hell. I'd never have another man in my life, and I'd always be impoverished. In the FLDS we believed in Armageddon, and when the final battles were unleashed, who would protect me and my children?

But I kept listening every afternoon. I was learning about a world beyond anything I could have ever imagined. I'll never forget the woman who called in and said she wanted to divorce her husband because he bought her a car that was the wrong color. Dr. Laura was not sympathetic to her; she was against divorce when it was for selfish reasons, especially when children were involved. But for me, the idea that a woman would even consider leaving her husband for something like that was mind-boggling. I was not used to women feeling they had the right to exercise that level of control.

Women called in who were frustrated by their husbands' refusal to help with housework or child-rearing. These women felt entitled to have genuine partners, and Dr. Laura agreed. She validated their feelings and encouraged women to stand up for their needs. She was adamant in her support for women who were in abusive relationships or who worried that their children were in danger of sexual or physical abuse. I'd never heard anyone take such a strong stand against violence toward children. Nor had I ever heard someone say that a mother who failed to protect her child was negligent. This was a radical notion of parenting but one I identified with immediately.

All my experience in the FLDS centered on the need to use harsh discipline to mold a child. The prophet Rulon Jeffs once said, "If you have not taught your children obedience by the time they are three years old, you may lose them."

The idea of allowing a child to grow and flourish creatively contradicted every FLDS notion of parenting. This attitude of control and domination over children goes right to the heart of the religion.

Brigham Young, the founder of the Mormon Church in the nine-teenth century, said, "I would rather see every child I have go into the grave this day than suffer them to rise up and have control over me."

Dr. Laura's ideas would be considered heretical in the FLDS, but they were welcome to my ears. The outside world that I had been taught to believe was evil was sounding exactly the opposite. But could I really reject the FLDS? I took seriously my birthright of six genera-tions in polygamy. I still believed I was a special spirit who'd been chosen in my preexistence to come to earth to do God's work. (The FLDS believes that spirits live before they are handpicked to incarnate into human bodies with a mission to fulfill. There is also a belief that in the afterlife a couple like Merril and Barbara can create "spirit chil-dren" who will then populate a planet that Merril will be God over.) For generations my mother and all my grandmothers had sacrificed their personal feelings in order to live the gospel. Wasn't I obligated to have as many children as possible to provide bodies to those waiting in the preexistence to come to earth and work on their salvation?

I listened to Dr. Laura regularly for almost a year. She helped give me the confidence I needed to begin to make serious plans to escape with eight children. I worried about how we would make it out safely, and I felt guilty about tearing my children away from the only life they had ever known. But I wasn't about to leave anyone behind.

The gravitational pull I felt toward the Dr. Laura show was intense. I *had* to keep listening to her. I knew I could not survive forever as a captive of the FLDS. Hearing Dr. Laura say day after day, in one way or another, that as a human being I had the right to protection was like a healing rain on my withered soul. I felt valued. The callers' direct questions and Dr. Laura's no-nonsense answers were penetrating the walls that I felt unable to scale. At that point I saw no way out of my prison, but every afternoon something vital slipped through the bars.

When she said that it is not only a mother's right but her obligation to protect her children, she was voicing something I felt intuitively but

could never express. Likewise, I always believed it was wrong to physically hurt a child. But in the FLDS children were routinely beaten
as a way to instill obedience to God and to offer proof of a righteous
mother. A woman who beat her children in rage, frustration, or desperation could honestly believe she was being devout and faithful.

When my daughter LuAnne was ten, Lorraine, one of Merril's
wives, took her out to the garden and beat her with a willow stick. Afterward LuAnne told me it hurt worse than being beaten with the
garden hoe, which she'd also experienced. (The garden was where children were often taken for beatings, and a hoe was often used.) I was
furious when I found out and let Lorraine know. From then on I turned
my back on her and refused to hug her after evening prayers when all
the wives were supposed to embrace. It was one way to stand up for my
daughter, even though it went against all my religious traditions.

I told Merril what had happened to LuAnne. He said I had absolutely no right to believe a child's story over the truth from one of his
wives. He insisted that Lorraine had not been involved in anything that
went against his wishes and that LuAnne had not been hurt. According to Merril, my accusations were what injured my daughter. I had
been standing up for my children for years and had gained practice in
becoming more assertive. From the moment my first child was born, I
had followed my heart about protecting my children. But I lived in a
world that insisted I do the opposite, and consistent feedback told me
that my actions were wrong. Dr. Laura was very logical, and her logic
matched my heart and my instincts. I knew I had been right to follow
my conscience. This was the first affirmation I had ever been given in
my life that I was doing the right thing in protecting my children. I
continued to make it clear that anyone who touched my children would
be held accountable. I drew boundaries. It might sound simple to someone who's always had that power in her life, but for me it was a radical
new step and one I owe to Dr. Laura.

Empowerment is contagious. Once I began examining my beliefs,

I could not stop. From Dr. Laura's program I gained a new understanding of the "evil" outside world. I began to think that maybe life would not spin out of control if I left the FLDS. My fears of "the buffetings of Satan" were dissolving.

Dr. Laura's show was also a tutorial in domestic violence. More than once I heard her tell a caller that she was involved in an emotionally abusive relationship. I knew what physical violence was, but I had not considered how damaging emotional abuse could be. Dr. Laura's stance was that crimes like abuse were unforgivable and that the only solution was to get out fast.

What Dr. Laura characterized as unforgivable were things I tolerated on a daily basis: lying, cheating, and failing to take responsibility for your own actions. Dr. Laura was adamantly opposed to men (and women) having sex outside of marriage. She disapproved of men who were overly controlling and put down women instead of valuing them. Once I started to understand how damaging this behavior was, I began to realize that the thinking that tied me to the abuse and abusers could change; it was just a construct of my mind.

As I listened to Dr. Laura, I heard about the different kinds of abusive personalities, and my eyes began to open. It was liberating to think that I had done nothing to deserve the abuse I experienced. What was happening to me was not my fault. I had to distance myself from those who abused me. These were not people who deserved to be in my life.

A turning point for me in overcoming the FLDS mind control was realizing that I had the right to choose the people I wanted to spend my life with. This was an enormous change for me and one that defied a very basic religious belief: that our sister wives were supposed to be our best friends. Often we had nothing in common and were decades apart in age. But in the FLDS the belief is that God chooses your husband and his other wives. So it's only natural for you to love those people God has placed in your life. Once you leave your father's family, you are to leave everyone else behind and concentrate on those people God chose for your life. Going outside your family for friendship was seen as being in rebellion not only against the prophet and your husband but also against God.

For thirty years I had lived in a culture that taught me to fear everything outside my religion. These fears had an irrational and phobic quality to them. I didn't think I could let them go and still survive. I was only taking baby steps, but I was moving in the right direction.

After the 439 children were removed from the ranch in Texas, the public couldn't understand why, when given a chance to get help, nearly all the women rejected it. What the public did not understand, and what the media could not explain, was the power of mind control. Every woman there had been brainwashed by the FLDS. I had had the advantage of a public school education and college; even so, the mind control I had to fight my way through had an intense hold on me.

I think the FLDS women in Texas might have been able to get help if their children had stayed in state custody. They needed a safe environment to break through the years of mind control they'd been under. They also needed a guarantee of long-term protection. These women had no reason to trust the Texas authorities, but if the state had kept the children long enough, the mothers might have been able to build some trust and take the steps that would have allowed them to change their lives permanently.

I did a lot of my best thinking while I was ironing. Bryson was born prematurely, and I knew that before we could flee, he had to be much bigger. Harrison also had to become stronger and more medically stable. With eight children, I always had more ironing than I could ever finish. But it provided me with wonderful solitude. No one had any idea that I was wrestling with new ideas and challenging lifelong beliefs.

The women caught up in the raid on the YFZ ranch, by contrast, were not only in the middle of a public and personal crisis but also in the national spotlight. The raid reinforced all their irrational beliefs about the outside world. Complicating everything was the fact that they were separated from their children and trying to get them back. The women felt threatened and defensive. It's unrealistic to think that anyone could have reexamined her values and beliefs during a time like that.

As Warren Jeffs exerted his control over the FLDS, I knew on a conscious level that it was disturbing and wrong. And unconsciously I began searching for answers. The help I needed came from a stranger on the radio, but it came.

Not until I began letting go of my religious beliefs did I fully realize the power they held over me. I needed a vision of a better world before we could flee. If I really believed I was condemning my children to hell, I never could have taken them from the FLDS. Listening to Dr. Laura, I was finally able to grasp that what was happening in my world was morally wrong. The physical abuse that was so rampant in the FLDS was a crime. I had to internalize this realization at the deepest level of my being before I made any moves. I had no guarantee of success, but eventually I knew I had to try.

Merril may have given me only one anniversary gift during our seventeen-year marriage, but it turned out to be the gift of a lifetime.

The Mind-Body Connection

It's impossible to think of transforming your life and leaving your body behind. That sea of pastel dresses I waded through at the Salt Lake City courthouse reminded me of how alienated FLDS women are from their bodies, which are nothing but baby machines. The prairie-style clothing desexualized them and made them all look the same. Individuality is dangerous in a cultish world. That's why when a small group of us started going to a Curves fitness center, we did it in total secrecy.

I never thought I'd want to add exercise to my to-do list. After Bryson was born, I was tired to the bone. My mother started to help me care for Harrison two days a week because she saw how worn out I was. Because Brycie was premature, I was breastfeeding him on demand while caring for Harrison and my six other children. My exhaustion was as overwhelming as it was unrelenting, but after a few months my two most vulnerable children were stabilizing.

One night when I went to pick up Harrison from my mother's, my cousin Lucy bounded into the room in leggings and a Curves T-shirt. I was shocked. Lucy had been at least one hundred pounds overweight her entire life and had finally had gastric bypass surgery. I couldn't believe she dared dress so provocatively.

"Oh, I just got back from working out, and I haven't changed my clothes yet," she said.

"You wear that when you work out?" I asked.

"I have to. It's impossible to use the machines wearing a skirt."

Lucy's attitude was contagious. She felt good about herself and was not at all embarrassed by the way she looked or dressed. Meanwhile I was so distressed and unhappy that I couldn't imagine ever feeling or looking that carefree.

"Do you want to come with me to work out? Several of us are going regularly now," Lucy said.

"I've never been to a gym before," I said. "I don't know how I'd like it. Don't you get tired?" I couldn't risk doing anything that might add to my exhaustion.

"No way!" Lucy said. "It's just the opposite. It gives you more energy and helps you feel better. Besides, it's a lot of fun. If you're able to come three out of four times each week, you'd be getting the recommended workout."

"Let me think about it," I said.

I checked around and realized that I might be able to get enough help with Harrison's care to go to Curves. Doing something forbidden appealed to me, but I could not afford to get caught. Merril would come down hard on me for such blatant rebellion.

I started going three times a week. At first I didn't say much to the other women who traveled in the van with me because I didn't want anyone to know I was sneaking out without permission. But gradually, as we began to chat, bits of information slipped out, and I soon realized that several of the others didn't have their husbands' permission either.

Lucy was an anomaly in the FLDS; she genuinely loved her husband, whom she called her "lord and master." Lucy had long-standing issues with obesity, which in the FLDS made her a less desirable wife to the more powerful men. Although he was born into generational polygamy, her husband didn't come from a powerful family. We always thought this was why the FLDS let her marry him when she'd asked; her husband was a good worker, and the cult wanted to keep him. Not only was he handsome, but he was a very decent guy who gave Lucy permission to go to Curves for health reasons in the aftermath of her gastric bypass surgery. A few other women in our group also had the blessing of their more liberal husbands, who liked the idea that their wives wanted to look good.

Going to Curves was like going to a party three times a week. The nearly hour-long round trip gave us time to talk in the van. Such opportunities were rare; several of us had been so busy in the past ten years that we hardly even saw each other. But after a few trips to the gym, our conversation deepened, and we discussed areas in our lives that were not working. For most of us, the big concern was the way our husbands treated us. Few of us were happily married or felt our lives were working out. Lucy's marital contentment was a novelty.

A few women believed the party line of the FLDS, that if a woman abides by the will of her husband, her happiness is guaranteed. But others among us were expressing frustrations. Even the women who had permission to go to Curves wanted it kept secret from the FLDS. If we were seen and reported, our husbands could be put in an uncomfortable position because they'd allowed us to engage in such utter nonsense. Those men could be interrogated about why their wives had encouraged other women to rebel against their husbands.

Curves was a symbol of just how cruel our world had become: in order to exercise for half an hour a few times a week, we had to act like secret agents.

But the men were onto something: exercise *is* dangerous. Once women start getting control over their bodies, they think about getting control over their lives. After a woman loses fifteen pounds and likes the way she looks, having that ninth or tenth child is less appealing. Getting in touch with her body puts her in touch with other areas of her life, like sexuality. Women who claimed sexual power were as threatening to the FLDS as women who claimed any other power. We weren't supposed to have sexual needs; we were merely the breeding stock that kept the cult replenished.

Curves was in Hurricane, a small town outside the FLDS community. We were at high risk of being seen there because a lot of FLDS went there to shop, do business, and eat. So when we pulled up to the gym, we established a lookout. Before we left the van, the scout checked to make sure the coast was clear. We all wore leggings under our skirts, so in the parking lot we removed our skirts. This was an ungodly act. Once we had our skirts off, we waited until the lookout said "Run!" and raced to the door.

Safely inside the gym, we acted like everyone else. We talked, laughed, enjoyed the music—a pleasure forbidden in the FLDS—and worked out on the machines. No one would have thought we were risking anything. We were discovering the real power of women free to be themselves.

We talked mostly to each other and avoided people who were not from our insular world. After the workout was over, we got ready to leave and waited. This was a critical moment because there could only be one dash to the van. When the signal was given, we ran for our lives. In my nearly fifteen years of marriage to Merril, this was the most outrageous act I'd ever committed.

We joked that if our husbands found out about Curves, we'd be forced to go on medication. It really wasn't a laughing matter; a lot of women did go to the clinic to get medication because they were miserable. At one point the state launched an investigation because so many prescriptions for antidepressants were being written in our area.

One day as we were leaving Curves, our game plan blew up. My sister Linda was the lookout. She was standing next to the door, looking in every direction, waiting to give us the sign to run to the van. She was very cautious and made us all feel safe. She gave the go-ahead, and we prepared to dash as a group.

Suddenly I heard screams from the front of our group. Linda grabbed the woman who had been first and shoved her back inside the gym. She looked like she wanted to yell "Oh, shit!" She couldn't even speak. Her face was red, and I could see her trying to get a grip on what was happening.

"Damn! We're in trouble now," said Jayne, who began talking almost nonstop. Jayne had the most to say because she was the least concerned. She had a job outside the community, and even though she didn't get along with her husband, he was pleased that she was working out. Those of us with more to lose were stunned into silence.

"Linda, what's going on?" someone asked.

"Our asses are grass" was all she said.

The manager of Curves noticed the commotion around the front door and wanted to know what was happening. We didn't dare tell her and insisted nothing was wrong.

What had happened was that, just as Linda gave the go-ahead, Joe Barlow, a prominent man in the community with several wives and more than fifty children, left the restaurant next door with ten of his sons. It would have been hard for us to be seen by anyone worse. Joe was a big deal in the FLDS, and his sons loved to gossip. In no time at all stories about us would spread around the community. So we hung around the door until Joe was gone, then hurried out to the van.

We were all worried about what might be waiting for us when we got back. Lucy broke the silence. "Well, I guess I might end up coming down here by myself," she said. "There is no way, even if this turns out to be a big problem, that I am going to stop." Several of us jumped on her. How could she be so indifferent to the trouble we might all be facing? Her attitude was that if our "lord and masters" didn't want us to exercise, we didn't have the right to do it. Within minutes we were talking about the FLDS and what we hated about it.

Most of us agreed that the only reason we weren't free to go to a gym was that our "work of God" was to be baby machines. Several of us confessed that we couldn't stand Warren Jeffs. We feared that if he succeeded his father as prophet, he'd suck up the last hope of our ever again having oxygen to breathe.

Lucy disagreed vehemently with a lot of what we were saying— then offered up a confession of her own. "Most of the principles of God are perfectly fine with me," she said. "The only one I don't understand is the principle of plural marriage. It makes no sense."

Dead silence. None of us could believe what we'd just heard. The principle of plural marriage was the bedrock of our belief system. Nothing was more sacred. I didn't know how to tell Lucy that this little principle that she couldn't grasp was the heart of our religion. Everything, including all the oppressive rules, made sense to Lucy except for plural marriage? Amazing.

Lucy, in all her righteousness, then started in on us for not having permission from our husbands to exercise. She was adamant in her defense of the FLDS. "Every one of us has a responsibility to look at why this is a problem for us," Lucy said in the van. "I am not worried about what my husband is going to say because I'm not keeping secrets from him. I think the problem isn't with our religion. It's with your relationships with your husbands."

"So you are saying that because your lord and master wants you to look good, you have that right, and if our lords and masters want us to look horrible, then we're supposed to just look ugly and be fat?" Jayne shot back.

"The real problem for me," I said, "is that I don't have the right to make any of my own decisions."

"It's not my fault that I have a good relationship with my lord and master and that he wants me to feel good and be healthy," Lucy said. "I also have health problems he has to be responsible for."

"It is not about your lord and master," Jayne said. "It's about Warren making our husbands our lords and masters. We should be able to make a few decisions for ourselves."

"My lord and master has nothing good to offer me," I said. "His only interest is in controlling and oppressing me."

"This is a problem between you and your husband, and it has nothing to do with Warren or the religion." Lucy was emphatic to the point of defensiveness.

"I think it has everything to do with the total power Warren gives to a man," I said. "I'm expected to submit. It has nothing to do with our relationship; it's about power."

The debate was heated all the way home. I got dropped off at the house where I'd left my van. I couldn't risk being seen with all the other women; it would raise suspicions. On the way home I decided I was going to continue going to Curves even if I was forbidden to. I was prepared to disobey. By going I was doing something good for me. It felt enormously empowering.

But somehow Joe Barlow and his sons must not have spotted us because we kept going and we kept talking more candidly about our lives. There was intense discussion about some of the most recent changes in the FLDS that Warren Jeffs had made. Although at that point Warren's father, Rulon Jeffs, was technically still the prophet, Rulon was old and ailing and Warren was the power behind the throne.

There was outrage that Warren Jeffs was kicking men out of the FLDS and assigning their wives and children to other men. Men were marrying their fathers' wives after Jeffs banished their dads. These practices had never happened before in the FLDS but Jeffs had no qualms about openly promoting them.

As the weeks went on, our conversations in the van moved from the abusive nature of our personal relationships (especially with our husbands) to what we felt was abusive about the FLDS in general. One day I brought up my fear that my family might be forced to move. "Warren is talking about taking the worthy to the center place," I said. "Because of Merril's position, I'm sure we will be one of the first to be taken."

"You should feel honored if you get to go," said Lucy. "I would."

"I will not go, no matter what," I told her. "I will find a way to never go."

Lucy jumped in again. "My husband might get called and if he does then my ass is getting hauled off to the center place."

"I hope you enjoy living in the jungle and being eaten by an anaconda," I said, "because the center place we are hearing about in church is not going to be a good place to go. Warren will take everyone to some isolated place where even if they tried to escape they'd never make it out."

"Jungle? Anaconda? Where did you get that from?" Lucy said in disbelief. "That's totally crazy. I will follow my husband if he chooses to follow the prophet."

"If he doesn't, you will be taken from him and given to another man who will," I said, "and you can say goodbye to love!"

"I am not talking about this kind of apostasy any longer. It's too crazy!" Lucy said, and with that, she closed off the conversation.

Speaking so openly about things I'd been afraid ever to mention before was a jolt of pure freedom, and it made me hungry for more. Most of all I wanted to be free from fear.

I had started exercising because it sounded like fun. I'd never worked out to music or on machines before. And before long I lived for the days when I could sneak out to go to Curves. Exercise was a healthy way to rebel; it gave me a physical outlet for my feelings. Before Curves I'd thought that nothing good could happen if I left my comfort zone. Now I saw that things might, in fact, get better. I felt stronger not only physically but also mentally. My view of the world was expanding, and so was my confidence. Unbelievably, a mere half hour of exercise, three times a week, was transforming my mood and boosting my energy. Eight babies in fifteen years had ravaged me. The idea of feeling powerful in my body was something I didn't know existed.

As I lost a little weight, I liked the way I looked and began to care more about what I ate. Starting to feel in control of my body made me think I could be more assertive in other areas. The more in control I felt, the less I was willing to let myself be controlled. No wonder the men in the FLDS didn't want their wives working out! I was breaking free in small steps. I no longer even cared if I was caught going to Curves. Much of my life continued to march along on the same path, day by endless day, but at least now I turned my eyes to the sky more often. I also began to see how I'd collaborated in digging my own rut. My reluctance to venture out of my comfort zone and experience something new had kept me firmly in my place.

Getting out of a rut can take a long time, but the beginning is simple: Do something you wouldn't typically do. Take a risk. Expand your world in some small way. The FLDS put limits on every aspect of my life, but after I escaped I realized that I had been limiting myself with my need to stay safe, to avoid risks. Unless I challenged myself to do things that made me feel uncomfortable (at least initially), I'd never fit into my new, unfamiliar world. I needed to change.

It's been said that the only difference between a rut and a grave is a few feet. After I escaped, I saw how many people get trapped in the same patterns, which become so familiar that change becomes harder and harder. We run from information, get angry when challenged by different opinions, and shut down in the face of things that make us uncomfortable. Our energy never breaks free to create new life.

When I first fled, I was afraid of everyone outside the FLDS. It took me weeks to feel confident even about the homeless coordinator who was working with us. One of the first big risks I took was allowing someone into my world who didn't understand where we were coming from but wanted to help us.

I also had to learn to look people in the eyes when I talked to them. In the FLDS, that was considered disrespectful. The first attorney who worked with me after I escaped still talks about how odd it was when we met because I wouldn't look her in the eyes, even though I was thirty-five years old. Something so natural to most people was really strange to me. But learning this simple skill changed my life. Not only did I appear more confident, I felt more confident.

Six weeks after I escaped from the FLDS, I started to go to Curves again, a different one this time. I trained myself to walk away from my house even when it was in complete chaos, because I needed to stay strong in my body and mind. I went several times a week. It took me fifteen minutes each way and then a half hour to work out. An hour a day all to myself! It was my way of saying, "I'm worth it."

Letting Love In

I have a hard time asking for help. I'm better at it now, but in the immediate aftermath of my escape, it was especially difficult because I'd been conditioned to believe that any form of need was a sign of weakness that could be used against me. In a matter of life and death I could reach out; otherwise I felt too self-conscious.

In August 2003, nearly four months after we escaped, the nine of us moved into one room in a homeless shelter for five weeks. The South Valley Sanctuary was noisy and chaotic. After being in a home with fifty-four siblings, my children didn't mind the confusion. But for Harrison, my handicapped son, it was life-threatening. I could see his condition worsening every day. The ATCH hormone drug that he desperately needed to protect his nervous system would also suppress his immune system; in a shelter, with germs everywhere, this would put him at great risk. Harrison's physician wouldn't even think of putting him on the medication until we had a stable living situation.

Meanwhile, Merril refused to pay any child support. He claimed that he was retired, with Social Security as his only income. I knew that was a lie. Before I fled, I had watched him move all of his assets out of his name to avoid paying a huge hospital bill he owed. But I could not prove in court that he'd fraudulently transferred his money unless I hired a private investigator and an attorney, which was out of the question.

Because I was receiving some Social Security for my children— Harrison got disability payments—the state of Utah did not see my case as an emergency. Even though I was homeless and destitute, state workers told me my case was not a priority and would have to be processed through "normal channels," which took three months.

After two weeks in the shelter, I went before a judge and filed for bankruptcy. Merril not only refused to pay any child support but also stopped making payments on a debt he had financed in my name to buy machinery and equipment. We also had some credit card debt we'd incurred as a couple. Because I had a restraining order against him, Merril wasn't allowed to call me, but he freely gave out my cell phone number to the creditors who were pursuing us. If I had called Merril to try to work out the debt situation between us, he could have gone back into court and argued that my contacting him was proof I wasn't afraid of him and that he therefore posed no risk to me. I also knew that Merril would agree to anything but then rarely follow through. Promises from him were meaningless.

Merril was trying to pressure me into returning by making it impossible for me to start a new life. He thought there was no way I could survive financially. By having creditors harass me, he was making the point that if I returned to the FLDS, he'd resume making payments on our debts. But I was never going back, even if it meant complete financial ruin.

The money we owed was a relatively small amount: $15,000. If Merril had paid even modest child support, I could have kept making payments and avoided bankruptcy. I wanted to pay what we owed, and it upset me that I couldn't. But when the judge stamped my bankruptcy agreement, I knew I was truly free. Bankruptcy was abhorrent to me, but afterward I realized Merril had lost the most powerful weapon he held over me. He was convinced that I needed his financial protection. But I walked away from that along with everything else.

Three weeks later I managed to find a landlady who would rent me a double-wide and a single-wide trailer that had been pushed together into one. It was shabby, with leaks here and there, but it was ours. The landlady was unbelievably kind to rent to someone with eight kids and barely any money. I told her I'd fled from a polygamous cult, but that didn't faze her at all.

I did not say a word about the move to the children until the afternoon I picked them up from my sister's, where they'd gone for a court-approved visit with their father. Because of the restraining order, my brother-in-law had to be the go-between each time they went from Merril to me. The kids piled into the van, thinking we were going back to the shelter. It wasn't until we got to the trailer that I said we had a new home.

Betty came unglued and immediately called her father on the cell phone he'd given her. Merril had been telling the kids that Dan Fischer wouldn't help me forever and that once he stopped, I'd have to come back to the FLDS and repent. Merril knew we couldn't stay in the shelter indefinitely, and he was sure our next move would be back to him. When he heard we'd moved into our own place, he was furious and encouraged the children to be more disruptive.

LuAnne started griping right away. "The shelter was a lot better than this place."

"LuAnne, I have worked very hard to get us moved in here, and people all over the city have donated furniture for us," I said. "I know you're disappointed, but there are far worse things than living in a trailer."

Betty went to the back of the second trailer and fell onto her bed crying. When LuAnne came into the bedroom they'd be sharing, she said, "Oh this is nice." She fell in love with the sky-blue bedspreads.

I had been lucky to get box springs and mattresses donated from a local furniture store, but I didn't have a bed frame, so the two beds were sitting on the floor.

"My bed is too short, and I hate these bedspreads!" Betty screeched. "Patrick and Andrew are not going to share a bathroom with us. This place stinks, and I am not going to stay here. Father is not going to approve of this. It's not right that we're living like this."

Betty killed LuAnne's mood, of course, and she began complaining, too. But I knew she was relieved to finally be out of the shelter, even though she also felt lost because she was cut off from the friends she'd made there.

"Oh, wow, my own bedroom!" Pat said when he saw the room he'd be sharing with Andrew. "Andrew, we have our own bunk beds! And a nightstand! I've always wanted one of those."

There were basketball bedspreads and pillow shams on the bunk beds and a white lamp on the nightstand. Leenie, Dan Fischer's wife, had purchased all the bedding for us and decorated each room individually. This bedroom was a novelty for Patrick and Andrew—as was the Nintendo that had been donated to us by another family. Pat kept saying, "This is so cool!"

The only thing Andrew remembers saying is "Wow!" He couldn't believe our good fortune.

Arthur, my oldest, just went into his room and shut the door. It was a full week before he checked out Betty and LuAnne's room. He told Betty to stop complaining because she had the nicest bedroom in the house. Arthur was the only one with his own bedroom and bathroom. He'd never had anything so nice in his life, and he realized it. I think it helped that the younger kids were excited about the trailer, which didn't look bad at all in the end.

The previous tenants had told me that my closest neighbor was a woman who was nearly eighty. A few days after we moved in, she came over and introduced herself. Venus had permed red hair and looked like someone who'd experienced a lot of life and could tackle almost anything. Her spirit was warm, generous, and compassionate, and the chaos of kids and moving boxes everywhere didn't bother her at all. I was relieved that she wasn't worried about the noise.

"I wanted to come over and welcome you to the neighborhood," Venus said that first day. "You'll like it here. We have a neighborhood watch, so this is a very safe place to live. About the only crime we have had here in years was when one family had something stolen out of their yard, but it was some kids who did it." Venus went on to explain that she was the oldest sister of a very large Mormon family, but that she'd left Mormonism years ago.

"I have some background with the Mormons," I said carefully. "I recently left a fundamentalist group that separated from the Mormon Church around a hundred years ago."

"Well, you certainly have your hands full here, and you look so young," Venus said, once again taking in my situation. "If you need any help, I'll do whatever I can."

I smiled at her in gratitude. "I'm not that young, but yes, I do have my hands full."

"I know what it's like to be out on your own," she said. "I've been married more than once, and in my second marriage I ended up raising some of my children as a single mother. So do let me know if there's anything I can do to help you with your kids."

I didn't understand how to talk to Venus at that point because I wasn't used to having women friends or trusting anyone who was non-FLDS. I didn't tell Venus the complete truth about our lives— just a minimal amount to explain how we landed in the neighborhood. I didn't enjoy talking about why I was in such a bad place; nor did I want anyone to know how desperate my situation was. Six of my children were in counseling, and so was I. Harrison had three appointments every week, and I had children in five different schools. It was a logistical nightmare. I had so much to do every day that I didn't see how I could find room for anything else in my life, least of all a friend.

Venus offered comfort and kindness whenever I saw her. Her attitude was always upbeat and positive, despite the tragedies she'd dealt with in her life. Yet I still resisted responding to her with openness. I was terrified of becoming dependent; I didn't want to rely on anyone else's strength. If I was going to survive, it had to be on my own. I believed that my need for approval in relationships had trapped me in a life of degradation. I didn't want to burden Venus with my pain or the staggering challenges in my immediate future. The easiest route was to shut down, isolate myself from the rest of the world, and focus my strength on getting through each day.

But at times I'd get stuck in traffic on the way home with the children and have to call Venus to ask her to meet Harrison's school bus. She'd sit with him until we arrived, which was a godsend. Venus continually offered to help with Harrison. I was astonished. None of my so-called sister wives had ever voluntarily lifted a finger when it came to caring for my sick son.

Her kindness touched us in other ways. Venus noticed that Patrick, who was then ten, loved to walk to the convenience store and buy a drink. So she'd ask him to do small jobs around her yard. She knew Pat would use the little bit of money she paid him to buy treats that I could never afford.

Once when Venus saw Betty sulking in the yard, she asked her what the problem was. Betty explained that she wanted to return to her father's family. Venus was sympathetic and told Betty that even at eighty she wished a lot of things in her life were different from what they were. Venus kept reaching out to Betty and encouraging her to stay strong and understand that disappointment is part of life.

Venus offered all of us a hand, but my hand was closed. I was so afraid of being needy that I missed the strength she had to give me. I was hung up on my vision of how things had to be and determined to stay in control. Now I realize that the dishes and laundry could have waited. I was robbing myself of something I really needed: human connection and love. My world was impoverished, and I contributed to that impoverishment by not appreciating the deep and abundant love that was right next door. Venus's wisdom could have given me ballast. I remained disconnected from the life support she offered.

Eventually we got to know each other a little better. Sometimes we'd sit down for a cup of coffee after I got Harrison on the bus in the morning. Four and a half years later, after she'd finished reading *Escape*, Venus called me in tears. "I wish I had known what your life was really like," she said. "I would have tried to do so much more for you!"

That's when it hit me: I'd cheated both of us by not reaching out to Venus with more honesty. My stubbornness and need for control had robbed her of the chance to help me and find greater meaning in her life. I'd thought being strong meant doing everything myself.

It would have meant so much to be able to talk to Venus when I was having a bad day. When you have no obvious answers and the way ahead is unclear, it's especially important to have someone in your life who genuinely cares about you and is willing to listen. Having a safe place to feel terrible is like having another oar in the boat.

Now I work on being realistic about what I can control and what I can't. I also remind myself that help may be closer than I think if I get out of my own way and just knock.

The Gift of Independence

The two women who raised my father were strong, independent, and devoted to their families. They also knew how to stand up for themselves and were very protective of each other. Grandma Gwen and Grandma Florence were full sisters who married the same man, Harold Blackmore. As far as I know, none of them were born into polygamy; they all chose to become Mormon fundamentalists at a young age and practice plural marriage. But it was a match made of love, and even after they eventually quit believing in polygamy, the three of them stayed together.

I realize now how much of my life has been shaped by these two remarkable women. Each taught me in her own way to focus on what I have and then do whatever it takes to make it work.

Gwen and Florence were completely enmeshed their entire lives. They were close in age, and their personalities complemented each other well. Gwen was short and stocky, upbeat and nurturing, with a wild sense of humor. She loved to laugh. Florence was taller and lean with a no-nonsense, let's-get-the-job-done attitude. She would always tell you exactly how she felt. What appealed to them about polygamy, initially, was that they would never have to be apart from each other if they lived in the same family. Since one of them couldn't have children (and to this day I don't know which of them that was), when the other had a baby, a second infant was adopted for the sister who couldn't conceive. My father was one of the adopted children. The two moms and a dad eventually had fifteen kids and were a genuinely happy family.

But while polygamy helped unite the family initially, my grand-mothers and their husband quit the FLDS after their children were nearly raised. They couldn't stand the abusive practices—and this was decades before Warren Jeffs came to power. Once they quit, they re-jected every aspect of the mainstream Mormon Church, too. But be-cause they couldn't bear the thought of living apart, the three remained together in a loving relationship until they died. (I assume that like most polygamists, each woman had a separate intimate relationship with her husband.)

I didn't know my grandmothers until after they'd left the FLDS. My father was the only son who stayed behind, and unfortunately this rupture caused tension and strain in the family. My father's par-ents were hurt when he distanced himself from those who had left.

Even though I didn't see a lot of my grandmothers, they shaped my life in important ways. Gwen was the more nurturing sister. She had been given two small goats when she was young and over a period of years raised a small herd. This enabled her to always provide milk for her family. She taught me how to milk a goat, taking my hand and showing me exactly how to pull and squeeze to release the milk. She also taught me how to feed and care for the goat after the milking was finished. Today Grandma Gwen would be making chèvre and selling it at farmers' markets.

My two grandmothers were a huge part of all our birthday parties. (Birthdays were still celebrated when I was growing up; they were later halted as the FLDS became more extreme.) Grandma Gwen would always bring us birthday pennies. We would get one penny for each member of the family multiplied by the new age you were. When I was five, I got ninety pennies. As I counted out my mountain of pennies, I felt like the richest little girl in the world.

Grandmother Gwen kept the home fires burning with her birthday pennies and her goats. Grandma Florence was passionate about her independence and felt women needed to be much more than just obedient to their husbands. She used to say that every woman should own her own backhoe. This became a mantra repeated throughout my childhood. Grandma Florence worked most of her life as a schoolteacher. Like me, she adored teaching but knew it would never create adequate financial independence for her. She saved her money and bought a backhoe, which she used to generate more income on weekends, digging out yards and driveways for people in the community. Instead of despairing about her small teacher's salary, Florence found a way to compensate for its limitations. She always focused on what she could do, not on what she couldn't.

Grandma Florence knew that unless she had a way to generate income, she could never be completely independent. Her backhoe guaranteed that no one could take her independence away. She did turn over some of her money, though not all, to her husband, but unlike most men in the FLDS, he kept track of it and later in life paid it all back, right down to the last penny. When I was young, I took her advice about backhoes quite literally—and it made me skeptical. If every woman had this implement, I thought, the suburbs would have to be a lot bigger, and women who lived in apartment buildings would have nowhere to park their backhoes. But after I fled the FLDS, I realized how valuable this concept was.

My grandmothers had been dead for years before I escaped, but if they'd been alive, they would have been outraged by my marriage to Merril. I hadn't thought of them much in the years leading up to my escape because I was so stressed out with everything else. But a housing crisis brought my grandmothers back into my thoughts in a dramatic way. During the first three years after I left the FLDS, I was always in a financially precarious situation. Each month I'd try to just make it to the next, and somehow I did. But after paying the rent and buying gas to get the kids to school, I often had nothing left to pay my utilities.

As winter drew near in 2005, I started to panic. Heating the trailer in the winter was always expensive. I had to keep the heat turned up high for Harrison, because I couldn't risk his catching a cold. Every time any kind of work came through or I managed to earn a little money, I hid it so I wouldn't be tempted to spend it. I hoarded my money and built an emergency fund. During the year I tried to save enough to ensure that we'd have heat in the winter. But in fall 2005 my emergency reserve was depleted. We were living on food stamps. Sometimes I'd find a little money here and there, but I knew I wouldn't have enough for my big winter utility bills.

One night both my grandmothers, Florence and Gwen, came to me in a dream. They were very concerned and working desperately to find a way for me to protect my children. Even though I was miserable, I could feel how worried and agitated they were about my family. They both appeared to be alive but living in a different dimension.

For three years I'd been on a waiting list for housing or rental assistance. Most women with children can qualify for low-income housing in a matter of months. I couldn't because of the size of my family. There were nine of us, and that was more than the number allowed in a three-bedroom apartment, which was the largest low-income housing available. My only recourse was Section Eight, a housing assistance program that helps pay the rent for qualified housing. Normally it took three years before anything became available; now, because a moratorium was in effect, the minimum wait was five years. That's a long way off when you're in a crisis.

Everyone I spoke with said that until my name moved up on the list, nothing could happen. I was not optimistic. I gave up all hope of ever getting Section Eight.

In the dream my grandmothers were talking to each other about how upset they were about my situation. They seemed determined to find the resources to help me.

The dream was both precise and imprecise. But when I awoke, I had a strong sense of peace and knew everything was going to be okay. Something had shifted. I didn't know how things were going to change, but I felt that they would.

I didn't tell anyone about the dream. But somehow, three weeks later, I was approved for Section Eight housing. My trailer qualified, so I didn't even have to move. Every month I received funds to help pay the rent. It was a miracle—literally, a dream come true!

I felt like my grandmothers, Gwen and Florence, had somehow blessed me with this great gift. I began to think about them on a daily basis, a lot more than I had in years. I remembered the firmness of my tiny hand in Gwen's as she taught me to milk and care for her goats. I thought of Florence and her backhoe. With the housing assistance, I could keep my family warm, safe, and fed. It seemed like it was time to find my backhoe. With one of those, I might reach my goal of getting off welfare.

The problem with state assistance was that for every dollar I earned, I lost two in benefits. It was going to be impossible for me to break free incrementally. I had to find a way to make enough money to get off welfare in one fell swoop. To really stabilize my life, I needed to be able to put a down payment on a house.

My backhoe, I realized, could be my story itself. Several people who had heard me speak about the life I'd fled suggested that I write a book. It would be a job that I could do on my own time. If I didn't have time during the day, I could work throughout the night. The project could adapt to the crazy demands of my daily schedule with eight children in five schools, plus karate, counseling, and sports.

I decided to carve out a small slot of time every day and start putting words on paper. Writing and publishing *Escape* did so much more than end my dependence on welfare. It gave me back my dignity on a level far beyond what I had ever thought possible. It gave birth to my life as an advocate for those trapped in polygamy and other degrading situations.

Escape was the backhoe that my grandmother Florence thought every woman should own in order to claim the right to independence and dignity.

Five years after fleeing the FLDS, I was able to make a down payment on a house in a suburb of Salt Lake City. My father had thirty-six children, and I was the first of his daughters ever to own her own home. No one in the FLDS, man or woman, is allowed to own their own home. It was one of the biggest moments of my life. I had accomplished something that even my father had been prevented from doing.

Merril's refusal to pay child support had pushed me into financial ruin. I didn't know how I would ever be able to dig myself out. Buying my house was a triumph. I was able to do it because of my book advance and because Brian was willing to cosign on my mortgage. It was a moment of genuine liberation from the mental and financial mess Merril had tried to make of my life.

Ironically, none of this might have happened if Merril had paid me child support. Had he shown more decency in fulfilling his obligations as a father, I probably would never have written *Escape*. I didn't write it to get even. I had no guarantee that the book would sell. If Merril had helped me pay off our debts and had supported our children, then writing the book would have been incredibly risky, since he would have cut off my support. I would never have risked losing it.

So in the end I'm almost grateful that he refused to meet his responsibilities. If he had done the honorable thing, I would still be chained to him. His lack of honor left me with nothing to lose by writing a book—and maybe something to gain.

I never could have imagined that *Escape* would spend twelve weeks on the *New York Times* best-seller list. I didn't know how to dream that big.

My Fight for Justice

Brian and I slept a little later than we'd planned. The night before, we'd stayed up late enjoying a real Texas pit barbecue at a party held in our honor by several members of CASA, the Court Appointed Special Advocates who worked with the children in the aftermath of the raid on the YFZ Ranch. I'd contacted CASA and made plans to get together when I found out that I was coming to San Angelo to meet Merril in court.

Merril had never paid a dime in child support. He was legally required to do so and had plenty of money, but after I won custody, I lacked the funds to pursue it. My attorney in the custody case advised me against going after Merril for support, because then he would hit back even harder for custody. She felt, as I did, that my first priority was keeping my children safe.

But after six years I finally wised up. As the leader of the Eldorado compound, Merril was one of the most powerful men in the FLDS. The FLDS was spending tens of thousands of dollars to assemble a team of high-priced attorneys to defend it in the criminal cases that resulted from the Texas raid. I realized that a river of money was still flowing into the cult.

Once I decided to move forward, my case proceeded quickly. We went to final trial in less than six months. I was sure that the FLDS would find a way to drag the case out for years. I was represented by Natalie Malonis, a lawyer I met when we were both guests on *Nancy Grace*. Natalie had been representing one of the children who had been taken from the ranch and was initially supportive of the FLDS. After our segment was over, we kept talking on the phone (we lived in different locations), and we continued the conversation in the weeks ahead. As Natalie began to understand how evil the FLDS really is, she became outraged. When she heard that Merril had never paid any child support, we discussed taking him to court. As an expert in family law, Natalie felt I had a strong case.

I was concerned that we were not adequately prepared for trial. Natalie is a tough and talented lawyer, but the case had come together with astonishing speed. We'd worked as hard as we could to mount our case, but I wondered if we were ready for the curve balls the FLDS would inevitably throw.

Brian and I were enjoying a leisurely morning before going to court when the telephone rang. Paulette Schell, a member of the CASA team whose home we were staying in, was speaking fast. She had gone into the office early.

"Three gunshots were fired around Debra's house at six-thirty this morning," she said. "A few minutes later three shots were fired near Angie Voss's house."

I was speechless. The first two nights Brian and I were in town, we had stayed at Debra Brown's house. Debra was the executive director of CASA, and she and I had become friends during the time the state had the FLDS children in custody. And Angie Voss, the lead child abuse investigator for the state, had told Judge Walther that there were serious problems on the YFZ Ranch. Angie has a stellar reputation, and Judge Walther knew that when she said there was a problem, it was for real. None of us thought it was a coincidence that gunshots were fired near the homes of two women who had been in the forefront of the effort to protect the FLDS children. I had been in town for three days, and it was certainly possible that the FLDS knew where I'd been staying.

"An eyewitness saw the truck that fired the shots," Paulette continued. "It was a white Ford F150 pickup with two people in the front of the cab. The police have been notified, and they found some of the casings from the gun that was used."

When Natalie learned about the gunshots, she alerted a Texas Ranger, who arranged for all of us to be escorted to court by state troopers. She and I both felt the FLDS was acting out more than anything else, but it was still wise to take precautions.

Merril had tried to have the case heard in Utah, where I lived. It was his best shot for evading justice because if I won, Utah would have no way to enforce its judgment against him—he and his assets were in Texas. Natalie felt that my odds were better in Texas because the court there had physical jurisdiction over him and could force him to pay or seize his assets, which were enmeshed with the ranch.

The case opened with Merril's attorney, Amy Hennington, arguing that Texas lacked jurisdiction over the case. Natalie argued that it had jurisdiction. The rear of the courtroom was filled with seven or eight FLDS men. They were snickering and acting like this was all a big joke. As I already knew from past observation, Judge Walther is not one to be intimidated. Confident in her right to hear the case, she ordered it to get under way.

Natalie called her first witness to the stand. Nick Hanna was one of the Texas Rangers who'd been involved in the raid. She asked him to authenticate some of the FLDS records that had been seized.

The second witness was Merril Jessop, who looked older and frailer since I'd last seen him in court, five years earlier. He answered almost every question by saying he couldn't remember, but this response seemed to amuse him because as he feigned forgetfulness, he could barely contain his smile. He claimed that he had no bank account, no

ATM card, and no income beyond his monthly thousand-dollar Social Security check.

Natalie questioned him about the businesses he'd been involved in. He couldn't remember much about any of them until Natalie mentioned a company he once owned, giving the wrong address. Merril said he couldn't remember the company but then corrected her about its address. His credibility was disintegrating.

By then Judge Walther was steeped in FLDS culture; she'd presided over all the cases involving the custody of the children seized from the YFZ Ranch. Merril's professed inability to remember anything about anything he'd ever done seemed not to surprise her in the least. Merril kept looking at me with a slick smile that said he was going to get away with what he was doing.

I wasn't intimidated. After living outside the FLDS for more than six years, I knew far better than he did that the court system takes child support very seriously. Finally he was going to have to answer to being a deadbeat dad.

Merril was living in a bubble, within which he was practically a god. His position in the FLDS let him do anything to anyone and never be held accountable. This position bred arrogance and convinced him that he was above the law.

Natalie's last question to him was "Mr. Jessop, why is it that you don't financially support your children?"

This time Merril had an answer. "When Carolyn was with me, I provided her with nice living conditions, and she didn't have to leave me," he said. "So I felt like that was all I could do."

The next witness called was my father, Arthur Blackmore, who at one time had been a business partner of Merril's. I was proud that my dad was standing up for me. He testified about money he had seen Merril receive, the most substantial being a check for $180,000 in 2004. If Merril hadn't incriminated himself enough already, my father's testimony added more damning evidence because it proved that he did have money to support his children. In November 2008 he had signed for a $900,000 lien against the ranch that named his attorney as the trustee. Merril had a hard time explaining it. He claimed he didn't know whether that lien was intended to pay for FLDS legal fees and that his lawyer had never billed him.

LuAnne, 18, took the stand next and answered questions about our living conditions after we escaped. Her father had been fully aware of how destitute we were, she explained to the court, when we were living in the homeless shelter and the trailer. She said she'd been too embarrassed to bring friends home from school when we were living there because she'd been used to living in a large house in good condition. She explained why she hadn't asked her father for things she needed during that time. "I didn't ask," she said, "because I knew what the answer would be."

I was proud of my daughter. She exhibited extraordinary poise and strength but conveyed real emotion and disgust about the way Merril treated our family. LuAnne firmly believed that she and all her siblings, especially Harrison, had been put at risk by Merril's callous disregard for their well-being.

In the months after we escaped, Merril had tried to persuade my children that they were being punished because of my wicked decisions. He tried to make them believe that if I went back, they'd be taken care of again. So my children all thought that if they made things difficult enough for me, they'd get to go back to the (superficially) better living conditions in the FLDS.

For roughly two years, this game worked. Then my children began to grasp that their father had a responsibility toward them regardless of my actions. By that point Merril was moving to Texas and was no longer a part of their lives. After I won full custody, he made no effort to see them, even when he was in Salt Lake City on business. Merril made a great show of wanting his children back, but it was all a facade. Once custody was decided, he essentially disappeared from their lives and made no effort even to arrange the visits I would have allowed. The kids got the message.

Merril looked shocked by LuAnne's testimony. He had always been able to abuse a woman by turning her children against her. This was quite possibly the first and only time one of his children had confronted him with the cruelty of his behavior, and people were paying attention. Judge Walther seemed impressed with LuAnne's composure and listened with great interest.

At one point Natalie asked LuAnne if she was attending college. LuAnne said she was a full-time student at a community college. "Who is paying for your tuition?" Natalie asked.

"I am paying for it," LuAnne replied. "I started saving for college when I was fourteen." LuAnne had done a lot of babysitting, and then when she was old enough, she got a job as a bagger at Albertsons.

I was the next witness called. Natalie had me read into the record some of the church material that had been seized during the raid. I read financial instructions from Warren Jeffs to Merril, in which Jeffs told Merril to get all of his financial interests out of his name so that I couldn't get anything from him legally. When Jeffs referred to me in the record, it was as the "apostate woman, Carolyn Blackmore."

I read these passages very matter-of-factly. It was clear to Merril that I was not intimidated, and I'm sure this really bothered him. Power in the FLDS is based on intimidation and fear. It was at this moment, I think, that Merril finally "got it." He realized that he no longer had any power over me—that I had escaped both physically and mentally. When the trial began, he behaved as if I were still his property. But after my calm reading of what Warren Jeffs had said about me, during which I offered no reaction, Merril was noticeably flustered.

It was nine o'clock that night before the judge called an end to the day's proceedings. We were due back in court twelve hours later, at 9:00 a.m.

Merril left with the other FLDS men who had accompanied him

to court, except for one—his son Danny Jessop. Danny was already gone: another FLDS member had advised him to leave the courtroom when LuAnne took the stand. I think they were worried that LuAnne might be asked about the sexual assaults that Danny had committed against her younger sister.

I was told that the courthouse police had photographed every FLDS vehicle that arrived at the courthouse. When Danny Jessop made his abrupt departure, he left in a white Ford F150. It matched the eyewitness's description of the truck used in the early-morning gunshots.

That morning the FLDS had entered the courtroom acting as if the trial was a big joke. But by the end of the day, the snickering had vanished. Perhaps they had finally realized that there was nothing funny about this case.

The next morning Merril's attorney approached Natalie and asked for some numbers. The FLDS wanted to settle. Natalie and I both knew we could fight forever and that there was a limit to the amount the judge would award. Legally, in awarding judgment, she was required to consider Merril's other children under the age of eighteen. (He had six in this category that I knew of, out of a total of fifty-four children.) Both attorneys talked with the judge several times, then reached a settlement by late afternoon. Judge Walther had indicated how high she was prepared to go if she ruled in the case. She also told both attorneys that she wanted adequate money for Harrison's care.

Merril knew that the judge was going to award child support and that I was eligible for six years of back support. The latter was a number he needed to bring down. It was a huge victory for me that Merril was required to pay *anything*. The settlement for Harrison was the main reason I made concessions in other areas. (For example, I agreed to be responsible for my children's health insurance and for any uninsured medical costs.) I was awarded $2,350 a month for child support, which would continue for the rest of Harrison's life, even after my other children turned eighteen. I had to deduct from that some of the Social Security income that I received from Merril's account. So for now my net monthly payment would be $1,500. The retroactive settlement from 2003 forward came to about $90,000 with an interest rate of 6 percent. Merril was to begin paying that in increments of $100 a month. But if he was ever more than thirty days delinquent, the entire amount would come due.

Eventually, if I can find Merril's assets and get a lien against them, I hope to set up a special-needs trust for Harrison. But that's a battle for another day. I know Merril illegally transferred assets out of his name. If I can prove that those assets are actually Merril's, I can make a claim on Harrison's behalf. My disabled son needs every additional layer of protection he can get.

As both attorneys read their agreement into the record, I could see that Judge Walther was pleased with the arrangements made for Harrison. Merril left the courtroom that day defeated and angry. I was stunned by my success. A court case I thought might take years to win had been settled in less than half a year. I knew the FLDS would willingly spend a million dollars to help Merril avoid ever paying me a cent. That was one of the main reasons I didn't go after Merril sooner. The timing had to be right, and after the raid it was. The FLDS had obviously decided that it had more to lose by fighting me than by settling. Based on questions I have been asked by authorities, I suspect that the church records seized by Texas during the raid are very damning in terms of what they reveal about FLDS financial and business dealings. The FLDS did not want any of that to see the light of day if it could be avoided. The longer it fought, the more likely that that damaging evidence would be released.

On Monday evening the FLDS contingent left the courthouse angry and concerned. On Tuesday morning they woke up to more bad news: a story in *The Eldorado Success* listed more details of the crimes that Merril's son Raymond Merril Jessop was accused of committing.

The news story was based on court documents filed in the case against him. I think knowing these storm clouds were ahead might have made the FLDS eager to get my custody case against Merril resolved.

Raymond's trial, which ended in conviction on November 13, 2009, was the first of the trials of the FLDS men indicted in the aftermath of the raid on the YFZ Ranch. Raymond was convicted of the sexual assault of a child, but the prosecutors also submitted court documents alleging illegal banking activity as "extraneous offenses" and "prior bad acts" that could be considered in the penalty phase of his trial—and they were. (He ended up with a sentence of ten years in prison.) The documents also contained allegations that Raymond, thirty-eight, had endangered his sixteen-year-old wife. During the sentencing phase of his trial the non-FLDS people in the courtroom listened with shock as prosecutors related how Raymond had allegedly refused to take his pregnant wife, who had been in labor for three days, to the hospital because Warren Jeffs had instructed him not to. The assumption was that Jeffs feared that hospital doctors might realize the girl was only fifteen when she got pregnant and report Raymond to authorities.

On September 29, 2009, I left the San Angelo courtroom victorious and filled with a sense of making history. From my perspective, the legal system had said, *Welcome to America. You're finally a full citizen of the free world*. At the ranch Merril may have been a god, but to the court he was just another deadbeat dad. His message from the court: *Welcome to America. You are financially responsible for your children*.

The ruling also sent an important message to all FLDS fathers: *No matter how many children you have, you must support all of them*. In the eyes of the law, it didn't matter if their children escaped or if they walked out of their lives and regarded them as apostates. The fathers would still be held accountable.

To FLDS women and children still trapped behind the compound walls, the court sent another message: *There is hope. You don't have to live without health care, food, clothing, or basic necessities if you find your way out of the cult.*

The far-reaching impact of my victory brought back memories of one of my grandmother Jenny's best stories. A man was traveling and came to a deep ravine. He knew he could still continue with his journey because he was young and strong enough to climb through the ravine to the other side. But once the man got to the other side, he realized that many subsequent travelers would not be strong enough to climb through the ravine and would thus be unable to complete their journey. So he halted and built a bridge, making it possible for others to complete their journey regardless of their physical strength.

Because of Harrison's medical condition, I was forced to face down the FLDS. Lisa Jones, the attorney who handled my custody case, was an incredible comfort during that time when I fought the massive resources of the FLDS. She and Natalie Malonis are two smart, tough, and determined women who use their legal training to fight for what they know is right. They are the engineers who made it possible for me to build my bridge.

Winning custody of my children built a bridge halfway across the ravine. Winning child support completed the job. I hope the landmark ruling in my case is an inspiration to all women in difficult or abusive relationships. You can stand up to a perpetrator and win.

Justice prevailed again on December 15, 2009, in the second FLDS trial when Alan Keate was convicted of the sexual assault of a child. I don't know Keate—he was part of the FLDS community in Salt Lake City—but it was my understanding that he'd been invited to move to the YFZ Ranch because he had many beautiful daughters. Keate, now fifty-seven, married a fifteen-year-old girl who gave birth to a child three years ago. It took a jury of nine men and three women only ninety minutes to find Keate guilty. The jury also heard evidence that Keate married off one of his underage daughters to Jeffs, and two more underage daughters to other men.

It took the jury a lot longer to sentence Alan Keate than it did to convict him. After deliberating for four and a half hours, the jury came back into Judge Barbara Walther's courtroom with its decision: thirty-three years. Keate must serve half of it before he is eligible for parole. At fifty-seven, this is practically a life sentence.

His sentence is three times that of Raymond Jessop who was convicted on the same charge. I was told that one of the jurors in the Jessop case wanted him to get only probation. The jury had to negotiate, which is how the relatively light sentence in that case was reached. Another factor may be that in the sentencing phase of Keate's trial, the jury heard testimony about the three other underage daughters Keate had married off to older men, including Warren Jeffs.

Keate's sentence sends a powerful message to FLDS perpetrators as well as to those women and girls they have harmed. I am thrilled at the severity of the sentence because I believe in the severity of the crime. It will never stop until men realize there are consequences for breaking the law.

I'm told Texas has spent close to twenty million dollars so far preparing these cases for trial. The state deserves a lot of credit for its aggressive prosecution and its determination to hold the FLDS legally accountable for crimes against underage women.

Keeping Hope Alive

My first meeting with Betty in two years came about suddenly. Moments after the settlement in my child support case, Willie Jessop, the unofficial spokesman for the FLDS, asked if I'd like to see Betty, adding that he hoped we could put the controversy of the case behind us. I always assume that an ulterior motive drives most FLDS actions, and this was no exception. Perhaps the meeting was Willie's idea, but I wouldn't be surprised if Merril wanted to make the point that by controlling Betty, he could still control me. He knew he could use her to try to hurt me. I didn't care whose idea it was; I wasn't going to pass up an opportunity to see my beloved daughter.

Betty looked pale and worn as she got out of the car, strikingly thin and fragile. Where was the old fire in her eyes? The moment she was close enough, I wrapped my arms around her in a tight embrace. My heart was racing. Betty gasped. "How are you, Mother?" was all she said.

When I hugged Betty, I realized that even though she looked weak and haggard, her power was undiminished. She was polite and unemotional. I knew she was on guard; her half-brother Rich had been sent along to monitor everything she said.

My relationship with Betty has never been easy, but I have always

loved my daughter deeply. I've always felt a special bond with her because when I was pregnant with her, we almost died together in an
automobile accident. But that didn't prevent the conflict the FLDS
stamped into our relationship. My desire to protect Betty ignited a rag-
ing hostility in her. As one of Merril's favorite children, about to turn
fourteen, she was furious when I fled. On July 4, 2007, two days after
she turned eighteen, she returned to the FLDS. I was heartsick, but
I couldn't stop her from going back.

Our communication was minimal, at best, after she left. What
little conversation we had, whether by phone or text messaging, was
brief and tortured. But after the first year I noticed a slight shift. She
became more communicative and wanted to know how her siblings
were doing. She told me more about her life. She had been assigned to
cook, clean, and iron for FLDS boys working construction in Arizona.
(I was quite relieved that Merril didn't ask her to join him at the ranch
in Texas, but I said nothing.) When she told me that she had started to
teach the boys to read and do math, I was proud and told her so.

To help break the ice at our impromptu reunion, Brian showed
Betty pictures of our family on his phone. She seemed to lighten up
and laughed as she looked at photos of her brothers and sisters. We
had just celebrated Bryson's eighth birthday with a Frankenstein cup-
cake cake. Betty disapproved of the cake—cartoons or any figurative
representations of literary or storybook figures are banned in the
FLDS—but she clearly missed her baby brother.

Moments later LuAnne arrived and pulled Betty into a big hug.
The girls hadn't seen each other for two years, although they had talked
occasionally by phone until the raid shut down all communication.
Brian took pictures of the two of them with his phone as they were
laughing, being silly, and teasingly pulling each other's hair. Then he
took pictures of the three of us together.

Betty and LuAnne had once been very close, but after we escaped,
their relationship became strained. Betty's anger disrupted our family,

and by acting as her father's emissary, she constantly tried to sabotage the stability I was trying to create. She would become abusive toward her siblings if they did something she thought Merril wouldn't like. "Father doesn't want you to do that!" she'd scream. "You will be in so much trouble!"

In the first six months after I won custody from Merril, Betty ran back to her father three times. The third time she took LuAnne with her. It was horrendous, but I acted swiftly. Gary Engels, who worked for Arizona as an investigator and was based in Colorado City for a time, went to the authorities and insisted they act. Merril's house was surrounded by police, who were ready to break down the door to get the girls. (This was before Merril moved his family to Texas.) Merril negotiated with the police and agreed to turn the girls over to them in the morning. Just twenty-four hours after they ran away, Betty and Lu-Anne were back home with me. Betty never ran away again because Merril stopped making the arrangements.

After about two years, because of the tension she created at home, Betty went to live with my brother, Arthur, in Salt Lake City. But we never stopped seeing her, and we certainly never stopped loving her. The day she returned to the FLDS broke our hearts; all of us wept, including Betty.

Betty and LuAnne made a vivid contrast to each other. Betty's hair was piled up on her head in the required FLDS style. She wore a long and frumpy dark green dress that made her look exactly like every other FLDS woman. LuAnne was wearing a tan pullover and a floral print skirt that stopped just above her knees. She radiated happiness. She told Betty about her college classes and caught her up on what their other siblings were doing.

I urged Betty to come to dinner with us, but she refused, saying she wasn't hungry. I didn't believe her—I suspected the FLDS had set a limit on the time she could spend with us. I wanted to prolong our visit as long as I could, so when she vetoed dinner, I asked her if we could at least go for ice cream. I knew this was something she couldn't resist. She loves ice cream, and it's rarely served in the FLDS.

As we were driving to Baskin-Robbins, LuAnne asked Betty if she was on Facebook. Betty said "No!" but then in a whisper she asked, "Is that like MySpace?" I knew she was curious, but with Rich eavesdropping, she couldn't pursue something so totally forbidden by the FLDS.

As LuAnne and Betty were chatting, Betty said, "You don't really understand what living really is until you go to bed at midnight every day and get up at four o'clock in the morning." She was bragging; maybe she felt like we were wimps, because she was able to live on such little sleep. But when LuAnne told me about their conversation, my heart sank. Off and on for the past five years, I had heard stories about acute sleep deprivation in the FLDS. Now I knew they were true. It was yet another sign of how extreme life had become in the FLDS.

When LuAnne asked her, "What have you been up to?" Betty said, "I've just been working, working."

My dad, who was with us because he'd come to Texas to testify on my behalf, asked Betty what she meant. Betty said, "I just go from one job to the next. I mean, look at my hands! They are so dirty and terrible. Isn't it wonderful?" No, it wasn't wonderful at all. The FLDS makes a virtue out of forced labor. Betty looked too weak and exhausted for me to believe she felt "wonderful" about any aspect of her life.

LuAnne told Betty that her hands just looked rough and chapped. Betty has always been fastidious about her appearance. She loved to pamper herself and always used to put lotion on her hands. Now her fingernails were dirty and cracked.

When Betty first went back to her father at the ranch, she had been greeted like returning royalty. When Oprah Winfrey's producers were doing preparation for the show on the YFZ Ranch, one of them told me she'd seen three young women there who seemed to be regarded almost like queens. Betty was one of them. But seeing how exhausted she looked in Texas, I suspected that she was being treated more harshly than when she first rejoined her father.

When we got to Baskin-Robbins, Betty ordered a starlight mint ice cream cone, her favorite. She had barely eaten half of it by the time the rest of us had finished our cones. Was she making it last to spend more time with us, or because she wanted to savor each lick as long as she could? I wondered.

I listened for any clues that Betty wanted our help. But I heard nothing overt. Could she be signaling something by talking about how little she was sleeping and how hard she was working? But then, how could Betty ever confide in me that she was unhappy in a life that she had fought me so hard to get?

I am often asked why Betty hasn't been married. At twenty, she is well past the age when most FLDS girls are given to an older man. I honestly don't know why, but I think it might be because she is my daughter. It's hard for someone who lives in normal society to understand how wicked the FLDS thinks I am for leaving. While Betty has a certain power as Merril's daughter, some may think she's tainted by her relationship to me, and that could make her less marriageable. It's also possible that by keeping her unmarried, Merril was attempting to undercut me by proving that my fears for my daughters if we stayed in the FLDS were unfounded. One of my main reasons for fleeing was that Betty was about to turn fourteen, and I couldn't bear the thought of her being forced to marry some older man. In effect, Merril was saying, *See, Betty is fine. We don't abuse our women. You were exaggerating.*

A loving and positive relationship with a child can be the source of a parent's deepest joy, whereas estrangement is a wellspring of pain. The helplessness I feel in not being able to protect Betty from the FLDS creates a terrible grief. It's hard enough when a parent must navigate the rocky terrain of estrangement from a child. But with Betty, I have to deal with another factor that only compounds the difficulty: the media.

Oprah's show from inside the YFZ Ranch was timed to coincide with the first anniversary of the raid. In her segment with Betty, Oprah asked her flat out if the FLDS was marrying girls younger than eighteen to much older men. Betty didn't look directly at Oprah; instead she looked in one direction and then in another, paused, and said, "Not any that I am aware of." Betty must have been under unbelievable pressure about that question. There was no way she could tell the truth. It hurt me to know she was required to give a misleading answer. Betty isn't good at deception.

My blood was boiling. I hated seeing her exploited by the FLDS. She was vulnerable, unprotected, and being asked questions she did not dare answer honestly in front of Oprah's audience of millions. After her show Oprah heard from many viewers who felt that Betty was lying. Viewers also apparently wanted to know where the teenage boys were on the ranch and why Oprah had not interviewed any of them.

Oprah and her producers decided a follow-up show was warranted and invited me to appear as a guest. One of the first things Oprah said to me was "I like Betty, but I don't believe her."

I understood exactly what Oprah meant, and I agreed with her. But I hated that my daughter was so manipulated by the FLDS that she was forced to be discredited in front of millions. I told Oprah that watching the interview was very painful, adding, "She's under a lot of scrutiny with what she says. She has to be very, very, cautious."

Betty told Oprah that I hadn't fled the FLDS because I feared that she would be involved in an underage marriage. She claimed I'd made that up later. I knew instantly this was more fodder from the FLDS spin machine.

The truth is that in one of my first interviews after we escaped, I told a Salt Lake City newspaper that the primary reason I'd left the FLDS was because of my concern about my daughters' vulnerability to underage marriage. Betty was almost fourteen, and LuAnne was nearly twelve.

Betty's accusation would have had little sting if it could have been made privately to me instead of to Oprah. A baseless accusation between two people usually can't gain much momentum. But when it's broadcast to millions of outsiders, it's more difficult for the accuser to back down because of the public humiliation. The mountain Betty and I both would have to scale in order to repair our relationship got significantly steeper.

When Betty went out with us for ice cream, it became clear that my suspicions were true: she was not being treated as well as she had when she first returned. The honeymoon was over, and now that the FLDS had accomplished its goal in driving us apart, it no longer feared that Betty would return to her family. The more the FLDS broke the bonds between us, the more enslaved Betty became, and the less the FLDS had to do to keep her there.

Betty knows that I am not angry with her, and I don't think in her heart of hearts she is angry with me. Confused and conflicted, yes. We had on-again, off-again contact after she first left, but in the period right before the raid things had improved greatly between us, and Betty and I actually talked once for forty-five minutes. She never told me much about her life, but she was sincerely interested and concerned about her siblings, particularly Bryson and Harrison. I was heartened by how much stronger our relationship felt. I dream that one day Betty will realize that a religion that requires a child to turn against her mother is not a religion of God, and I look forward to welcoming her home with open arms.

I'm often asked if I think Betty will one day leave the FLDS. I don't know. What I do know is that Betty does not have a personality that will do well with an abusive relationship. If she somehow ends up in a marriage that is loving, she might stay. But if she ends up in one as abusive as mine, she will eventually find it intolerable and will try to get out. Fortunately, she's so strong-willed that I know she will succeed. Betty and I are a lot alike, and once she sets her mind to something, she is as determined as I am.

When we first escaped, I was able to get Betty into counseling with a skilled and sensitive therapist. But it didn't last long. Merril's attorney got a court order to have all my children see a court-appointed "neutral" counselor who was handpicked by Merril's lawyer because he was sympathetic to the FLDS. The court-appointed guardian who was monitoring our situation soon realized that the therapist was biased in favor of Merril and said that I wasn't required to have my children continue their therapy with him. But I was still fighting for full custody of my children, and if I took them out of therapy, I ran the risk of the FLDS putting the therapist on the stand to testify against me.

I was in a classic no-win position. The therapist could damage my children and disrupt our efforts to become a family, but if I lost custody—or won only partial custody—my children would be forever at the mercy of the FLDS.

At one point the therapist encouraged Betty to write a letter to the judge listing every bad feeling she'd ever had toward me. The letter was upsetting. Merril's attorney, Rod Parker, told my lawyer he thought the letter would turn the tide in Merril's favor. My lawyer, Lisa Jones, understood family law far better than he and knew the judge would see it for what it was: a father manipulating a child to fight her mother.

When the judge received the letter, he expressed concern about protecting Betty's relationship with me. He ordered that the letter not be recorded into the public record because this was in Betty's best interest as a child. (But Merril's attorney defied that order by attaching the letter with a court pleading.) Ultimately the letter bolstered my case against Merril. When the judge ruled, he allowed Merril regular visitations with his children but prohibited him by a court order from taking them into his home or outside the Salt Lake area. Lisa told me she'd never seen a Utah judge do that before. She also presented evidence of the pressure my children were under during their visits with Merril, such as being required to fast and pray for my death.

Betty was drafted in a war between her father and mother before she was capable of making responsible decisions on her own. The cruelty that tore us apart during the first year after we escaped was brutal for us both. Writing that letter made Betty feel empowered and superior to me. She was hostile and defiant, and parenting became almost impossible. I didn't fully comprehend how much had been stolen from us until I went to a bat mitzvah in California with Brian on April 4, 2009. Emilie, the thirteen-year-old daughter of one of Brian's college friends, was marking the Jewish rite of passage with her family and friends.

Unforgettably, at one moment in the celebration Emilie's mother read a poem about her daughter and how much she meant to her. Then she placed a brightly colored woven fabric over her daughter's shoulders and invited her to take her place in the world. A wave of grief washed over me: at that moment I realized just how much I'd lost with Betty.

No young woman in the FLDS was ever invited by her mother or anyone in the group to experience the wonders of life. We were taught to fear life, not to embrace it. Growing up, I was continually warned of the dangers of the outside world. Fear kept us confined to the small boxes of our lives.

Emilie, by contrast, was being invited into a world of enchantment and beauty. She was also expected to give back to life with generosity. To me, the rich colors in the fabric that her mother placed on her shoulders represented the tapestry of life with all its joys and sorrows. In the fabric of our own lives, sometimes there are colors we don't want and threads we didn't choose, but the pattern that emerges is distinctly our own.

Watching Emilie's mother inviting her daughter to accept life—

all of life, with its pain, sorrow, and joy—was wondrous for me. Her mother assured her of the steadfastness of her love and hoped it would provide ballast for her daughter.

Love as a compass to guide a life was revelatory for me. I had been taught that obedience and submission were all that would protect and guide my life. If I surrendered myself, there would be nothing to fear. Romantic love would have no place in my life. The vibrancy that comes from a life well lived was never an option. My life was to be cut from plain, drab cloth designed to make me invisible.

I left the bat mitzvah in California wishing I could give Betty a life rich in freedom and opportunities. I wanted to cover her in the warmth of my love and invite her into a world waiting to receive her gifts. I dream one day of again being able to nurture and support her mind and heart. But instead I am forced to watch my daughter continue with choices that lead her farther along on a pathway of pain.

I have to work strenuously to accept that regardless of how much I want to protect my daughter, it's her life. Letting go is wrenching. This is not the way I want life to be, but for now it is the way life is. All I can do is keep my heart open and love and believe in her from afar.

The moment I knew I was pregnant with my first baby, my life stopped being about me. Year after year, like millions of other mothers, I made sacrifices that were in the best interests of my children. After giving so much, it's hard not to feel entitled to have a say in the choices your child makes. But sometimes we have to step back and let them make choices, even if we feel like they are wrong.

Children need to fail sometimes in order to learn. What is crucial is that our children know we are there to support and encourage them when they get back up again.

The helplessness I feel in being unable to rescue Betty is probably similar to the feelings of parents whose children become addicted to drugs. But there can be no meaningful change until Betty decides it's what she needs to do. It has to come from within her. A parent can spend a lifetime loving and protecting a child, but once a child is legally old enough to make her own decisions, the power of parental protection skids to a virtual halt.

When a child makes tragic choices, a parent's every waking moment is consumed with fear and worry. All I can say to a parent trapped in a cycle of anguish like mine with Betty is, do not question the past. Let it go. I have asked myself over and over what I could have done differently to make Betty stay with us. Maybe the answer is nothing. What I do know is how unproductive it is to beat myself up with the what-ifs. As parents, we leave a large footprint on the lives of our children. But we also have to realize we are human and we make mistakes. We all do things we later regret.

I can't change the past, but if I stay mortgaged to it, I will fail to build the most productive life I can live in the present.

When my son Harrison was diagnosed with an aggressive and potentially fatal cancer at fifteen months, I had to deal with my fear that he might die. But as devastating as the day of his diagnosis was, it wasn't nearly as painful and frightening as the day Betty returned to the FLDS. It was easier to face my fears with Harrison's cancer. I could fight back. I could care for him 24/7 in the hospital. I could figure out how to get the help he needed. There was a lot I couldn't control, but there was also a lot I could do. But I never felt as powerless and as vulnerable with him as I did with Betty. I could protect Harrison; I was helpless to protect Betty.

Until the bat mitzvah in California, I don't think I could honestly name all I'd lost with her. She had rejected every aspect of the embrace of my love and cut me out of her life. I buried my deepest fear of never being in her life again. Facing that reality was hard, but after I did, I found the strength to stand again and a determination to learn and grow through my pain.

In the years of upheaval with Betty I have asked myself uncomfortable questions: Why go on? Why keep trying? Why love against the odds? The best reason I know is that life matters, and what makes life matter is love.

Even when the outcome is not what we'd hoped it would be, I have learned that love is never wasted. Despite the heartbreak, the love we've shared means everything to me. She will always be my daughter. Even if she rejects my love forever, I am a better person for having loved her.

I refuse to give up hope. Although I had to wait two years, a moment came when I could hug my daughter and buy her a starlight mint ice cream cone. She knew in the short time we had together that her family's love is still there for her, as steadfast as ever. Even if she cuts herself off from our love, I believe it still counts for a lot.

Every night before I go to bed, I make sure to leave the light on above the front door. It's a moment of hope. As long as my Betty is still absent from our family, I will leave the light on so she can find her way home.

The Unconditional Love
of a Good Man

In my life the bridge from survival to triumph has been built with my children and Brian Moroney. Brian is my "true north," my moral compass and invaluable guide to the world outside the FLDS. He and I are inseparable, and because of him I finally understand what it means to love and be loved unconditionally.

Our first meeting was as unexpected as it was improbable. Brian was a substitute teacher in a GMAT prep class that I was taking on Saturday mornings. We ended up having lunch after class, which segued into dinner. Both of us were recently divorced and had no interest in getting married anytime soon. In addition, Brian, a businessman, was working part time in California. That built brakes into our relationship from the start because it meant he was only back in Utah twice a month.

Brian was my first foray into romance and intimacy, ever. I was thirty-six years old, had eight kids, and was living on welfare. My primary goal was survival. I had no time to invest in a real relationship, whatever that was. But there was an undeniable chemistry between us, and going out to dinner a few times a month when he was in town sounded like fun.

I'd never met a man like Brian. He was handsome, intellectual, and passionate about life. Most gratifying of all, he took me seriously. He wanted to know what I thought about things. It was stimulating to talk to him about everything from politics to football to art. I knew nothing about professional sports, which Brian loves. He took me to Utah Jazz basketball games and taught me about football. We rented classic movies I'd never seen, like *Casablanca*. I'd barely heard of the Beatles, the Rolling Stones, James Taylor, and Earth, Wind & Fire, but Brian introduced me to all of them. He welcomed me into an interesting, sophisticated world I never expected to experience. But what made him magical to me then, as now, is his huge heart. He adores his two sons and was devastated when his divorce meant he wouldn't be with them every day.

One of Brian's closest friends is a psychologist, Mitch Koles. Mitch helped Brian cope with the painful aftershocks of his divorce and helped him put the pieces of his life back together. After Brian had been divorced for a year and a half, Mitch urged him to start dating.

Imagine, then, how overjoyed Mitch was when Brian told him he had met "the most amazing woman I've ever known." Mitch was delighted and confident that Brian had reached a milestone in re-engaging with life after his divorce. Now imagine his reaction when Brian told him I'd escaped from the largest, craziest polygamous cult in America and had eight children, one of whom was severely handicapped. Needless to say, Mitch thought Brian had lost his mind. He urged Brian to slow down. Be realistic. Think about the obstacles. For the first and only time, Brian ignored his best friend's advice.

Happily, when I began meeting Brian's friends, we hit it off. Mitch and I clicked right away, and he realized how much less anxious Brian was when he was with me. Brian had lived in a fast-paced, high-pressure world of success and achievement. He felt I was at peace with my world, and that provided a balance he didn't have before.

After about a year Brian became the CFO of a small public Utah company and returned from California. That was when our relationship really took off. At last we could be with each other every day. Except I had eight children and was living in a trailer. My kids didn't know about Brian, and there was no way I could afford the babysitters I'd need to see him as often as I'd like.

Brian had an idea: What if he came by after I put the kids to bed? They were usually in their rooms by ten, so around ten-thirty, rather than knock on the front door, he would tap softly on my window.

I'd hand him a small stool and pull him through the window. We'd pour two glasses of wine, talk about our day, and watch the Sci-Fi channel. On weekends I'd spring for a babysitter, and we'd go out on a conventional date. But during the week, we'd do the knock-and-pull routine. He's probably the only Harvard MBA ever to climb through a trailer window to meet a girlfriend with eight kids.

Brian wouldn't park in front of my trailer because we didn't want to alarm the children. My low-income neighborhood was iffy. One night Brian parked a few doors down, and a woman yelled. "Don't park next to my trailer if you're cheating on your wife with some whore in this neighborhood."

Brian fired right back, "You should know what you're talking about before you start attacking people."

Trying to build a relationship with a man I desperately loved was frustrating because I couldn't put my children on the back burner to be with him. After we'd been together about a year, I knew it was time for my children to meet him and understand what he meant to me.

One reason I'd put off this introduction was that my kids had been raised in the FLDS to believe that a woman who has an intimate relationship with a man outside of marriage has committed a crime punishable by death. According to the bizarre theology of the FLDS, the nine new wives Merril had married shortly after our divorce brought him closer to God. But my dating was a capital crime.

And once I told my children about Brian, they would realize we were never going to go back to the FLDS. My "sinning" would rule it out forever.

One morning Brian and I overslept. When Merrilee came knocking on my door, he ducked into my walk-in closet. I went to get something in my bathroom, and Merrilee opened the closet door looking for socks. They were so shocked at the sight of each other that both were speechless.

I reassured Merrilee that Brian had come over early to look for something, but she didn't buy that explanation. Later she told me she had thought he was in the closet because he was spying on me.

That's when Brian and I decided we had to stop hiding the fact that we were in love. I had met his boys a few months earlier. I told my children one by one, and it did not go well. Arthur was sulky and uncommunicative. Betty and LuAnne were furious; in fact, the next time Brian came over, LuAnne threw a ball at him.

Without missing a beat, Brian said, "LuAnne, do you need attention?" Today the two of them are extremely close, and he has had an enormously positive impact on LuAnne's sense of herself. My younger boys responded to the news of our relationship by acting out and throwing tantrums, but I knew that what they really yearned for was a dad.

Slowly Brian became an integral part of our family. My children were amazed to see a man truly love and value their mother. He also intervened when my children behaved abusively toward me. It was hard for him to stomach at times. I explained that women in the FLDS were seen as doormats and that my kids had been routinely encouraged to mistreat me by Merril's other wives. Brian continually told them how special I was and how much he loved me. If one of them asked Brian for something, his first response was "Is your mother happy? If Mom isn't happy, then nobody is happy." He set a powerful example by being so respectful toward me.

Most of all, Brian is fun. He's athletic—he used to run marathons in New York and Boston—and always up for an adventure. My children had never had a man in their lives who was eager to do things with them. They quickly got used to the idea!

Brian also let my children know that we were living in poverty because Merril was irresponsible. Brian told the kids flat out that a father is responsible for supporting his children. Period. He explained that it was wrong for a man to think of a woman, or any person, as property.

After the kids were used to us as a couple, Brian invited his mother, Edith Moroney, to visit. Edith had raised six children but worried about her son getting involved with a woman with so much baggage. Brian's dad was a military man who was devoted to his wife and children, and Edith always hoped Brian would find a woman he loved as much as his dad loved her. One of the few regrets Brian and I have is that his dad died before I could meet him. Brian always says that his dad would have loved me.

Before Brian took us all out to dinner with Edith, we sat in my living room, and he introduced her to each of my children. When he was finished, Edith said, "Brian, every one of them looks just like you." I was stunned by her generosity and acceptance.

Like any couple, Brian and I have our ups and downs. We acknowledge our disappointments with each other and try to confront them head on. When I was writing *Escape*, Brian was enormously supportive of me and tried hard not to resent the time it took away from him. After the book became a success, he was its biggest cheerleader.

Before I left on my book tour, he was driving me to the airport and asked what I'd do if someone showed interest in me while I was on the road. I said I had no idea.

"Let me tell you exactly what to say: 'I have eight kids.'"

I reminded him that this was one of the first things I told him when we went out to lunch.

"Most men are not like me," Brian replied. He's so right—and that is exactly why I want to share my life with him.

By the time *Escape* was published in paperback, Brian and I were living together. When I traveled to promote the book, he'd hold down the fort at home. I remember returning one night from Kansas City, dead tired but elated by the hundreds of people who had turned out to meet me and get their books signed.

I called Brian as soon as my flight touched down. He didn't answer. I tried calling again before reaching the baggage claim. Still no answer.

Brian was usually early, and if he was running late, he'd be sure to answer his phone. I arrived at the baggage claim and looked around, disappointed, exhausted, and demoralized. I couldn't understand why he wasn't there. Then as I turned back to watch the luggage tumble onto the conveyer belt, I felt Brian's hands grabbing my waist. He was laughing as he pulled me toward him and began kissing me. He hadn't answered his phone because he wanted to surprise me. Little romantic moments like this are a part of life I never really knew existed before.

My life now sometimes zigzags between the ridiculous and the sublime. Two days after winning my child support battle against Merril and seeing Betty, for example, I flew with Brian to Boston to celebrate the twenty-fifth anniversary of his graduation from Harvard Business School. It was surreal to begin the week testifying against Merril in a courtroom in San Angelo, Texas, and to end it walking across the Spangler Lawn at Harvard holding hands with my true love. The leaves were turning from green to gold, and the Harvard campus was even more beautiful than Brian had described. I could barely comprehend that a few years earlier I was a single mom of eight on welfare struggling to keep a roof over our heads. Now I was a best-selling author visiting one of the world's most prestigious universities with my lover, a distinguished alumnus. Harvard epitomizes everything the FLDS tries to destroy: self-expression, academic rigor, and intellectual freedom.

When I first fled the FLDS, I was completely disoriented, as if I'd landed on another planet. And in some ways I had. Similarly, Harvard left me feeling wonderfully disoriented. I had never been in an environment where so many had achieved so much. I felt like I was floating inside the world's most exclusive bubble.

We went to lectures, parties, and receptions. Brian's friends were all type As who had been fast-tracked from an early age. They had soared far above the ordinary achievements that the rest of us are content with.

That weekend helped me understand Brian in a way I never had before. He is a perfectionist who sets the bar very high for himself. Like his Harvard classmates, he is used to being at the front of the line. Brian always tries to come in first, and when he doesn't, it upsets him.

My approach is much less intense. I go with the flow, trying to control what I can but accepting that I'll be disappointed a lot of the time. I am far less self-critical than Brian. I've learned that no matter how high you fly, life will reach up, grab you, and slam you back to earth. Brian gets disappointed far more than I do because his expectations are so much higher.

My rare glimpse into privilege and power at Harvard was both liberating and grounding. It was a potent reminder that my life experiences are radically different from most people's. In the FLDS, I was forced to pay constant attention to everything and everyone just to survive, but in doing that I learned a lot.

Shortly after we escaped in 2003, my children and I went to San Diego with Dan Fischer, the former polygamist who was instrumental in helping me begin my life again. It was the only vacation we had ever taken, but we were all so battered and worn out that we didn't really enjoy it.

After *Escape* was published, I had enough money for a family vacation but not enough time. Two summers went by, and finally in the summer of 2009, I told Brian we needed to take a trip as a family. He and I voted for Yellowstone National Park. It would be an adventure and educational. But the kids overruled us. They wanted to go back to San Diego to enjoy what had felt too foreign and strange the first time. It was a *long* drive from Salt Lake City. Yellowstone was much closer. But the kids pleaded, so off we went.

Neither Brian nor I would ever describe a two-day car trip with six kids (Arthur stayed home because he had a summer job) as restful, but everyone was so excited that the kids bickered only occasionally. With all of us on good behavior, we were simply grateful to be together and have a week away from our daily routines.

Brian had bought tickets on the Internet for Sea World, the San Diego Zoo, and the Wild Animal Park and had arranged for his mother to meet us in San Diego to help out with Harrison. She couldn't have been more wonderful. She pushed Harrison in his wheelchair and was as enthusiastic about Sea World and the Wild Animal Park as the kids. Clearly Brian inherited his irrepressible spirit from his mom. Edith has infused our lives with kindness, support, and love.

Our hotel was a particular highlight of the trip. It had several saltwater swimming pools, each only four feet deep. Every night after dinner a huge screen was set up by one of the pools for a kids' movie, complete with popcorn for everyone. My kids had the time of their lives. After they went to bed, Brian and I had some quality time in the Jacuzzi. Relaxing there together gave me a chance to take stock of how far I'd come in the six years since my escape.

What a joy it was for me to realize that, with the exception of Betty, my children were all thriving beyond my wildest dreams. Arthur, 22, had just transferred from the University of Oregon to the University of Utah and was working hard to save money. He has his private pilot's license and is working toward getting his commercial one.

LuAnne, 18, is an athlete with a brown belt in karate. She worked her way onto the honor roll in high school and stayed there. Now she is enrolled in community college. After two years, she plans to transfer to Mount Holyoke in Massachusetts—a college she and I both fell in love with after I spoke there in 2008 and again in 2009. It seems unbelievable that six years ago LuAnne told me it would be a privilege to marry Warren Jeffs. Now she's horrified when she remembers that and understands how distorted her sense of reality was. These days she dreams of being an attorney.

Merrilee, 12, who for years wanted nothing more than to be a princess, has settled into the seventh grade and loves spending time with her friends. Her personality is one constant smile. She has earned her green belt in karate and caught up academically in school.

Patrick, 16, and Andrew, 14, were both distraught when we fled. Pat thought the world would come to an end and he would be destroyed if he stayed with me. Now he is a typical high school junior who loves text-messaging his friends and playing sports. Pat hates inequality and never fails to stand up for people in need.

Andrew has nearly doubled in size since 2003, when he was convinced I was taking us all to hell. He missed the siblings he left behind and was terrified of not doing what his father wanted. Today he is a well-adjusted high school freshman whose passion is football. (He's a wide receiver.) He would never consider missing a single practice, and, like Pat, he has earned a junior black belt in karate.

Bryson, who's eight, is remarkable because he alone has grown up entirely outside the FLDS. He was just a year old when we escaped and is an academic star because he never experienced the educational neglect of the FLDS. Bryson taught me the thrill of being a one-on-one mother—with him, no one ever told me not to hug or kiss him and no sister wives disciplined him behind my back. I learned how rewarding and joyful it is to raise a child and shape his values in accordance with my own.

Brian is the only dad Bryson has ever known, and they adore each other. Brian is an avid golfer, and one day he came home with a miniature set of clubs for Brycie. For me, watching the two of them go off together to "golf" is another chapter in the miracle of love.

And then there's Harrison, sweet Harrison, who couldn't hold his head up when we first arrived in Salt Lake City and needed a high-calorie formula to maintain his weight. A few years ago it felt like a miracle when he managed to sit up; now he's walking. At ten, he still doesn't speak, although he once said "Mama." His school bus driver says he is the happiest child on the bus.

Taking Harrison to Sea World was the high point of our trip to San Diego. We went as a family to see the show with Shamu, the whale who is Sea World's biggest star. The younger kids wanted to be in the splash zone and get wet, so Brian, Edith, LuAnne, and I sat with Harrison in the handicapped area. He was fascinated watching the stadium fill up with people. When the show began, he looked confused. He had no idea what was happening or what to expect.

First, Shamu's trainer talked about how he had become involved with whales. Then suddenly Shamu leaped high out of the water. Harrison nearly jumped out of his wheelchair. He began to laugh and laugh and laugh. When Shamu burst through the surface of the water again, Harrison became more excited than I'd ever seen him. Each time the whale soared up from the water, Harrison was over the moon with delight. He was jumping around so much in his wheelchair that even with the brakes on it began to move.

Brian and I looked at each other in pure wonder. Who knew there was so much joy in Harrison waiting to be unleashed? What a triumph.

He just wanted a decent book to read ...

Not too much to ask, is it? It was in 1935 when Allen Lane, Managing Director of Bodley Head Publishers, stood on a platform at Exeter railway station looking for something good to read on his journey back to London. His choice was limited to popular magazines and poor-quality paperbacks – the same choice faced every day by the vast majority of readers, few of whom could afford hardbacks. Lane's disappointment and subsequent anger at the range of books generally available led him to found a company – and change the world.

'We believed in the existence in this country of a vast reading public for intelligent books at a low price, and staked everything on it'
Sir Allen Lane, 1902–1970, founder of Penguin Books

The quality paperback had arrived – and not just in bookshops. Lane was adamant that his Penguins should appear in chain stores and tobacconists, and should cost no more than a packet of cigarettes.

Reading habits (and cigarette prices) have changed since 1935, but Penguin still believes in publishing the best books for everybody to enjoy. We still believe that good design costs no more than bad design, and we still believe that quality books published passionately and responsibly make the world a better place.

So wherever you see the little bird – whether it's on a piece of prize-winning literary fiction or a celebrity autobiography, political tour de force or historical masterpiece, a serial-killer thriller, reference book, world classic or a piece of pure escapism – you can bet that it represents the very best that the genre has to offer.

Whatever you like to read – trust Penguin.